THE OLYMPIC CHALLENGE

THE OLYMPIC CHALLENGE

Bill Toomey
and
Barry King

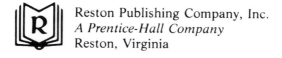

Reston Publishing Company, Inc.
A Prentice-Hall Company
Reston, Virginia

Photographs: World Copyright All Sport Limited

Library of Congress Cataloging in Publications Data

Toomey, William Anthony.
   The Olympic Challenge.

   1. Olympic games.   2. Olympic Games (23rd : 1984 :
Los Angeles, Calif.)   I. King, Barry John.   II. Title.
GV721.5.T66 1984   796.4'8'0979494   83-24605
ISBN 0-8359-5222-3

Editorial/production supervision and
typesetting by Professional Publications Limited

© **1984 by William A. Toomey
and Barry J. King.**

10 9 8 7 6 5 4 3 2 1

Printed in the United States of America

CONTENTS

ACKNOWLEDGMENTS

We would like to thank the following people who assisted in the creation of *THE OLYMPIC CHALLENGE*. In particular, we thank Bob Paul of the U.S. Olympic Committee, who approved the manuscript. Bob contributed his wisdom and experience directly, as one of the nation's leading Olympic historians.

Numerous federation officials have willingly given their time and understanding to the cause, proving extremely responsive in the editing process. Our special gratitude to Colonel Don Hull (Boxing), Bill Steinkraus (Equestrian), Samual Merrick (Yachting), Carla Mae Richards (Fencing), and Rolf Engen (Volleyball). Their comments and corrections greatly enhanced the level of accuracy and clarity of the manuscript.

The enormous task of putting it all together was shared by Laurie Carman, Beth Waltman, and Penny Barton. Deanna King and Marjorie King proved very effective in their proofreading of early drafts. The KayPro word processing system supplied by Professional Publications made extensive revisions possible.

Professional Publications typeset the book using the word processor diskettes, so rekeying errors were eliminated.

Fortunately for all, the research and composition was done at our beach office, mostly during the Southern California summer and fall with the ocean lapping at the doorstep—an invigorating environment which, it is hoped, is reflected in the healthy tone of the book.

INTRODUCTION

This book has been compiled in eager anticipation of the 1984 Olympic Games in Los Angeles. They are supposed to be games, merely sports events, 220 contests for gold, silver, and bronze. But not all the excitement will be in the arena. The Games are a happening, a global festival, which in size and splendor have become an important world institution. No other event brings together so many of the world's people, across geographical and ideological boundaries, to share a common and positive experience.

The 1984 Games will be an unprecedented sports and entertainment spectacle, the world's biggest media extravaganza and the most covered event in history. The American Broadcasting Company plans to televise 187½ hours of programming in the U.S., and an estimated two billion people worldwide will see some of the Olympic broadcast. Los Angeles expects to host over 10,000 athletes from more than 150 countries, competing in 21 official sports. Seven million tickets will be sold, returning only a portion of the budgeted $472 million cost of staging the Games.

This book is a guide to the gala occasion, intent on providing the spectator and viewer with the information necessary to understand, appreciate, and fully enjoy their Olympic experience. The emphasis is on the events, and the athletes' pursuit of performance. A chapter on each sport provides the historical background and the Olympic highlights, as well as the basic rules and strategy of each event. We have looked ahead to 1984 to indicate the general trends and spotlight individuals when they have evidenced clear potential for striking Olympic gold.

The opening five chapters chart a straight course through the historical development of the Games, from their ancient heritage to the present day. A sketch of Los Angeles as host city details the Olympic preparations and the unique business deals that provide most of the funding. "Faster, Higher, Stronger" explores the uncompromising quest of the athlete for the superior performance.

The Games exist at the focus of a vast network of national Olympic committees and sports federations, whereby millions of youth throughout the world have the opportunity to practice and compete in a set of the most basic physical skills. The athletes build their strength through years of training, dedicated to a singular ambition: to do their best in the most important test, at the Olympic Games. Only a few get the chance, but for all the others, the hope of making an Olympic team inspires the same energetic and healthy pursuit. The value of the Games is this process, the years of goal-oriented adventure that benefit young people regardless of whether they win gold or even make the team.

This book shares the positive view toward the Games. We subscribe to the ideal, promoting the notion that humanity should be able to come together peacefully to demonstrate their excellence in competition and abide by principles of fairness. Athletes from practically every nation joyfully mingle in the village and engage in serious contests in the arena.

In terms of international understanding, the Olympic Games have emerged as a major force contributing to world peace. Yet increasingly, they have become a stage for political bickerings of global proportions, which stir nations to boycott. The Olympics are a mirror reflecting the troubled state of world affairs. As a symbol of peace, they have become a game piece in the arena of diplomacy, dependent on the moves of the major powers. The struggle to maintain the Games in their continuing sequence is a crucial part of *THE OLYMPIC CHALLENGE*.

Bill Toomey
Barry King

Capistrano Beach, California
December, 1983

THE OLYMPIC CHALLENGE

1

THE ANCIENT GAMES

Nor let us think to praise a place
of festival more glorious than Olympia.

—Pindar Oder (476 B.C.)

Today, the ruins at Olympia are quiet and melancholy. A peaceful charm exists where once there was great festivity and excitement. Carpets of wild flowers grow amid the fallen columns, creating a mosaic of soft colors. Around the remains, the pillars of once great monuments lie scattered among the trees. Nearby, a museum houses the few remaining statues of gods and athletes not damaged or stolen.

A ceremonial archway opens onto an enormous rectangle of sunbaked dirt, 200 meters long and thirty-five meters wide. Here, the heroic contests were held. Spectators watched from the slope of a pine-forested hill to the north and from an earthen mound to the south. Many an exuberant visitor has run the length of the empty stadium and heard the distant echoes of the festive Greeks, their poets and politicians cheering their favorite athletes.

The rest of Olympia consists of a small village, a few hotels and a row of shops, many selling reproductions of classical art. The storekeepers wonder why more tourists don't make the five-hour, 220 mile journey from Athens. Those who do include modern-day athletes making their pilgrimage of sport. While there, many visit the Olympic Academy, the International Olympic Committee's conference center, situated about a mile up the road from the ancient site.

The origin of the Ancient Games has been lost in the mists of time. Human beings seem to have an innate desire to test their physical strength and skill. Organized sports events took place in the ancient civilizations of Egypt and China and among the first cultures arriving on the American continent. Practically every society has practiced some sort of organized athletic activity throughout the ages.

At Olympia in western Greece, sports events and religious ceremonies are known to have occurred long before the first recorded date of the Olympic Games, 776 B.C. The events were provincial affairs and the first recorded Olympic victors were local athletes. Only the winner of the sprint was recorded. Coroebus, a cook from nearby Elis, raced one stade (the length of the Stadium) about 190 meters, to become the first champion in recorded history. The Greeks later dated their calendars by this event, charting their history by Olympiads. In this way the four year cycle between Games began a tradition that would continue uninterrupted for a thousand years.

In the early days, facilities at Olympia were few and the program of events limited. Beginning in the sixth century B.C., a great cultural upsurge began and continued for two hundred years until Olympia became a major center of classical Greek culture and the focal point of the Mediterranean world.

The ancient Greeks worshipped the earth and the sun, and idealized clarity of mind and youthful vigor. They believed that man's physical prowess and athletic skills should be honored along with the capability of his mind. Thus, it was natural to combine athletic contests and religious ceremonies in their great festivals.

The Games at Olympia honored Zeus. As the importance of the Games grew, beautiful temples were built. The earliest was dedicated to the goddess Hera and later came the great Temple of Zeus. Set on sixty-foot pillars, this impressive edifice housed a forty foot statue of the seated Zeus, inlaid with gold and ivory. It is regarded as one of the seven wonders of the ancient world.

Men went to Olympia to witness the heroic athletic contests. Greeks were fascinated by sport and their favored athletes were honored in art and poetry. "There is no greater glory for a man as long as he lives than that which he wins by his own hands and feet," wrote Homer in The Odyssey.

Nothing was more important to the Greeks than the Games. Every four years a truce was declared, all wars ceasing for the month in honor of the festival at Olympia. Tens of thousands made the pilgrimage to Olympia and camped out in midsummer heat along the beautiful banks of the Alpheus River. They witnessed almost every kind of contest imaginable: running, jumping, throwing, equestrian, and wrestling. In addition to the athletic events, contests of poetry, drama, and music were also held.

Each Greek city-state sent its best men, determined by local elimination trials. The athletes sought only victory. Second place was equivalent to failure. The winner was decorated with a simple branch of wild olive, but the rewards were great in other ways. A victory at Olympia was the highest honor attainable in Greece. When the athletes returned home, cities voted huge payments to the victors. The crowds idolized them, poets wrote odes to their triumphs, and sculptors perpetuated the great moments in bronze and stone.

In the sixth century B.C., the Games were at their height of splendor. About twenty events were contested during the five days of the Games. Many events tested military skills and warrior qualities. The most important events were combined to form the five event pentathlon.

The first pentathlon event was the long jump, in which the athletes carried weights known as halteres in their hands like dumbbells. The halteres were released in midair, supposedly to propel the jumper forward. Modern jumpers have yet to discover how to use them to gain distance. Legend says that Phaylos of Croton leaped fifty feet using halteres. Today, a triple jump is necessary to span such distance.

The second event in the pentathlon was the discus throw. The ancient discus was a circular plate of metal or stone usually two to three times the weight of the modern discus which is 2 kilograms (4.4 pounds).

Next, the pentathletes competed in the javelin throw. A leather strap was wound around the shaft, rotating it upon release. This strap increased stability and provided greater distance. Accuracy, as well as distance, was a factor in determining the winner. The fourth event was the one-stade (190 meters) run, the length of the stadium.

The pentathlon was designed to narrow the field to two finalists who would compete in a final wrestling bout. Wrestling was one of the most popular sports in ancient Greece, a fitting head-to-head struggle to decide the overall pentathlon winner.

Several foot races were held at Olympia. The one-stade sprint was the most glamorous and determined the swiftest runner. Longer races used a turning post (kampter) so the contestants ran up and down the stadium as many as twenty-four times, about 2.75 miles. There were no marathon races at Olympia.

There were boxing events at the ancient Games. These were exciting and dangerous attractions. The philosopher, Plato, who visited Olympia when he was seventy years old, observed training procedures and described a sport very similar to modern boxing.

Wrote Plato: "Surely, if we were boxers, we would practice for days beforehand, trying out the punches and parries which we were going to use on the day; and to make it as real as possible. Instead of the usual leather straps we would put on boxing gloves, so that we could try out the punches at full strength without hurting anybody. And if we ran out of sparring partners, we should be so afraid of being defeated and laughed at, that we would hang up a dummy and have a go at that. Or, failing all this, we would resort to shadow boxing by ourselves. How else can the art of self-defense be practiced?"

The brutality of the fighting events increased after the sixth century B.C., giving rise to the Pankration, a life and death struggle. Everything was allowed except biting and eye gouging.

Milo of Croton was one of the most famous and jovial of the wrestling victors. He developed his great strength by carrying a calf every day. As the calf developed into a full-grown bull, Milo carried a greater weight, growing stronger until his power grew to legendary proportions.

Most of the events were held in the main stadium before as many as 50,000 spectators. The stadium was longer and narrower than those used today and the floor was composed of sunbaked dirt and sand. Only the judges had the luxury of sitting on permanent stone seats. The large crowds sat on grassy slopes, the hillside to the north, the mound to the south. Competitors performed naked and no women were permitted inside the stadium.

Outside the stadium, toward the river, was the hippodrome, where horse and chariot races were held. As many as ten four-horse chariots raced together, simultaneously negotiating the tight turns. Accidents were the chief thrill for the crowd. Women were allowed in the hippodrome and actually were victors of some equestrian events, as the championship was awarded to the owner of the horse or team.

Remains of the stadium at Olympia and 1980 decathlon champion Daley Thompson.

The ancient stadium at Delphi, site of the Pythian Games.

Athletics reached a peak of popularity between the fifth and sixth centuries B.C. Almost two hundred years after the first recorded festival at Olympia, another major sports festival, the Pythian Games in honor of the god Apollo, were established at Delphi. The Isthmian Games were begun near Corinth the same year, honoring the god Poseidon. With the addition of the Nemean Games, the fourth major festival of the circuit was established.

The great ambition of the Greek athlete was to win the crown at each festival. Many became professionals, living off the rewards bestowed by the state and aristocracy. They traveled the circuit of contests and trained year-round.

The glory of the Games peaked at the zenith of classical Greek culture, but the subsequent period of decline and degradation was long and slow. As the center of world power moved to Rome, the ideals of Olympia became less important.

The death blow to the Games came with the ideas of early Christianity. Glorification of the body was scorned and the celebration of the Greek gods was viewed as pagan ritual. Finally, the emperor Theodosius decreed the Games forbidden in A.D. 394.

Shortly thereafter, the looting of Olympia began. The statue of Zeus was carried off to Constantinople where it was later destroyed by fire. The great temples were dismantled by looters and toppled by two earthquakes in the sixth century. Finally, spring floods of the river Alpheus slowly buried Olympia, leaving the most revered site in the ancient world under a layer of silt. This once great and honored place was forgotten for a thousand years.

Europeans rediscovered the site in the eighteenth century. In 1805, Captain Leake began digging in the area of ancient Olympia, stirring up interest that provoked a series of visits by British archaeologists. By 1813, the first plan of the ancient site had been drawn. Still, much remained to be done and little had been uncovered to tell the long-forgotten story of the ancient Olympic festivals.

The majority of the unearthing and reconstruction was supervised by German archaeologists under a 1874 contract with the Greek government. Soon, the full magnificence of Olympia was being revealed. Students of the classics at universities in Europe were speculating on the nature of the Olympic Games. A few idealists even began to talk of their revival. One was Pierre de Coubertin.

2

THE EARLY
OLYMPIC MOVEMENT

— 2 —

The revival of the Olympic Games and the development of the International Olympic Committee (IOC) which monitors them, is credited almost entirely to French aristocrat Baron Pierre de Coubertin. The first modern Olympic Games at Athens in 1896 took place as a result of his ceaseless campaigning and single-minded devotion to the Olympic cause.

Pierre was born in January 1863. He traced his ancestry to Louis IX and the powerful families of Normandy. Although a rather frail youth, he participated in sports such as rowing, fencing, and boxing. He also read, traveled extensively, and developed his skills as a writer, philosopher, and educator. Coubertin was inspired by the classical Greek ideal of a sound body and mind, and the importance of physical training in building a nation and an individual to their fullest extent.

In 1871, France experienced the humiliation of defeat in the Franco-Prussian War. Turbulent times followed. France suffered from low national esteem and a depressed economy, while the imperial fortunes of England and Germany prospered. To Coubertin, it was the strength of the British educational system and the role of sports in the public schools that were responsible for Britain's national strength. The public schools were the foundation of the far-reaching British Empire. The schools built an elite educational system which developed a quality called "Muscular Christianity" that fashioned young Britons both politically and militarily.

Pierre de Coubertin visited several of these public schools, including Rugby School, which was famed for developing Englishmen of leadership potential. In 1890, he visited Much Wenlock in Shropshire, where Dr. Brooke had established the Olympian Society and conducted an annual sports festival at a site called Olympia Fields. Popular sports fairs such as this had historical roots far back in medieval times. These sports fairs inspired and motivated Pierre de Coubertin to put his Olympic ideas into actuality.

Returning to France, Coubertin wrote and lectured about the importance of physical education and the possible advantages of restoring the Olympic Games as an international sports event for promoting world peace. He wrote, "Nothing in ancient history has given me more food for thought than Olympia, this dream city." Coubertin campaigned tirelessly for his dream.

In 1894, at an International Congress in Paris organized to discuss and define "amateurism," Coubertin managed to add the agenda item, "On the possibility of restoring the Olympic Games and under what conditions could they be restored?"

Spiridon Loues won the first Olympic Marathon for host country Greece at Athens 1896.

Coubertin staged a dramatic presentation, inspiring the seventy-nine delegates from twelve countries with a performance of the ancient "Hymn to Apollo," which had recently been discovered at Delphi. The Assembly voted unanimously to support the restoration of the Games. At last, Baron de Coubertin had a framework, the support, and an agreement to try launching the Olympic revival in Athens in the spring of 1896.

When Coubertin initially sought to find a local organizing group in Athens, he encountered only indifference and rejection. The Greek government was bankrupt and lacking an existing sports program, they did not wish to see Greek athletes embarrassed.

Coubertin's idea finally gained the support of Crown Prince Constantine, who helped the Frenchman create a fund-raising group. A donation from Greek merchant Georgius Averoff provided the funding to rebuild the ancient Athenian Games Stadium as the principal venue for the 1896 Games.

ATHENS 1896: Games of the Ist Olympiad

King George of Greece proclaimed the first Olympic Games open in Athens during the first week of April. The opening ceremony was witnessed by 70,000 enthusiastic spectators. There were 295 competitors on hand, 214 Greeks, and 81 foreigners, representing thirteen nations.

It was a modest beginning. Foreign athletes came to Athens at their own expense. They did not represent the best athletes of Germany, the United States, or Britain of that time, but rather the athletes who could afford the time and cost.

No world records were set in the athletics events, not only because of the level of the competitors, but also because of the extremely tight turns and soft surface of the 400-meter track. The track had been built to its ancient proportions, extremely long and narrow. To make matters worse, runners ran in a clockwise direction, opposite to the standard direction of both then and now.

U.S. athletes dominated the track events, French the cycling, Swiss and German the gymnastics. Greeks also had their share of victories, doing particularly well in the shooting and gymnastics. They had eight victories overall.

As the final day dawned, no events had been won by Greeks in their athletic stadium. The disappointment of the hosts and their possible opposition to the future of the Olympic Games evaporated, however, when tiny Spiridon Loues, a Greek peasant, trotted into the packed stadium on his way to victory in the marathon. This was a most important event for the Greeks, a link to their ancient heritage. Thus, the Games concluded on a happy note.

Unfortunately, the 1896 Games in Athens were more magnificent in their pomp and ceremony than in the brilliance of athletic performance. Yet, because no other event of such a multinational scope had been held, it was still a profound beginning. It was a great step forward for the development of international sport.

Robert Garrett USA won shot and discus in Athens. 2nd in high jump and 3rd in long jump.

PARIS 1900: Games of the IInd Olympiad

The Games that followed in 1900 in Paris were a setback for the fledgling Olympic movement. In Paris, Coubertin could do no better than attach the Olympic Games to an international exhibition already scheduled to take place.

In Paris, the name "Olympic Games" did not even appear on the official program and competitors weren't sure if they were even competing in the Olympics. It was some time later, when a commemorative Olympic medal was sent to all of the competitors by Baron de Coubertin, that the matter was clarified. French organizers did nothing to provide competition facilities. There was no track, so runners sprinted around the undulating turf at the Racing Club de France.

Still, there were some notable athletic achievements, most far superior to Athens. The cause of international sport had benefited from a second major event. Perhaps the most brilliant performer of the Paris games was Alvin Kraenzlein of the University of Pennsylvania, who showed great versatility by winning four events: both hurdles races, the 60-meter sprint, and the long jump, setting Olympic records in all.

ST. LOUIS 1904: Games of the IIIrd Olympiad

The 1904 Games in St. Louis were attached to the exposition celebrating the Centennial of the Louisiana Purchase (1803). Because few foreign athletes crossed oceans to compete in the Exposition, it was really a U.S. collegiate event. Many athletes even competed in their college uniforms.

The distance from Europe was such that few international athletes could attend, the journey being too far and too costly. The United States, represented by collegiate athletes, won seventy-eight of the ninety-six gold medals in events contested under the Olympic banner.

Archie Hahn was the winner of three sprints in St. Louis. His 200 meter victory (21.6 seconds) set an Olympic record that stood until 1932. In this race, Hahn's three principal opponents were all penalized one yard for false starts, an arbitrary act of a judge, reflecting the lack of standardization of rules at the time.

The Games were strung out over seventy-five days and it was not always clear which events were part of the Olympic program. Among the most questionable of the non-Olympic events staged at St. Louis were those called "Anthropology Days."

Native groups, mostly from the sideshows of the exposition, participated in athletic contests with which they were totally unfamiliar. Under the watchful eye of several anthropologists, aboriginal groups from Africa, Patagonia, the Far East, Turkey, Mexico, and Sioux Indians from the United States, competed in what was really a mockery of the sport, essentially a sideshow exhibit.

Martin Sheridan USA twice won discus title, first in St.Louis 1904, again in London 1908.

Ralph Rose USA two-time shot champion, St. Louis 1904 and again in London 1908.

LONDON 1908: Games of the IVth Olympiad

In 1908, while organizing for the London Olympic Games, the British Olympic Council created a plan that became the basis for all subsequent Games. Each international sports federation formulated regulations, selected officials, and conducted events in that sport within the broader context of the Olympics. This planted seeds which aided the growth of several international sports federations, which still have direct responsibility for the conduct of individual Olympic sports.

A magnificent new 70,000-seat stadium was built, containing both cycling and running tracks and also a pool for swimming events. Over 2,000 athletes from twenty-two nations competed, far more representative of international interest than the first three Olympics.

London 1908 tandem winners Schilles and Auffray of France.

For the first time, the United States team had to share the track and field medals. Several major squabbles between the U.S. delegation and the British officials were given considerable attention in the press. Most celebrated was the walkover 400-meter victory of Windom Halswelle, a British Army Lieutenant, the only Olympic victor ever to win by a walkover. Having won his semifinal in an Olympic record 48.4 seconds, Lieutenant Halswelle faced three U.S. athletes in the final.

In those days, runners did not run in lanes and on the final turn, there was a skirmish as two of the U.S. runners appeared to cut in front of Halswelle. The chief judge jumped on the track and broke the tape before declaring the race invalid. One U.S. runner was disqualified. In protest, the other two refused to participate in a rerun; thus the Englishman trotted around the track alone, in a leisurely 50 seconds.

Johnny Hayes USA the eventual winner of the 1908 London marathon.

Another media controversy raged over the disqualification of Pietri Dorando in the marathon. Dorando, upon entering the stadium well ahead of the eventual winner Johnny Hayes, staggered and fell. British officials, urged on by the sympathetic crowd, jumped onto the track and assisted Dorando across the line. Only later did they realize that because of this act, Dorando was automatically disqualified.

These controversial events, and the numerous brilliant performances in the London Olympics, captured the public's imagination and media attention as never before, helping to instill the Olympic ideal of international competition firmly in the public's mind. On the track, Mel Sheppard of the United States achieved the most outstanding performance, setting a world record in the 800 meters, and completing the middle distance double with a victory in the 1,500 meters.

Pietri Dorando ITA strides through North London leading the 1908 marathon field.

STOCKHOLM 1912: Games of the Vth Olympiad

In Stockholm, over 2,500 contestants representing twenty-eight nations kept the Olympic flame burning despite rumors of war in Europe and political disunity within the IOC. The new Olympic Stadium, with a capacity of 30,000, was dedicated by King Gustav during the opening ceremony.

Among many brilliant performances, one athlete's achievements stood out. Hannes Kolehmainen was the first great Finnish distance runner, beginning a long and proud tradition that continues today. He won three gold medals in Stockholm, setting world records in the 5,000 and 10,000 meters and leading his team to victory in the 8,000-meter cross-country event.

The 5,000-meter race was the highlight at the Stockholm Games. For 12½ laps, Kolehmainen and Jean Bouin of France battled stride for stride, leaving the rest of the field far behind. The battle continued down the final straight, first one, then the other forging ahead. At the tape, it was Kolehmainen, who won by inches in 14 minutes, 36.6 seconds.

The 1912 free pistol shooting event in Stockholm.

In the 100-meter final, there were seven false starts before the race finally got underway. Ralph Craig pulled ahead near the finish to win in 10.8 seconds and later made it a double with a victory in the 200 meters. Craig would reappear as an Olympic competitor thirty-six years later as a yachtsman in 1948. He had the honor of carrying the colors of the United States in the London opening ceremony.

The decathlon and pentathlon events were introduced in Stockholm and their outcomes helped create the legend of Jim Thorpe. A native American Indian,

Thorpe won both by huge margins. He was hailed by King Gustav as "the world's greatest athlete."

This great triumph soon turned into one of the great tragedies of Olympic history. The following January, Thorpe's medals were stripped as a result of Thorpe having earned a few dollars playing baseball two summers prior to the Olympics. The medals were returned to Thorpe's family in 1983.

The Stockholm pentathlon produced another athlete who would become a legendary figure. Avery Brundage finished fifth in the pentathlon and competed in the decathlon. In 1952, he would become president of the IOC and firmly defend its principles for twenty years.

Around the new swimming pool, Duke Kahanamoku of Honolulu was noted for his exuberance and friendliness as much as his brilliant 100-meter freestyle and relay victories. His relaxed attitude made him a popular figure in the pool as well as in the streets of Stockholm.

The Stockholm Olympic Games were known as the innovative Games. Many events were added to the program, while several more traditional sports took on their current form. The modern pentathlon was introduced for the first time. Stockholm also saw the longest endurance event in Olympic history: the cycling roadrace, which was conducted over 320 kilometers (199 miles). Rudolph Lewis of South Africa was the eventual winner in 10 hours, 42 minutes and 39 seconds.

The Stockholm Games were everything that Baron de Coubertin had envisioned for the Olympic Games. With none of the disputes and controversial decisions that gave rise to nationalistic feelings in London, the Games were conducted flawlessly and generated enormous positive feelings. They were indeed a milestone for the Olympic movement, without which the Olympic movement may not have survived the calamity of World War I.

BERLIN 1916: Games of the VIth Olympiad (canceled)

In Stockholm, Berlin was chosen as the host city for the Games of the sixth Olympiad to be held in 1916. The Germans, like everyone else, thought the European conflict would be short, and continued to make Olympic preparations. Many new facilities were built. Soon it was too late to find an alternative, neutral site and for the first time the Games were canceled. Instead, the youth of the world spent the summer of 1916 behind opposing artillery.

Although he was fifty-one years of age when war broke out, Pierre de Coubertin enlisted in the Army. Believing the IOC should not be headed by a soldier, he asked to resign as president. The request was rejected. The IOC, however, did decide to move its headquarters to Lausanne in neutral Switzerland, away from the ravages of war.

ANTWERP 1920: Games of the VIIth Olympiad

No one knew what to expect from the competition. It had been eight years since the Games in Stockholm, and international sport had been virtually suspended due to the war. Many of the great names in Olympic sport had disappeared from competition and many, like French track and field star Jean Bouin, had lost their lives on the battlefield.

Tug of War was contested for the last time at the Antwerp Games 1920.

The track had been hastily built and due to almost continuous rainfall, became slow and heavy. As a result, performances suffered. Olympic records from Stockholm survived in all of the individual running events. Off the track, Hannes Kolehmainen returned to tackle the classic marathon event, finishing his magnificent career with a brilliant victory, covering the distance in 2 hours, 32 minutes, 35.8 seconds.

The 5,000 meters saw the Olympic debut of a young Finn named Paavo Nurmi. Throughout the race, Frenchman Joseph Guillemot followed at his heels until, halfway down the final straight, Nurmi was outsprinted. Three days later, during the 10,000-meter final, the circumstances were reversed. Nurmi followed the Frenchman and, in the final straight, rushed past him to win by eight yards.

Thus began the Nurmi legend. Before the Antwerp Games were over, Nurmi added the individual title in the 8 kilometer cross-country race and helped Finland win the team championship as well.

Swimmers from the United States and Sweden took all the honors in the pool. Once again, Duke Kahanamoku won the most prestigious title, the 100-meter freestyle, as well as earning another gold in the relay. In a preview of things to come,

Susanne Lenglen of France won the singles & mixed doubles at Antwerp Olympics 1920.

two children captured diving medals at Antwerp. Thirteen-year-old Aileen Riggin of the United States won the springboard diving championship, while Nils Skoglund of Sweden, also thirteen years of age, won the silver in the plain high diving.

In the final football (soccer) game, home team Belgium faced Czechoslovakia before 40,000 spectators. The game of football was still young and high standards of sportsmanship and officiating had not yet arrived. The referees' decisions were constantly disputed until the Czech team walked off the field in protest and was disqualified.

Albert Hill GBR achieved a brilliant 800/1500 meters double in Antwerp 1920.

The Belgian victory failed to satisfy the crowds. The selection of the team had been bitterly criticized because hometown favorites had been left off the national team. Throughout the game, Belgian players were resoundingly hooted by disgruntled fans, most of them their own countrymen.

Overall, the 1920 Games produced somewhat disappointing performances. However, the mere fact that the Games took place had major significance. Even the world's most destructive war, lasting more than an entire Olympiad, could not retard the modern Olympic movement.

PARIS 1924: Games of the VIIIth Olympiad

Following the turmoil of the war, the Games at Antwerp had been necessarily austere. The world was better prepared for Olympic festivities in 1924. More than 3,000 athletes from forty-four nations came to Paris to compete in the Games. The track and field events were held in Colombes Stadium, where six new world records were established.

Start of 1924 5,000 meters. Paavo Nurmi (inside) about to win his fourth Paris gold.

Athletically, the Paris Olympics were the Olympics of Paavo Nurmi, the legendary middle and long distance runner. Nurmi was indomitable on the track, capturing four gold medals. His efficient stride was perfectly paced. As he reeled off the laps, he would glance at the stopwatch he carried in his hand. The great Nurmi won the 1,500-meter and 5,000-meter championships within two hours, setting Olympic records in both and receiving little opposition except from Ville Ritola in the 5,000.

Earlier, Ritola, a resident of the United States but a native Finn, had won the 10,000 meters with a world record 30:23.2. Nurmi was extremely bitter that he was not entered in this race, which he believed he would have won. Nurmi had beaten Ritola in the 10,000-meter cross-country and also helped Finland win the 3,000-meter team race, four gold medals in all.

It's almost impossible to think of the Paris Olympics without recalling images from the highly-acclaimed movie *Chariots of Fire*. The film accurately depicts the contrasting personalities of British athletes Harold Abrahams and Eric Liddell.

Liddell was a stern Scot. A rather stocky figure, he had a peculiar running style, throwing his head back, pumping his arms vigorously in front of him. Liddell thought his best event would be the 100 meters, but the heats were scheduled on Sunday. Competing on the Sabbath was a violation of his strict religious beliefs, so Liddell did not run in the 100 meters. He chose, instead, to enter the longer races, the 200 and 400 meters.

The 100-meter finalists included favorites Charlie Paddock, who had won in Antwerp, and Jackson Scholz both from the United States. They moved out quickly, but at the 50-meter mark, Harold Abrahams, a student from Cambridge, edged past a rapidly fading Paddock, who finished fifth. Abrahams barely beat Scholz to the tape in an Olympic record of 10.6 seconds.

Harold Abrahams GBR streaks to his "Chariots of Fire" 100 meters victory in Paris 1924.

Paavo Nurmi, Finland's great distance legend, won nine gold medals between 1920 & 1928.

The sprinters met each other again two days later in the 200-meter final, this time joined by Eric Liddell. The co-favorites, Scholz and Paddock, were now watching Abrahams, but from the start he was never a factor. It was Paddock who led all of the way until, at the tape, he was nipped by the narrowest of margins by the rapidly finishing Scholz. Liddell finished third, Abrahams last.

Liddell successfully progressed through the 400-meter heats the following day and in the final faced J. Imbach of Switzerland and Horatio Fitch of the United States. Both had set Olympic records en route to the final. Liddell ran like he'd never run before. He led all the way, chased by Fitch, and held on to win in a world record 47.6 seconds.

For Liddell, victory was a triumph of religious devotion. He had been born into a family of missionaries in China and returned there to do his own missionary work before his early death. Harold Abrahams went on to become the athletics correspondent for the London Times and later the head of England's Amateur Athletic Association, the organization that governs track and field.

In Paris, the track and field events were dominated by the United States and Finland. The United States won twelve gold medals in the twenty-seven men's events. The distance heroics of Paavo Nurmi, Ville Ritola, and marathoner Albin Stenroos, garnered a total of ten gold medals, a phenomenal achievement for the tiny nation.

In the pool, Johnny Weissmuller of the United States won his first Olympic gold medal in the 100 meters. He was followed by the durable Duke Kahanamoku, then in his twelfth year of Olympic swimming and Duke's brother Sam Kahanamoku, who captured the bronze.

A year after the Paris Games, at an IOC congress in Prague (May, 1925), Baron De Coubertin resigned, handing over the helm to Henri de Baillet-Latour. The success of the Paris Olympics enabled the baron to say, in his official letter of farewell, "The world institution that we have built is ready to face any eventualities."

AMSTERDAM 1928: Games of the IXth Olympiad

The Amsterdam Olympic Games were attended by 3,015 athletes from forty-six nations. For the first time, Baron de Coubertin could not attend. He was ill and sent a message of regret to the athletes. However, he would have been satisfied with the performance of the Amsterdam organizers and the smooth, successful running of the Games.

There was a noticeable widening of participation from the nations on distant continents. Uruguay won a second football (soccer) championship. Argentina earned two gold medals in boxing and one more in the pool. India began to dominate field hockey. Chile gained its first medal, a silver by Miguel Plaza in the marathon. Japan emerged in track and field, led by Mikio Oda's 49 feet, 10¾-inch leap to win the triple jump. Egypt earned a gold in Greco-Roman wrestling and another in weightlifting. Haiti's Silvio Cator won a silver in the long jump.

Amsterdam also marked the return of the central powers to Olympic competition. The aggressors of World War I had been prevented from competing in Antwerp and Paris and had seen no Olympic competition since 1912. Germany did very well, winning ten gold medals distributed across the entire sports program. Hungary also showed some power, collecting four gold medals, two in its traditional stronghold, fencing.

In track and field, the story of the Games was one of great success for Finland and a relatively poor showing by the United States. The U.S. team could manage only three golds in the twelve running events—the two relay events and the 400-meter victory of Ray Barbuti.

Finland swept the four distance running events, this time with four athletes. Nurmi was still brilliant, although not quite the "peerless Paavo" of 1924. He started with an Olympic record in the 10,000 meters, his seventh Olympic championship in three Games.

Perhaps the heats of the steeplechase and 5,000 meters took some spring out of Nurmi's thirty-two-year-old legs, for he had to settle for a silver behind Ville Ritola in the 5,000 meters and followed countryman Toivo Loukola in the steeplechase. In twelve Olympic finals, Nurmi concluded his incredible career with nine gold and three silver medals.

Percy Williams CAN, surprise winner of 100 meters in Amsterdam 1928 while just nineteen.

The Finns have a word for willpower and endurance. It's called *sisu*, a quality that is essential in distance events of 1,500 meters and farther. Nurmi and the stoic Finns cornered the market on "sisu" throughout the twenties and beyond, which is why they continue to produce some of the world's greatest distance runners.

Perhaps the outstanding individual performance in track at Amsterdam came from Percy Williams, who achieved the prestigious 100 and 200 meter sprint double. A powerful nineteen-year-old college student from Vancouver, Canada,

Paavo Nurmi stalks Ville Ritola FIN in Amsterdam. Nurmi won 10,000m, Ritola the 5,000m.

Williams was a virtual unknown when he left the starting line in the 100-meter final. Four days later, after achieving his double, Williams was being hailed as the world's fastest human. He would underscore this honor two years later by recording the world's first 100-meter clocking of 10.3 seconds.

In the swimming pool, Johnny Weissmuller added two more gold medals to his collection, again winning the 100-meter freestyle and assisting the United States in the 4 X 200-meter relay.

The Games of Amsterdam were a great success. Those who had fought so hard to establish the Games on a sound footing had to be delighted with the institution that had come into being. It was somewhat sad that Pierre de Coubertin could not be at Amsterdam or the next Games. The distance to Los Angeles in 1932 would be too far for the aging Frenchman; his life was already waning at the time of the Berlin Games.

In his later years, Coubertin devoted himself mostly to his writing, including an influential commentary on the Olympic movement. On September 2, 1937, during a walk in the park in Geneva, Coubertin had a heart attack and died. As he had requested, to the astonishment of many, his heart was removed and buried at ancient Olympia.

3

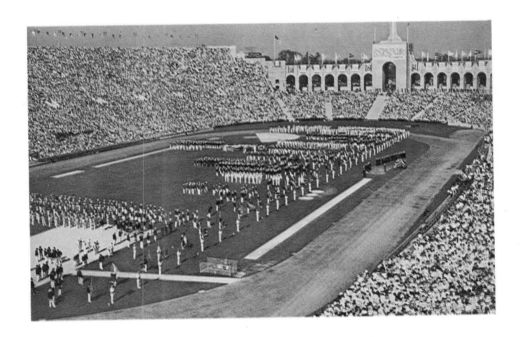

LOS ANGELES—1932

— 3 —

In 1932, Los Angeles was one of the more youthful cities in the world. The Gold Rush of 1849 had brought population and development to Northern California. Seemingly lost in the shuffle was the dusty adobe settlement to the south, just a day's ride inland from the Pacific Ocean. Fifty years before Los Angeles held the tenth Olympic festival, the city had a population of fewer than ten thousand people, most of whom were still engaged in the Mexican pastoral economy. Then came the railroads.

The 1887 population boom began as a price war between the Southern Pacific and Santa Fe railroads, in which the fare from Kansas City to Los Angeles was slashed from $100 to $25. Then on March 6, after a frenzy of price-cutting competition, Southern Pacific offered a transcontinental railroad journey for just one dollar. After a few days the rate rose back to the twenty-five dollar level. Nevertheless, many Easterners, fascinated by the idea of purchasing inexpensive land in the West, decided to take the opportunity to see the Pacific.

Southern Pacific claimed to have transported over 100,000 people to California in 1887. Many stayed and, soon, the number of developers and real estate agents carving up the land equaled the total population prior to the boom.

By 1932, Los Angeles was experiencing another population explosion, brought on by the ravages of the Great Depression in the East and Midwest. It was another time of migration westward. The Southern California climate attracted people who had been uprooted elsewhere and the population of the Greater Los Angeles area climbed to over 1¼ million by the start of the Games. Images of Southern California were propagated by the movie industry via the "silver screen," which portrayed the idyllic Hollywood lifestyle to the rest of the nation and the world.

Into this almost frontier town setting, far from the old capitals of Europe, came the Games of the Xth Olympiad. William May Garland, a successful Southern California developer, first appeared in Antwerp in 1920, carrying his bid for Los Angeles to host the Games. But Pierre de Coubertin and the International Olympic Committee (IOC) were firmly committed to Paris for the 1924 Games and Amsterdam had been waiting in line for more than a decade to become an Olympic Games host. Los Angeles would just have to wait.

The IOC, however, was very impressed with Garland and his Los Angeles bid. As a result, Garland was elected to the esteemed group in 1922. At the IOC session the following year, the delegates gave the City of Angels the nod for the 1932

Olympic celebration. Coubertin had long felt the Games must be global in scope, so the IOC firmly endorsed the plan to bring them to the New World for a second time.

Garland mobilized and headed an extremely strong, energetic, and imaginative organizing group, the Community Development Association. The group led construction of the huge Los Angeles Coliseum, which was then one of the world's finest stadiums.

Then the world fell into one of the worst economic crises in history. Fears arose worldwide that the expense of sending athletes such a great distance would prove prohibitive and, consequently, that participation would be severely limited. But Garland and his committee went to work, seeking lower fares from steamship and railroad companies. With the creation of the Olympic village concept, Garland also announced that Los Angeles was prepared to provide room, board, and local transportation to competitors for just two dollars a day.

Fifteen hundred athletes from thirty-seven nations made the long journey to the shores of the Pacific. For many, it was an arduous and expensive task. The Brazilian team had no money, so arrived on a ship loaded with coffee, which the athletes had hoped to barter to pay expenses. Upon their arrival, however, the Brazilians encountered import restrictions and only a handful of members were able to come ashore.

In the midst of the depression, people made their way to Los Angeles as best they could. Don Hull, a nineteen-year-old boxing enthusiast from Loveland, Colorado, described one popular means of cheap transportation:

"There were many visitors in town. They had great crowds—and quite a lot of them, like me, had bummed their way out on the rails. But they pulled me off in Needles (California). Some of the bulls (railroad detectives) weren't too bad. They knew we needed the ride."

What Hull saw in Los Angeles inspired a lifelong involvement with Olympic sport. Today, he presides over the development of boxing as head of the Association Internationale de Boxe Amateur (AIBA).

Male athletes were housed in the Olympic village, where 250 prefabricated units were assembled in a spacious circle atop the Baldwin Hills. The village was just ten minutes from the Coliseum and in those days commanded a panoramic view of the Pacific Ocean. It was built for $165 per unit and sold after the Games for the same amount. Much of the village was reconstructed fifty miles south in Laguna Beach, California. It is now a rather exclusive resort where some of the units remain as parts of half-million dollar homes.

The concept of an Olympic village had been talked about during previous Games but was never realized. The gathering of so many people from diverse cultures into a world village was unique. The concept proved popular and, indeed, became an integral part of the Olympic movement. The 200 women athletes, enjoying more opportunities on the 1932 program than ever before, stayed at the

Chapman Park Hotel on Wilshire Boulevard, which was the town's main thoroughfare.

On July 30, 1932, the athletes of the world paraded into the sunlit stadium before 101,000 spectators, the largest Olympic audience ever. United States Vice-President Charles Curtis, substituting for President Herbert Hoover who was starting his re-election campaign, welcomed the youth of the world and declared open the Games of the Tenth Olympiad. The next day, records began to fall.

The Olympic Village in Los Angeles 1932.

Los Angeles saw the most complete revision of world and Olympic records in history. Twenty Olympic records were set in the twenty-three men's athletics events. There were fifteen world records in track and field events, including records in all seven of the women's events.

One of the Games' greatest contests was the 400-meter duel between United States' team members Ben Eastman of Stanford University and William Arthur Carr, a sprinter from the University of Pennsylvania. They lived up to their billing as the two greatest 400-meter runners in history. Carr, at twenty-two, was the younger and less experienced, but was probably the more gifted of the two. Eastman had experience and the world record to his credit.

Prior to the Games, running in Palo Alto, California, "Blazing Ben" Eastman caused the world to rethink how the event should be run. At the time, Emerson "Bud" Spencer held the world's 400-meter record at 47 seconds flat. In the previous thirty years, the record had been reduced only eight-tenths of a second.

On this March day in 1932, Eastman took off and blazed the first 220 yards almost flat out, passing the halfway point in 21.3 seconds. He continued to drive hard around the turn, into the final straight. As he passed the finish line, the judges' watches stopped at 46.4 seconds. It was a dramatic breakthrough, six-tenths of a second better than Spencer's record.

Eastman became regarded the favorite in the 1932 Olympic Games. But, when the collegiate championships were held in June, also standing at the starting line was William Arthur Carr. Carr was relying on the words of his coach, the 1932 Olympic coach, Lawson Robertson, who said, "Stick to Eastman, he'll show you what to do." Carr followed the advice perfectly. He came into the final straightaway a yard behind Eastman and began narrowing the distance, forging ahead just before the finish in a time of 47.0 seconds.

The race was considered inconclusive, Eastman claimed a sinus infection had slowed his performance. It remained speculative as to what would happen when the two met again. At the U.S. Olympic trials, Carr again defeated the record holder by two yards in a time of 46.9 seconds, a fast time, but still slower than Eastman's record.

Then came the Olympic final, the race that would determine the ultimate champion. Carr had improved upon the Olympic record in his first heat, a 47.2 performance, but the experts thought Eastman's experience might pay off in the final. At the gun, Eastman came out flying. He gave it all he had, passing the first hundred meters in 10.8 seconds and the 200 meter mark in 21.9. Carr was a few yards back.

When they came into the final straight, with 100 meters to go, it was still Eastman by a yard, but Carr's running stride still appeared effortless while Eastman was beginning to fade. Fifty yards from the finish, Carr breezed past his struggling opponent to win in 46.2 seconds, a world record. Eastman was clocked at 46.4 seconds, equaling the old mark.

The race was regarded as one of history's greatest exhibitions of running and was fully appreciated by the 90,000 spectators in the Coliseum. The *Los Angeles Times* wrote: the spectators, "fell back into their seats . . . limp with exhaustion after watching Wee-Willie win the greatest 400-meter race ever run on this planet."

Another athlete renowned for her outstanding Olympic performances in the '32 Games was "The Babe." Mildred Didrikson was born in Texas to parents who were great sports enthusiasts. Rather than bring their seven children up on dolls and toys, the Didriksons introduced them to the joy of foot racing, jumping competitions, and weightlifting. As in most large families, sibling rivalries were quite fierce, and Mildred had to work extra hard to keep up with her five older siblings.

"Babe" Didrikson threw the javelin a world record distance to win in Los Angeles 1932.

Jean Shiley USA won high jump gold when Didrikson's diving style was declared illegal.

Mildred "Babe" Didrikson USA out-leans Evelyne Hall USA in 80 m hurdles at Los Angeles.

Her first competitive sport was basketball and before she was twenty, she had led her team to three straight national AAU championships. From there she moved on to baseball. Her athletic strength and skill were so outstanding she was able to compete with men on an equal basis.

When Babe turned her attention to track and field, no woman could challenge her on all-around skill. In the 1932 Olympic trials, Babe competed in eight of the ten events, winning five, and setting three world records in the process.

In the Coliseum, Babe began her legendary Olympic saga with a javelin throw of 143 feet 4 inches, a world record, but only 7 inches farther than the runnerup. The 80-meter hurdles final was also very close. Babe threw her left shoulder at the tape and barely outleaned Evelyne Hall, who thought she had won. The judges gave the victory and the gold to Babe even though both women were given credit for the world record of 11.7 seconds.

In the high jump, both Babe and Jean Shiley cleared 5 feet 5¼ inches, a world record that would endure for several years. In the tie breaking jump-off, when the bar was lowered to 5 feet 4 inches, Babe's diving style clearance was ruled illegal and she was awarded the silver medal. Today, her technique would be perfectly acceptable.

Babe endeared herself to the crowd with her self-confidence and physical exuberance. Her fresh attitude toward the Olympics was summarized when, according to the *Los Angeles Times*, Babe said after the Games, "It was a good meet and everybody was swell."

After the Olympics, Babe turned her attention to a new sport, golf. Her greatest success came in the early 1940's, when she had a streak of seventeen straight tournament victories. In 1947, when Babe accepted a $300,000 motion picture offer, she lost her amateur status. As a result, she focused her attention on getting women's professional golf on its feet, then went on to win the professional women's world championship three straight years.

Babe underwent cancer surgery in 1953, but heroically managed to come back the following year to win the U.S. Women's Open. Babe, who rarely allowed anything to foil her goal of victory, succumbed to cancer in 1956 at the age of forty-three.

Another brilliant performer was Eddie Tolan, who earned the distinction of an Olympic sprint double. In the 100 meters, the judges waited for a photograph to be developed before proclaiming Tolan the winner by inches over Ralph Metcalfe. Both were credited with a time of 10.3 seconds, equaling the world record. It was the first time a photo-finish camera had been used in the Olympics. Tolan had less trouble winning the 200 meters in 21.1 seconds, the fastest time ever around a curve.

The other big news in track was the end of a decade of Finnish distance running supremacy. The first blow to the Finns took place the week before the Games, when thirty-five-year-old Paavo Nurmi, entered in the marathon, was

Helene Madison USA starts the 100-meter freestyle, wins first of her 3 gold medals.

Wilhelmina von Bremen carries relay baton to USA 4x100 meters victory over Canada.

banned from the Games for professionalism. It was the conclusion of a three year inquiry by the athletics federation into Nurmi's excessive expense payments. For several years, Nurmi attracted great crowds wherever he ran. To encourage him to compete, event organizers reportedly would offer Nurmi a generous share of the gate.

The Finns had won every Olympic distance race over 1,500 meters in Paris (1924) and four of five in Amsterdam, four years later. In Los Angeles, they settled for two.

The first of these, the 5,000-meter victory of Lauri Lehtinen, raised a chorus of boos from many of the 50,000 spectators. Lehtinen and Ralph Hill of Oregon came off the final turn together. As they battled stride for stride toward the finish, Lehtinen, on the outside, cut across Hill, causing him to lose his stride. Hill was still only a foot short at the tape.

Most experts thought it was an obvious foul, but no formal protest was made by U.S. team officials. After a two-hour debate, the officials announced their decision. It seemed the generosity and diplomacy of the hosts worked in Lehtinen's favor.

Finland's second gold medal came under lighter circumstances, when an official lost count of the laps and the steeplechase finalists ran 460 yards too far. Not that it made any difference, since Volmari Iso-Hollo was ahead after 3,000 meters and continued to extend his lead throughout the extra lap.

"My heart bleeds to end my career by winning the marathon," Nurmi pleaded. But he could only watch as the trumpeters announced the arrival of nineteen-year-old Juan Zabala of Argentina, who entered the stadium ahead of the marathon field and won in Olympic record time.

In the Olympic pool, adjacent to the Coliseum, Japanese swimmers caused a sensation by dominating the men's events. In four of the five individual races, Japan went one–two, a streak broken only by Clarence "Buster" Crabbe, who won the 400-meter freestyle for the United States. The Japanese also won the relay, with a world record.

The U.S. women, however, had little competition in the pool. Led by Helene Madison's three gold medals, the United States captured four of the five races and both diving events.

The newly emerging Olympic stars were quickly absorbed into the Hollywood social scene. The film industry was in its heyday and the athletes were welcomed as celebrities in this star-studded town.

The stars came out to the Coliseum: Douglas Fairbanks, Gary Cooper, Cary Grant, Buster Keaton, and many more watched the events. But for once, leading men and women played supporting roles to the athletes. Their presence was hardly noticed by the crowd, unless someone's view of the athletic action was obstructed.

The fans had come to cheer their Olympic heroes. Among the actors, only Johnny Weissmuller was applauded when he made his frequent poolside appearances. Even so, he was popular not as Tarzan, but rather as an Olympic swimming legend.

The Olympic Games helped everyone forget the depression for two happy, eventful weeks. Although full economic recovery was still far away, the period during which the Games were held brought positive news from Wall Street. "Wild Frenzy of Buying Booms Price of Stocks" declared a *Los Angeles Times* headline on August 7, sharing the front page with Olympic news. It seemed the bullishness was inspired by positive hope and good cheer, more than any real change in market conditions.

America's foremost spokesman, Will Rogers, observed the closing ceremonies and expressed the optimism that was inspired by the Games. He wrote, "It was the best managed and attended big affair you ever saw. Seeing or reading about the exploits of the youth of the whole world for the last few weeks has been a good thing for everybody."

4

OLYMPIC CHALLENGE
(1936—1980)

— 4 —

While the International Olympic Committee (IOC) tries to keep political upheavals from affecting the Games, such skirmishes have long been part of the Olympic story. We have come to expect each Olympiad to be disrupted by an array of ideological struggles and political demonstrations, accompanied by fears of terrorism. Massive security costs have prompted many people to say the Games are too expensive and just too big.

In retrospect, the Los Angeles Games of 1932 seem to be the last of the relatively innocent Olympics. The Games were becoming too important not to influence international relations. Because of the importance of the Games, politicians would be tempted to abuse the Olympics for purposes beyond the realm of sport.

The IOC could not have anticipated the ambitions of the Third Reich and its desire to dominate world affairs when they voted in 1931 to award the Olympic Games to Berlin. While the '32 Games were underway in Los Angeles, elections were held in Germany. Adolf Hitler began moving his National Socialist Party toward power.

BERLIN 1936: Games of the XIth Olympiad

What would become an Olympian growth toward gigantism began in Berlin in 1936. At first reluctant to host the games, Hitler's propaganda machine soon recognized the value of the Olympics as a means of displaying Germany's philosophy and national strength to the world.

In the summer of '36, the nations of the world were talking peace while preparing for war; the storm clouds were gathering. Hitler had sent troops to repossess the demilitarized Rhineland in March. The Western Allies, led by Britain and France, considered a boycott of the Games, their only way to protest this act of aggression. The United States team also came precariously close to a boycott for a different reason—the issue of anti-Semitism.

Hitler had pronounced the Nuremberg Laws in September 1935, depriving the Jewish populace of their German citizenship. Many immigrated to the United States with stories of Nazi terrorism. The New York Times said, "Sport does not transcend all political and racial considerations," and warned against sending a U.S. team to Berlin.

Chancellor Adolf Hitler, the presiding head of state at the Berlin Games.

Holland's happy 4x100 meters swim relay team following their gold medal performance.

Avery Brundage, then head of the United States Olympic Committee (USOC), declared, as he would many times, that politics must not interfere with the conduct of the Olympic Games. The Berlin Olympics went on unaffected by the numerous threats of boycott.

On August 1, the flame, carried by relay from Olympia, arrived in Berlin to open the Games. The stadium, unequaled throughout the world in its magnificence, was packed with 110,000 people, many of them young soldiers. Chancellor Adolf Hitler, the head of state, declared the Games open with the simple sentence, "I declare open the Olympic Games of 1936 celebrating the XIth Olympiad of the modern era."

The next day, before a capacity crowd, the young German athlete Hans Woellke stepped into the shot put ring and unleashed an Olympic record throw of over 53 feet. With this throw, he won the first medal of the 1936 games. Evoking frenzy from the partisan crowd, he was the first German male athlete ever to win an Olympic athletics title. Lina Radke was the first German female, having won the women's 800 meters in 1928.

For the first time, the Nazi swastika was raised to the top of the flagpole. Hitler, caught up with the nationalistic fervor and excitement of the crowd, gave a personal greeting to the victor in his box. The 10,000-meter event followed. It was a clean sweep for Finland. The victors were again escorted to a personal audience with the Fuhrer, as were two German girls, Tille Fleischer and Louise Kruger, who had finished one-two in the javelin throw.

Hitler congratulated the first three winners of the Olympic Games, but when the high jump was decided and black Americans Cornelius Johnson and David Albritton climbed the victory stand in first and second place, Hitler was nowhere to be found. Some Olympic historians have suggested that Hitler hurried away when he saw the two American blacks climb the stand. By congratulating them, Hitler would have made a mockery of his racist theories. The Aryan supremacists regarded the twelve blacks on the U.S. team as nothing more than "black auxiliaries." Others say Hitler left because the high jump was going on and on, as it tends to, and he simply had to leave for another appointment.

We may never know whether Hitler's action was a racist statement or pure coincidence. Regardless, Count Latour, then president of the IOC, sent a message to Hitler following the day's competition, saying that unless he was willing to congratulate every winner at the Games, he should not recognize any.

It is believed that subsequent German victors met with Hitler under the stands, out of sight of the crowd. This way, the issue had already been resolved before Jesse Owens first stepped atop the victory stand.

The 1936 Games affix the symbols of Naziism in our minds. At that time, they appeared to only be symbols of nationalistic propaganda, but ten years later they were symbols of a war-beaten enemy and racial terrorism. Those who attended the Games can still visualize the enormous number of soldiers in the stadium, the sea

Jesse Owens USA at the start of the 100 meters, about to win the first of 4 Berlin golds.

Kitei Son of Korea, running in the colors of Japan, wins the Berlin 1936 marathon.

As star of the Berlin Olympics, Owens exploded the Nazi myth of Aryan supremacy.

of swastikas, the outstretched arms of the Nazi salute, the haunting chants of "Sieg Heil! Sieg Heil!" and the presence of Hitler at almost every session of athletics competition.

Athletically, the Berlin Olympics were the Games of Jesse Owens. With his success, Owens denied and mocked Nazi racial theories. Although Germany won the unofficial medal count over the United States, eleven of the twelve blacks on the United States team brought home medals. Thus, Jesse Owens and the "black auxiliaries" became champions who struck a major blow against the Nazi propaganda scheme.

This brings up the great irony of the Berlin Games. In Berlin, the black athletes were well received, did not feel discriminated against, and had enjoyable experiences. As Mack Robinson, silver medalist in the 200 meters and older brother of famed baseball player Jackie Robinson, says; "In Germany, the people treated us very well and on the rest of the tour of that summer, at other track meets in Norway and England, we were held in high esteem. What was difficult was returning to the United States and again having to sit at the back of the bus as a second class citizen."

1940: Games of the XIIth Olympiad (canceled, WW II)

The 1940 Olympics were awarded to Tokyo while the Games in Berlin were underway. The Tokyo organizers proceeded with their plans even as the Japanese military command was committing the country to imperial adventures in the Far East. In the summer of 1938, Tokyo was forced to withdraw its bid. Helsinki then offered to organize the 1940 Games and the IOC optimistically chose London as the site of the 1944 Games.

Helsinki built a new stadium and continued to prepare, still hoping for peace until May of 1940, eight months after war had been declared. But nothing could stop the momentum of international animosity that marched the world into history's most widespread and horrible conflict.

1944: Games of the XIIIth Olympiad (canceled, WW II)

LONDON 1948: Games of the XIVth Olympiad

The fourteenth in the series of modern Olympics set the movement on track once again after two cancellations due to World War II. Although the war had created worldwide shortages and economic difficulties, fifty-nine nations were represented in London, more participants than any prior Olympic Games.

Germany and Japan were excluded from these Games because of their roles as aggressors in the recently concluded war. The exclusion of the countries

Highboard diving medalists, left Kohler GER, Dunn USA, champion Dorothy Poynton USA.

probably had a considerable effect on the outcome of the Games, particularly in swimming, where the Japanese had shown great ability in '32 and '36, and in fencing, canoeing, and shooting, where the Germans were traditionally strong. Some officials tried to disallow Japan's prewar Olympic swimming records, but when Japanese champion Furhashi advanced several world records shortly before the London Games, he reaffirmed Japan's swimming prowess and the attempt to disqualify prewar performances was abandoned.

Laszlo Papp of Hungary KO's John Wright GBR in London 1948, Papp's first of three golds.

These Games were to be the first for Israel, which had recently achieved statehood and wanted to symbolize its new status with Olympic participation. But several Arab nations threatened to boycott the Games if Israel was permitted to compete. Thus, Israeli athletes had to wait until 1952.

The London Games are remembered for numerous superb athletic performances rather than any serious political disturbances. Having survived many years of war, people looked to the Games to provide some entertainment and diversion from the tragedies of recent times, and the '48 Games succeeded as never before. The Games were broadcast on television for the first time and watched by nearly one-half million people throughout Britain.

Holland's Fanny Blankers-Koen, who competed as a teenager in Berlin, waited out the war for her chance to collect four golds at the age of thirty. Seventeen-year-old schoolboy, Bob Mathias of the United States, won the most demanding of events, the decathlon. It was an event he'd never heard of until just a few months before the Games.

The British watched in amazement as an unknown from Czechoslovakia, Emil Zatopek, ran seemingly in pain, his face contorted, his style the worst they had seen. Yet, as the 10,000 meters progressed, Zatopek extended his lead to 48 seconds to beat Alain Mimoun of France, the largest victory margin in Olympic history.

HELSINKI 1952: Games of the XVth Olympiad

The Helsinki Games were opened by Finland's legendary distance hero, Paavo Nurmi, who carried the Olympic torch into the arena on the last leg of its trip from Greece. The fifty-five-year-old Nurmi drew a tumultuous roar and many tears from the crowd before he handed the torch to another Finnish distance legend, Hannes Kolehmainen, who ignited the Olympic flame atop the stadium tower.

West Germany was invited back into the Olympic fold and only minor political skirmishes marred the Games. Communist China showed up uninvited, but its forty athletes were allowed to compete. Several Eastern bloc nations separated their athletes in a very non-Olympic gesture. The Soviet team stayed on a ship, while Hungary, Poland, Bulgaria, Romania, and Czechoslovakia set up their private Olympic village where the athletes kept to themselves, away from the influences of the other athletes.

The Soviets entered the Games for the first time since 1912, and earned twenty-one gold medals. They provided the state of the art in wrestling, gymnastics, and weightlifting and showed great promise in track and field. Soviet newspapers claimed an overall Olympic victory by virtue of the total medal count, a claim which the American team refuted. Thus began a new dimension in the "Cold War" based on Olympic success.

IOC President Avery Brundage reprimanded both the USSR and the United States for political and nationalistic abuse of the Olympics, an event which was meant to supersede all national boundaries and to treat athletes as individuals.

Nearly 100 Olympic records were broken at Helsinki, which also became known as the Games of Emil Zatopek. Zatopek, a Czechoslovakian, won the 5,000 and 10,000 meters in Olympic record times, then entered the marathon, which he had never before run. Speeding along in his awkward, on-the-verge-of-collapse style, Zatopek collected his third gold medal of the Games, producing the only sweep of the three longest distances.

These were also the Games of decathlete Bob Mathias, who improved greatly upon his 1948 winning score and came through with a world record and a second successive Olympic gold.

MELBOURNE 1956: Games of the XVIth Olympiad

The Melbourne Games came during a period of worldwide political turmoil and it was inevitable that, despite the IOC's best efforts, politics would drift into the Olympic arena. The Suez Canal controversy had by this time exploded into a full-scale war and Egypt, Lebanon, and Iraq withdrew as a sign of protest.

Young Ron Clarke lights the 1956 Olympic flame high above the Melbourne cricket ground.

Communist China boycotted the Games to protest the Olympic Committee's recognition of Nationalist China, which sent no athletes anyway. The invasion of Hungary by the USSR sparked boycotts by Spain, the Netherlands, and Switzerland. Surprisingly, the Hungarian team did compete, even though many of its athletes had been forced to prepare for the Games under difficult conditions, while Soviet tanks took charge of Budapest.

The Hungarian team achieved a small measure of revenge when it beat the Soviets 4-0, in a water polo qualification match which, not surprisingly, was a vicious and vengeful game. The Soviet team had to be escorted under heavy guard from the pro-Hungarian crowd in the arena.

The German Democratic Republic had sought to reenter the Olympic Games since its exclusion following World War II. The IOC hesitated to grant membership to a state that was not recognized by a large part of the world. The IOC turned to member Karl Ritter von Halt to find a solution. For years, von Halt had dreamed of

Vladimir Kuts USSR leads Pirie and Ibbotson (both GBR) in 5,000 meters at Melbourne 1956.

reuniting West Germany and the German Democratic Republic (East Germany) under one flag.

Miraculously, he did just that, by negotiating an agreement under which both East and West Germany would compete in the Olympics as one team. Thus, German victors in 1956, and in the two subsequent Olympiads, received their medals under a compromise flag and a compromise "anthem," a hymn by Beethoven.

The first Games ever held in the southern hemisphere opened on November 22, off-season for the European and North American athletes. Vladimir Kuts of the USSR replaced Emil Zatopek as the iron man of distance running. Bobby Morrow of the United States achieved the first sprint double since Owens in 1936. Young Al Oerter, also of the United States, surprised the experienced discus favorites with his first Olympic win.

The Australian athletes did themselves proud in front of their hometown crowd. Led by Murray Rose and Dawn Fraser, Australian swimmers won eight

Following sprint double, Betty Cuthbert anchors Australia to win relay in Melbourne.

golds, while the rest of the world shared honors in the remaining five events. Betty Cuthbert from Sydney became the teenage heroine of the Games with a track sprint double and a third gold medal as anchor on Australia's relay team.

Laszlo Papp achieved his third successive boxing title. As a member of the Hungarian team, he received sympathy and the support of the crowd, who cheered his win on points over Jose Torres of the United States.

ROME 1960: Games of the XVIIth Olympiad

There was a merging of the ancient and the modern at the Rome Games. Many of the events were contested on historic soil where 2,000 years before the Romans held their sporting contests. The wrestling, for example, was held among the ruins of the Basilica di Massenzio.

Abebe Bikila of Ethiopia ran the fastest marathon ever, gliding barefoot, as gracefully as a deer, along the Appian Way, finishing at the Arch of Constantine. The imposing ruin of the ancient Baths of Caracalla was refurbished to hold 5,000 spectators. They watched as Larisa Latynina and others demonstrated the graceful art of gymnastics against a dramatic background.

The Rome Games set a new standard for Olympic splendor, with the Italians as perfect hosts. The world had settled down, fully recovered from World War II and various postwar disputes. The jet airplane transported more athletes than ever before. Over 5,337 from eighty-four nations competed. Performance standards had risen greatly and sport, not politics, was the essence of the Rome Games.

Lovely Larisa Latynina USSR won two all-around titles and seven more golds from 1956-64.

The story in track was the sweep of three middle-distance events by runners from the southern hemisphere. Within an hour, New Zealand's Peter Snell and Murray Halberg had won gold medals, which was quite remarkable considering New Zealand's remoteness and population of only three million.

Halberg won the 5,000 meters using a courageous kick with three laps to go and the 800 meters announced the arrival of the era of Snell's middle-distance supremacy, a reign which would extend beyond the Tokyo Games. Herb Elliott of Australia put on one of his renowned power surges with 600 meters left in the 1,500 meters and ran away from his opponents to win by an enormous 20-yard margin in a world record time of 3:35.6.

Wilma Rudolph of the United States left the field behind in winning the 100 meters in a world record 11.0 seconds. She went on to capture two more gold medals in the 200 meters and sprint relay. A young and confident Cassius Clay of the United States won the light-heavyweight boxing championship, and lovely Larisa Latynina of the USSR won medals in all six women's gymnastics events.

TOKYO 1964: Games of the XVIIIth Olympiad

Japan became the first Far Eastern nation to conduct the Games. The Japanese saw the Olympics as a chance to regain national esteem, which had suffered badly as a result of World War II, and they more than succeeded. Nearly $2 billion was spent for staging the Olympic events and hosting of the many foreign visitors.

The only political entanglement concerned South Africa and its racist policies for team selection. In 1956, a law was passed in South Africa requiring white and nonwhite athletes to be segregated with regard to team selection. In addition, no racially mixed teams were permitted to leave or enter the country.

To compete against a South African team, in a sense, implied acceptance of these segregation laws. With a rapidly growing number of black nations joining the Olympic movement, the IOC was pressed to ban South Africa from competing in Tokyo rather than risk a boycott by Third World nations.

Nevertheless, the Tokyo Olympics were described by journalists as the "Happy Games." The Japanese were brilliant organizers. All aspects of event productions were superlative and, as with every Olympics, there were superb athletic performances.

Abebe Bikila of Ethiopia made history by retaining his Olympic marathon championship. This time it was even more of a waltz than in Rome, as Bikila strode away from the field to win by more than four minutes.

Iolanda Balas of Romania collected her second high jump gold with 1.90 meters (6 ft. 2¾ in.), four inches higher than second place and just one centimeter under her world record.

Peter Snell of New Zealand achieved the ultimate in middle distance running, the 800 / 1,500-meter double. Al Oerter of the United States won his third straight discus title. At the ripe old age of twenty-seven, Dawn Fraser of Australia swam to

Dawn Fraser AUS won straight 100-meter freestyle titles in Melbourne, Rome and Tokyo.

victory in the 100-meter freestyle for the third consecutive time. Vera Caslavska of Czechoslovakia became the world's preeminent woman gymnast, collecting three golds.

MEXICO CITY 1968: Games of the XIXth Olympiad

In 1963, when the IOC selected Mexico City as the site of the 1968 Games, concern immediately arose about the 7,300-foot altitude of the ancient Aztec capital. Little was known about the effects of the thin air on endurance events. The possible physiological consequences to distance runners and swimmers evoked considerable alarm.

As usual, Avery Brundage made the IOC's position quite clear; "The Games belong to the world: hot and cold, dry and humid, high and low, east and west, north and south."

Most endurance runners resigned themselves to careful preparation, visiting high-altitude training camps to acclimate themselves to the thin air of Mexico City. Runners from the high plains of Kenya looked forward to the chance to perform at high altitude and sprinters everywhere anticipated their best performances on Mexico City's fast, synthetic track.

In the months before the opening of the Games, the organizing committee suffered through the threat of a simultaneous boycott by forty nations over South Africa's participation in the Games. In a practical step, the IOC voted to withdraw South Africa's invitation and finally dropped South Africa from the Olympics altogether in 1972. With another threat overcome, preparation for the Games went ahead confidently.

In the end, it was not the altitude nor a boycott, but Mexico's internal strife that almost led to the cancellation of the Games. For months there had been unrest in Mexico. National University students and their sympathizers demonstrated at the university, located directly across from the Estadio Olympico. They focused on their nation's poverty, their discontent with the regime, and the extravagance of the Games. As the Games drew near, the demonstrators garnered a worldwide audience for their cause.

On October 2, just ten days before opening day, a demonstration was called at the Plaza de las Tres Culturas and was attended by over 10,000 supporters. Suddenly, the army opened fire on the demonstrators, armed for such a conflict. In the ensuing five hours of street battle, the students and followers were overwhelmed. No one knows how many were killed. The government estimated a few dozen, but most other accounts placed the figure at 260 dead, thousands injured. There were no more demonstrations in Mexico; the opposition had been crushed.

Lee Evans, left, leads protest of 4x400-meter relay runners following USA win in 1968.

The era of the late sixties was marked by worldwide student unrest. In the United States, civil rights leader Martin Luther King was killed in the spring of 1968. In the early summer, the Democratic Convention in Chicago was disrupted by rioting. Student unrest focused on the United States' involvement in Southeast Asia.

Throughout the spring, a group of black athletes attempted to organize a U.S. Olympic team boycott to protest racial discrimination, in the United States and throughout the world. But the athletes eventually chose to attend the Games, where their cause would have an enormous audience.

Onto this stage stepped the finest sprinters the world had ever seen. The world record charts for sprints and relays would be completely revised in Mexico City. Among the record-breakers were Tommie Smith and Lee Evans, both San Jose State University students. They also shared a common background, having grown up in large families of farm laborers in California's Central Valley.

The hard physical labor produced many fine, strong athletes, who escaped the laborious cycle of poverty and despair, while giving other youngsters a spark of determination and hope for a more promising future by using their athletic talents.

Following brilliant victories in world record times, Smith at 200 meters, Evans over 400 meters, both chose to express their feelings toward their country, during the raising of the flag and playing of the anthem at their victory ceremonies.

On the 200-meter victory stand, Tommie Smith and bronze medalist John Carlos held their black-gloved fists aloft, their eyes cast downward. It was a militant posture that struck anger and fear into many spectators and, as intended, communicated to the United States by television, their feelings as blacks—their unity and power, their demand for change. The IOC acted swiftly and expelled Smith and Carlos from the Olympic village.

The United States swept all three medals in the 400 meters. On the victory stand, Lee Evans, Larry James, and Ron Freeman wore black berets and black socks, but refrained from the black-power salute. The three were also members of the 4 X 400-meter relay team which brought another gold medal on the final day of the Games and a second chance to communicate with the world from the victory platform.

The Mexico City Games were notable, not only for brilliant performances by the sprinters, but for the domination of distance running by athletes from Kenya. Few people noticed when Kip Keino and other Africans waved one finger, an African black power gesture and a further show of unity among black athletes. Keino ran an extraordinary 1,500 meters in the thin air of Mexico City. His 3:34.9 was an Olympic record that has withstood three 1,500-meter Olympic finals.

Bob Beamon of the United States turned in a climactic long jump of 8.90 meters (29 ft. 2½ in.) which surpassed the world record by an enormous margin and was justifiably described as the most astonishing athletic feat in history. Al Oerter produced the best throw of his long career, throwing the discus 64.78 meters (212 ft. 6½ in.), winning his fourth consecutive gold medal, the longest Olympic winning streak ever.

Vera Caslavska was crowned the queen of Mexico City. The glamorous Czech gymnast first captured the all-around event, then won three of the four apparatus finals for a total of four individual golds. In repeating her 100-meter victory, Wyomia

Tyus of the United States became the first sprinter, male or female, to capture back-to-back titles.

The 1968 Games were the first to be broadcast to the world via satellite. Television and the Olympics combined to bring the world together like never before.

MUNICH 1972: Games of the XXth Olympiad

The Munich Olympic Games began brilliantly. The training and competition facilities were the best in the world, set throughout Olympia Park adjacent to the Olympic village. The organization and officiating were the finest and the opening ceremony was the most spectacular ever. In light of the tragedy that followed, few remembered that these great successes were also part of the Munich Games.

It was 4:30 A.M. on September 5, when eight Palestinian terrorists from the "Black September" faction, dressed as athletes, broke into the Israeli quarters at the Olympic village. Some athletes escaped, two were killed in the ensuing struggle, and the nine who remained were held hostage until just after midnight the following night.

Throughout the ordeal, 15,000 spectators sat on the banks across from the Olympic village, their eyes glued to the position of the terrorists. The whole world, linked by television, waited for the drama to unfold. Throughout the Olympic village, athletes in the midst of their most important competition seemed stunned, almost uncomprehending, unable to ignore the tragedy, yet knowing they must put it out of their minds to compete.

Athletes tossed in their sleep as helicopters flew overhead, carrying the terrorists and hostages away from the village to an air force base on the outskirts of Munich, where the plane demanded by the terrorists was waiting.

German police, with the concurrence of the Israeli government, had no intention of allowing the terrorists to leave the country. Just before midnight, having awaited an opportune moment, German sharpshooters opened fire on the terrorists. Many terrorists were shot, but their leader managed to pull the pin on a hand grenade and lob it into the helicopter where the Israeli athletes were strapped into their seats, unable to escape a fiery death. Nine Israeli athletes, five terrorists, and a Munich policeman were killed at the airport.

At dawn, decathlon competitors, up early for a 10 A.M. start, heard the tragic news. They wondered if their event could possibly take place, but warmed up anyway. Instead, all events were postponed for twenty-four hours and athletes gathered at a memorial service hastily organized in the packed Olympic stadium.

Athletes assembled in the center of the arena, the Berlin Symphony played the funeral march from Beethoven's "Eroica" symphony, and Avery Brundage spoke. "We have only the strength of a great ideal. I am sure the public will agree that we cannot allow a handful of terrorists to destroy this nucleus of international cooperation and goodwill we have in the Olympic movement."

The following morning the Games went on, displaying cooperation and friendly competition, the true spirit of the Games, in spite of terrorist attempts to destroy it.

A few days later, Vince Matthews and Wayne Collett of the United States, who had gone 1-2 in the 400 meters, stood on the victory stand slouching and chatting, snubbing the all-important flag raising ceremony. Seeing this as another abuse of the Olympics for political reasons, the IOC suspended the pair for life from future Olympic competition.

Their suspension prevented the United States from forming a relay team for the 4 X 400 meters, in which they were overwhelming favorites. It also deprived their relay teammates, Lee Evans and a replacement for the injured John Smith, from almost certain gold medals. The suspension was a much greater punishment than had befallen Tommie Smith and John Carlos for their more militant demonstration on the Mexico City victory stand four years earlier.

Not everything at Munich was as depressing to the Olympic Movement. On the track, Lasse Viren showed the indomitable Finnish spirit of endurance with victories at 5,000- and 10,000-meters. Valeri Borzov proved himself the perfect running machine, achieving the coveted sprint double, the 100- and 200-meter gold medals.

In the pool, Mark Spitz won seven gold medals, more than anyone had ever achieved at a single Olympics. The United States lost its first Olympic basketball game to the Soviet Union, and the elfin beauty and charm of Olga Korbut created a worldwide passion for women's gymnastics.

The Munich Games were a splendid production. They were brilliantly organized, the facilities were perfect, and the Bavarian people were wonderfully hospitable. The athletes enjoyed the Games and were perhaps less affected by the tragedy than the general public, who had stared transfixed at their television screens as the tragedy unfolded. Munich stands alone in Olympic history as having suffered the most wanton and senseless of atrocities. Eleven young athletes, murdered in their prime.

MONTREAL 1976: Games of the XXIst Olympiad

In the four years between the Munich and Montreal Games, there was much media speculation about the future of the Olympics. When athletes and visitors left Munich, they passed through the massive security at the airport. Somehow, automatic weapons and the Olympic Games didn't go together.

In Montreal, construction delays and cost overruns proved most threatening to the Games. When Montreal was awarded the Games in 1970, Mayor Jean Drapeau said the city would conduct the Games without costing the taxpayers one penny. That was before poor management and labor troubles intervened.

Construction workers went on strike, causing work on the Olympic facilities to fall behind schedule and costing triple overtime pay to complete them in time for the opening ceremony. The construction site around Olympic Park was cleared a scant two weeks before the start of the Games.

As the events proceeded, a giant crane could be seen hovering over the stadium roof, which would remain unfinished. It stood as a symbol of mismanagement. The city was left with an enormous $1.3 billion debt, most of which was passed along to the taxpayers of Quebec.

As athletes and officials began to arrive in Montreal, unresolved political arguments began to rage. There was the pressure exerted by the Canadian government, a trading partner with the People's Republic of China, to prevent Taiwan from competing under the name Republic of China. Due to the political maneuvering, even United States' participation was threatened. Finally, Taiwan rejected a compromise and went home.

Then the problem of South Africa resurfaced, like a recurring nightmare for the IOC. Overnight, twenty black African nations and a few from the Caribbean, pressured by governments back home, withdrew. Some of the world's greatest distance runners packed their bags.

Officially, the countries withdrew because New Zealand had played a touring South African rugby team the previous winter. In reality, the Olympics were victim of large-scale international politics. African nations withdrew in order to place international focus on the apartheid policies of South Africa and further isolate them from the rest of the world. The withdrawal accomplished nothing, but saddened the hearts of millions of fans who wanted to see the great Africans run.

Perhaps Lasse Viren's task became a little easier without the presence of the athletes from Africa, but he seemed invincible anyway. He won the 5,000 and 10,000 meters, as he had in Munich, achieving a monopoly in distance running over two Olympiads. Then he tried his first marathon and stayed with the leaders for 30 kilometers before fading to fifth.

The darling of Montreal was fourteen-year-old Nadia Comaneci, who exhibited what gymnastics judges confirmed as perfect motion, scoring "10's" seven times during her sixteen routines. Nadia's performances thrilled the world and brought her three gold medals. Nikolai Andrianov was equally brilliant in men's gymnastics. The Soviet won four individual golds, including the all-around title.

The meteoric rise of the East German women, in swimming and track and field, was a major theme of the Montreal Games. Their swimmers had won nothing in Munich, but over a four year period of concerted national effort, they came to Montreal to win eleven of thirteen golds in women's swimming. In track, they improved on their already recognized prowess, capturing nine of fourteen golds and 50 percent of all medals.

Red Army soldiers display Misha the Moscow Games mascot, at 1980 opening ceremony.

MOSCOW 1980: Games of the XXIInd Olympiad

It was New Year's Eve of 1979, when word reached the United States that 80,000 Soviet troops had stormed across the Afghanistan border and spread out across the helpless country. The next day, West Germany called upon NATO countries to respond to the invasion with a combined boycott of the Moscow Games and two weeks later the United States and Britain, responding to this call, began discussing the possibilities of a boycott.

President Jimmy Carter sent Muhammed Ali as his special Olympic envoy to visit Africa and promote the boycott with those nations, where many resisted the idea. Amazingly, Ali's views changed during his mission and he decided against continuing his journey.

With the battle lines drawn, Lord Killanin, presiding over a February, 1980 IOC meeting, said, "The very existence of the Olympic Games, the Olympic movement, and the organization of sports is at stake."

When President Carter's deadline for the Soviets to withdraw from Afghanistan expired on February 20, Carter told the world, "Our decision is irrevocable, we will not participate."

So, for the first time in Olympic history, the United States stayed home. More than thirty other nations also chose to boycott the Games, including powerful teams from West Germany and Japan. The boycott had an enormous effect on the outcome of the events, but did little about the Soviet presence in Afghanistan.

The USSR spent $9 billion to stage the Games and impress the athletes, media, and television viewers of the world. The entire look of Moscow was altered in the process.

Alcoholism, a major problem in Moscow, compelled the authorities to remove all drunks from the streets and intern them in camps out in the countryside. Many young children were sent to traditional summer camps, but many believe it was actually an effort to shield the young Soviets from the influence of Western athletes and visitors. The USSR completely dominated gold medals with eighty. East Germany earned forty-seven and Eastern bloc nations earned the next four places in the medal count.

From an athletic point of view, the Moscow Games were held in first class facilities and produced some brilliant performances. Britain's Sebastian Coe and Steve Ovett each won a middle distance event, their dramatic 800- and 1,500-meter duels attracting the most media attention. Aging Miruts Yifter won the 5,000 / 10,000-meters double, having waited eight years between Olympic Games due to the Ethiopian boycott in Montreal.

The top gymnast was Alexandr Ditiatin of the USSR, who won a medal in each of the eight men's events, the most medals ever won by an individual in any sport at a single Olympics. East German women again dominated the swimming, winning eleven of thirteen events as they had four years earlier. They swept six events, claiming gold, silver, and bronze awards.

Sara Simeoni of Italy, Olympic high jump champion, Moscow 1980.

Steve Ovett GBR defeats teammate Sebastian Coe in Moscow 800 meters final.

Teofilo Stevenson of Cuba duplicated Laszlo Papp's previously unique boxing accomplishment, winning his third straight Olympic title.

During the evening closing ceremonies of August 4, the Moscow Olympic flame was extinguished. The president of the IOC, Lord Killanin, stood in the center of a hushed Lenin stadium, and declared the Games of the XXIInd Olympiad closed. As required by tradition, he called upon the youth of all countries to assemble in four years in Los Angeles. But, for a few words he departed from the required text and implored, "the sportsmen of the world to unite in peace before the holocaust descends."

As the Olympic Games of 1984 approach, the four-year frantic cycle of media and political hype resumes. That the Games survive gives testimony to the strength of the ideal on which the Games were founded. The Olympic ideal survives because the human search for excellence always seeks a way to test its achievements. The world loves sports; the vast majority of people still believe the money and effort of staging the Games is worthwhile. During each Olympiad there are those who dedicate themselves to bringing athletes of all nations together once again.

5

LOS ANGELES 1984
—THE HOST CITY

— 5 —

Los Angeles is the largest of a cluster of cities that merge to form Southern California's great urban expanse. Set on a wide coastal plain and encircled by tall mountains, the megalopolis spreads up and down the Pacific coast, spills into adjacent valleys, and supports a total population of 12 million.

The youthful energy of its people and the climate combine to make Los Angeles one of the world's sports capitals. Sports can be played year-round and people can be found enjoying every type of recreation and fitness activity. The invigorating environment produces far more than its share of Olympic athletes, as well as those who fill the ranks in all professional sports.

It seems Los Angeles has always been an Olympic city. In 1923, it was appointed to host the 1932 Games. Before those Games were over, many Southern Californians were working to bring the Olympics back.

After World War II, a plethora of cities lined up to host the Olympic Games, so Los Angeles would have to wait its turn. For many years, Detroit was favored over Los Angeles by the United States Olympic Committee (USOC) for the right to bid for the Games as the sole U.S. representative. Following the incidence of terrorism in Munich (1972) and the gigantic financial burden of Montreal (1976), the line of potential Olympic hosts suddenly got very short. In October, 1977, after Teheran withdrew, Los Angeles was left as the only candidate willing to host the 1984 Games.

In October, 1978, the contract was finally signed awarding the Games of the XXIIIrd Olympiad to Los Angeles. The deal was concluded despite the refusal of the Los Angeles city government, acting on public referendum, to provide the financial responsibility required by IOC rules. The 1984 Games are, therefore, privately financed, supported only by U.S. business interests.

Olympic venues are dispersed throughout the Greater Los Angeles area. Sixteen of the twenty-one official sports will be held within a twenty-five mile radius of the Coliseum, the hub of activity. The outlying venues, Lake Casitas (rowing and canoeing) and Coto de Caza (modern pentathlon), are separated by over 140 road miles.

Only two new facilities were built specifically for the Games. These are the Olympic velodrome on the campus of California State University, Dominguez Hills, which is the only world-class cycling facility west of the Rocky Mountains, and the new swimming stadium on the campus of the University of Southern California.

The Los Angeles Coliseum, the first stadium to twice be principal Olympic venue.

New Olympic pool at USC campus.

Both were built with funds provided by corporate sponsors: Southland Corporation paying for the velodrome and McDonald's donating the pool.

Many other venues, especially the Coliseum, were badly in need of refurbishing to become satisfactory sites for the Games. The Coliseum is a very old stadium and the site of many prestigious athletic events during its sixty year history. But a stadium sustains a lot of wear and tear, and the Coliseum is not one of the more glamorous places to host an Olympic Games.

Of the millions of dollars spent by Atlantic Richfield (ARCO) to renovate the Coliseum, most went into upgrading the stadium floor, the field, and the synthetic track, to the highest level possible. Otherwise, the Coliseum is not spectacular, but rather a utilitarian stadium, built inexpensively a long time ago to hold a lot of people.

The Coliseum stands as a symbol of the low-budget Olympics. It is no match for the stadiums of recent Games, especially the architectural accomplishments of Munich and Montreal, monuments to an era of unnecessary Olympic extravagance.

The Coliseum stands a few miles from south-central Los Angeles, the site of the infamous Watts riots of 1965. Although tremendous improvements have been made, the area still remains a troubled place, a far different picture from that which visitors have come to expect from the Hollywood image of Los Angeles.

Perhaps such problems are inherent in the nation's second largest urban area. A short drive south of the Coliseum reveals much urban decay. Boarded up windows, run-down buildings, and many street residents with little hope for jobs and proper housing. The unemployment rate among black teenagers in Watts is extremely high, and you won't see many buying tickets to the Games which will be taking place in their neighborhood. Aware of this problem, Olympic organizers chose to distribute 100,000 free tickets to disadvantaged youths and will utilize Olympic athletes to explain the excitement of the Games in neighborhood schools.

To the west of the downtown area the prosperity of the neighborhoods tends to increase. Westwood, where UCLA is situated and where half the athletes will stay, is surrounded by the most affluent areas. The beach communities exhibit the relaxed lifestyle that thrives at the edge of the sparkling Pacific. At freeway exits along the way to the scattered Olympic venues, franchise restaurants and palatial shopping centers display Southern California's mobile world-class economy which continues to exert a magnetic attraction on people everywhere.

Los Angeles is one of the most ethnically diverse cities in the world, a melting pot of energetic peoples attracted by hopes of a better life in the sunshine. At the time of the 1932 Games, Los Angeles was filled mainly with white Americans of European ancestry, who had drifted west, driven by the Hollywood image and the hope of work in the productive environment. Since then, more than ten million people have been attracted to happy, sunny, Southern California and its zestful economy. The bursting energy of its people make for an innovative society, recognized worldwide as a trendsetter.

In 1960, only one in nine L.A. county residents was Hispanic. Today, one-half of the population is Hispanic. Of the almost eight million residents in Los Angeles county, one million are Asians, a fourfold increase since 1970. Since 1970 more than two million people, many from of the most exotic parts of the globe, have settled in Los Angeles. There are Japanese, Korean, Thai, and Filipino neighborhoods, often existing as separate cultural enclaves. As a result, every type of national cuisine can be found.

The Los Angeles Olympic Organizing Committee (LAOOC) was formed to take on the gigantic task of organizing the 1984 Games. It is an ever-growing entity, built from scratch by Peter Ueberroth with the sole purpose of producing a fifteen-day sports extravaganza, and then dissolving itself. The growth of the LAOOC can be compared with the task of building a Fortune 500 sized corporation in just five years.

Ueberroth has gathered some of Southern California's top-flight executives on his blue-ribbon management team. Through the sale of television rights, funding from over thirty major sponsors, a coin program with the U.S. Treasury, and ticket sales, the LAOOC has projected a half-billion dollar budget with which to conduct the Games.

At one time, Ueberroth was hopeful of a $100 million profit. But he soon discovered the cost of getting things done is always more than expected. The organization, having grown larger than anticipated, grew out of its first administrative building at UCLA into a former aircraft hangar in Venice.

Cost estimates for security have continued to escalate. The LAOOC has said it will pay only for what it orders, but pressures exist to buy more and more security services. However, the organizers say, they will not reimburse any of the massive $68.9 million the federal government budgeted for the Games, ($18.9 million for security services and $50 million for military contingencies). The Reagan Administration says providing this protection is part of the nation's reasonable responsibility to the Games.

It is estimated that close to 17,000 security personnel could be employed to deal with problems as varied as traffic tangles to threats of terrorism. The LAOOC plans to hire 3,300 people to provide security inside Olympic venues, villages, and official vehicles.

Security planning is of such Olympian proportions that it involves dozens of agencies from local, county, state, and federal levels. All are engaged in planning for various scenarios, and working out jurisdictional responsibilities, such as which agency will react to what problems. In reality, it's virtually impossible to anticipate how terrorism may strike. The Federal Bureau of Investigation (FBI) is conducting pre-Olympic intelligence in the hope of predicting sources of danger. But, an open city like Los Angeles is very vulnerable, perhaps even indefensible and, in the end, it will probably be the quick-reacting local police who will be on the front line if problems occur.

Optimists point out there has been only one act of terrorism in Olympic history. Peter Ueberroth says the Olympics are merely a series of sports competitions and hopes this understanding will lower everyone's anxiety and help people focus on the positive aspects of the Olympic festival.

In his job as president of the LAOOC, Ueberroth is a prime target for the mud-slinging and political flak that is aimed at the Olympics. He seems to have done a good job at defending the Games. This is clearly demonstrated by the flood of U.S. blue-chip corporations that have joined the Olympic partnership. Indeed, it is Ueberroth's ability to arrange innovative financing for the Games that is his greatest asset. With financial projections well in the black, the majority of the logistical problems solved, and their public image very positive, there is only one major source of concern for the LAOOC—the specter of boycott.

At the time of the Moscow Games in 1980, Los Angeles had been the designated host of the 1984 Olympics for almost two years. It seems surprising that the Soviet Union, deeply injured by the U.S.-led renouncement of their Games, has not seriously threatened to boycott Los Angeles. However, the Soviets have yet to formally accept the invitation to compete, and will probably postpone the decision until the June 2, 1984 deadline. Peter Ueberroth said it was within their rights to wait to respond, yet, "many nations, to be helpful, will accept their invitations earlier."

One source of comfort was the $3 million television contract signed by Soviet broadcasters in August, 1983. Marrat Gramov, President of the Soviet Olympic Committee, has said, if the Soviets do not come to Los Angeles, it will be because of problems of security, not punishment of the United States for its boycott of the Moscow Games. The Soviets have a great deal to gain from Olympic competition. Their entire sports system is based on the incentives provided to youth, and the opportunity to show the world their national athletic prowess through the unofficial medal count.

Still, there are limits. In the period following the downing of Korean Airlines flight 007, U.S. public animosity arose toward the USSR. Soviet sports teams canceled planned rowing and volleyball events in California. Los Angeles organizers hope no international incident of such negative proportions will occur in the final months preceding the Games. Otherwise, the Soviets seem certain to attend.

Another distant rumble was heard from China in early 1983. Peking suspended all cultural and athletic exchanges with the United States for twelve months, following the defection of China's top female tennis player in the spring. The threat to the Olympics was obvious, causing anxiety within the organizing committee concerning the possible withdrawal of China from the Games. The return of China to the Olympic fold is one of the greatest accomplishments of the Los Angeles Games. The success of an Olympic Games is measured by the number of nations participating, as is the performance of the host city.

In 1932 China brought one participant to Los Angeles. A few Chinese athletes were entered in 1952. But for thirty years, nearly one fifth of the world's people has not been represented in the Games. China's participation in 1984 will be an important milestone in the Olympic Movement. The Chinese are probably as anxious to enter the Games as Los Angeles is to have them. With many great athletes to exhibit, they will contend for many medals, particularly in gymnastics, volleyball, and diving. The LAOOC, and Olympic fans everywhere, can only wait, hoping for an improved climate in international affairs.

The task of actually producing 220 world-class sports events, and handling all the athletes and spectators, is incredibly complex. It requires use of the latest management techniques and state-of-the-art information systems. It is estimated that 12,000 people will be hired for the month of the Games.

Los Angeles is famous for its climate, the movie industry, aerospace technology, and freeways. The freeways are comprised of over 700 miles of concrete and asphalt arteries that will carry the majority of Olympic athletes and spectators to their events. These fifty-five mile per hour conveyor belts of bumper-to-bumper vehicles can prove quite intimidating to any out-of-towner.

Since the freeway experience is becoming a way of life in most U.S. cities, it's the uninitiated foreign visitor who should be most careful. He should be prepared, without warning, to face a sudden unmoving wall of red brake lights of the famous and deadly "stop and go" traffic.

Without a doubt, the Olympic Games will bring more traffic to Los Angeles than ever before. Already there are more vehicles per capita in Los Angeles than any other place on earth and the freeways are choked to capacity. Some fear that Olympic traffic conditions will be awful, perhaps disastrous. Others point out the main venues are regularly full of spectators for football, baseball, and basketball, and perhaps many people will stay off the streets to watch the ceremonies and various finals on television.

Most venues are so well dispersed that the effect on traffic will be slight. The real problem spot will be the vicinity of the Coliseum where three events, athletics, boxing, and swimming, will take place, with the village and press center nearby. As it is, traffic becomes clogged on nearby freeways on a daily basis as commuters go to and from work in the downtown business centers. Efforts have been made to schedule events around the work hours, but it isn't possible to avoid the enormous convergence of vehicles that the Olympics will bring.

The well-prepared Olympic spectator must have a detailed set of maps. Freeways may be choked with traffic, but wide surface streets which parallel them offer alternative, sometimes faster routes. The successful Olympic visit requires an ingenious navigator.

The main form of Olympic transportation is the jet aircraft. It's fortunate that the biggest construction job in local history, the $700 million terminal renovation at LAX, was completed just in time and on budget. Practically every athlete and visitor must fly the busy skyways to get to Los Angeles. The Olympics will bring a much needed boom to the airline industry, highlighting the commercial impact of the Games. United Airlines can benefit from the association with the 1984 Olympics, and through a very unique business arrangement, help provide the funds required to host them.

THE CORPORATE GAMES

The Los Angeles Olympic Games are the first to be funded solely through private enterprise, independent of government subsidy. The projected $472 million operating budget is being provided by television revenue, sponsorship income, and ticket sales. Should the LAOOC make a profit, it is required to allocate the surplus to the development of Olympic sport.

While some of the recent Olympic Games have cost billions of dollars, Los Angeles is unique in already having most of the world-class sports facilities needed. As a result, it will be the least expensive Olympics in two decades, although little of the Olympic splendor will be missing.

The American Broadcasting Company (ABC) is paying $225 million for U.S. television rights and to produce the signal that the LAOOC sells to foreign broadcasters. The European Broadcasting Union (EBU) and Japan each have chipped-in $20 million. The LAOOC is charging according to a country's capacity to pay; thus the forty-three nations of an African broadcasting consortium are getting their rights for a bargain $200,000. Not all income is retained by the LAOOC. One-third of the television revenues go to the IOC.

Television has been a major partner in the Olympic Games since Rome (1960), although some of the Games were broadcast throughout Britain as early as 1948. The 1936 Games were shown through an experimental closed-circuit system in Berlin. It was not until 1968, however, that significant coverage was received in the United States and began to attract the imagination of a huge audience.

ABC raised the ante to $15.5 million for U.S. rights to broadcast the Munich Games. The audience sat transfixed throughout sixty-six hours of coverage, athletic triumph, and human tragedy, providing two weeks of riveting programming that received enormous ratings. ABC also had a chance to promote its new fall season shows. Its sudden growth from the perennial third network to number one has often been attributed to the ability of the Olympic telecast to change the network's image and influence viewing habits.

ABC increased its coverage to seventy-nine and a half hours, paid $25 million for the rights to the 1976 Games, and remained number one in the ratings. Shortly thereafter, the National Broadcasting Corporation (NBC) entered the bidding for the 1980 Games and finally won the rights to the Moscow Olympics with an offer of $85 million. However, the network's plan for 150 hours of coverage was demolished by the boycott. Although an insurance policy with Lloyds of London offset a reported $50 million of the loss, the boycott cost NBC dearly.

The rights deal for the 1984 Games was concluded on September 26, 1979, three months before the USSR invaded Afghanistan. The subsequent boycott showed the great risk of Olympic television. Producing the Games on home turf greatly reduces ABC's risk and the network has shown nothing but satisfaction with its opportunity to broadcast the Games once again.

By the start of the Games, the '84 Olympics will be the most thoroughly promoted event in history. During prime time telecasts, other networks might as well take the night off. The Los Angeles Olympics are expected to attract a huge audience.

ABC hopes to recoup its $225 million rights fee and enormous production costs with the sale of some of the highest priced commercials in history. Hundreds of prime time spots are virtually sold out at prices as high as $250,000. This compares with the record $400,000 paid for thirty seconds during the 1983 Super Bowl. ABC expects to sell in excess of $600 million worth of time for its coverage of both winter and summer Games, about equal to the cost of rights and production. What ABC stands to gain during the 187½ hours of Olympic broadcasting is mostly continued prestige and a chance to promote new shows. In terms of its vast scope and technical ingenuity, ABC's coverage will be an historical achievement in the field of communications.

U.S. viewers will be bombarded with approximately 2,000 commercials. The Olympic fan will experience the largest sales assault that consciousness can endure, with up to twelve minutes of commercials an hour.

Television serves the Olympics not only as a business partner, but as a contributor to the Olympic ideal of communicating across national boundaries. Television unites the world and it is estimated some 2.5 billion people, more than half the world's population, will view some of the Olympic events. The television medium is inextricably tied to the modern Games. In fact, much of the Los Angeles schedule has been designed with prime time television in mind. Many of the important finals begin in the early evening in Los Angeles, prime time on the East Coast.

Much of the representation of the Olympics is in the hands of a television director, who ultimately decides what goes on the air. This might tend to fuel the politicization of the Olympics at the expense of pure sport, as commentators tend to relish political saga and international intrigue. The imbalance in the exposure of various sports is another problem.

ABC's 1976 Montreal telecast had almost no coverage of archery, handball, shooting, soccer, yachting, or hockey, along with many other sports considered "minor" in the United States. Equally exasperating to the purist is the lack of first time sports coverage, versus the endless repeats of the highlight events. Still, for the Olympic fan, the telecast offers a rich indulgence in exciting action—the most covered event in history.

With less than a year to go, the LAOOC was well in front of its income projections. Peter Ueberroth's greatest contribution has been his ability to sell the Olympic Games to major U.S. corporations. Thirty-two sponsors have signed up at a minimum fee of $4 million to join this most exclusive sports club in history. The sponsorship agreement allows each corporation to exploit the 1984 Olympic Games through the use of LAOOC symbols in its advertising, marketing, and promotional activities. The symbols of the 1984 Olympics, the "Star-In-Motion" and "Sam the Eagle" (the official mascot) will appear on everything from Snickers candy bars to Buick automobiles.

The Coca-Cola Company and Anheuser-Busch are among the corporations who have paid premium prices for sponsorship rights. Cans will carry the Star-In-Motion as a stamp of excellence. Coca-Cola has been supporting the Olympic movement since 1928 when a boatload of soft drinks showed up in Amsterdam to quench the thirst of athletes. The company has also been a consistent and major contributor to the U.S. Olympic Team. "There is no better way," said a Coca-Cola executive, "for our company to align ourselves with youth and healthy activity."

Many corporate sponsorship fees were designated for specific tasks. Atlantic Richfield Company (ARCO) was one of the first on board, paying $9 million to become the Games' official petroleum products. Much of this fee went to refurbishing the Coliseum and providing nine other synthetic surfaces for nearby running tracks to serve as training facilities during the Games. Southland Corporation, the Dallas-based owners of 7 Eleven convenience stores, provided the funds to build the Olympic cycling velodrome at California State University, Dominguez Hills. McDonald's Corporation built the Olympic pool at the University of Southern California (USC). During the Games however, no corporate signage whatsoever is allowed inside the venues.

Other corporations will provide less permanent, but equally important services for the Games. Levi Strauss Company, the official outfitter, will provide uniforms for the tens of thousands of officials and also outfit the U.S. Team through a separate agreement with the USOC. In return, Levi's will market a leisurewear line emblazoned with Olympic symbols.

American Telephone and Telegraph will manage the torch relay run, assuming the responsibility of escorting the Olympic flame across the continent to the opening ceremony in Los Angeles. Pacific Telephone designed and installed the telephone system for the Games. Transamerica will provide insurance coverage, Xerox will supply the official copiers, IBM the Olympic information system, and Sports Illustrated will publish the official souvenir program. Vons supermarket will supply $15 million worth of food, at cost, to feed the athletes in the Olympic village. Meanwhile, Arrowhead will provide mountain spring drinking water to quench their thirst.

The LAOOC is anticipating total income from corporate sponsorships to reach $150 million, far exceeding original projections. Corporate America was extremely enthusiastic about joining the Olympic effort, sharing a sense that the 1984 Games will be a "happening." It is the world's most enormous media event, something which may never happen again in this country. For a corporation, it provides a chance to tie-in with an historical event while preventing competitors from doing the same.

The "Star-In-Motion" will certainly be the most imposing symbol of 1984, adorning countless products, pieces of paper, and video images throughout the months of build-up to the Games. The use of the symbol denotes membership in an exclusive club which brings the benefit of association with other prestigious companies, carefully selected to be noncompetitive. Only one company can fulfill a product category, and each is among the top companies in its field. Membership is both image-building and practical. It opens doors, fuels joint promotions, and allows corporate chieftains to go to the Games in style. But most importantly, the association with the Olympics is designed to sell products.

The LAOOC sponsorship fee, however, is just the first payment. Companies must also communicate their Olympic association to the public. Coca-Cola, perhaps the most experienced of companies in the Olympic marketplace, has a total Olympic budget of about $74 million, much of which pays for commercial spots on the telecast and the production of Olympic advertising. Buying television time on ABC is almost obligatory. It wouldn't do to let a competitor sponsor the broadcast of the Games after contributing money to ensure their success.

Fuji Film, having become the official film with the LAOOC, was out-bid by Kodak for ABC commercial time. Now Kodak, an official sponsor of the telecast, gets to use the ABC Olympic logo which incorporates the Star-In-Motion.

The majority of sponsors have purchased the LAOOC logo, the television time, as well as sponsorship of the U.S. Olympic Team. ARCO didn't expect to sponsor the team until it realized Mobil Oil might step in to help the USOC.

The USOC pays the bills for preparing and managing the United States Olympic Team and has thirty-seven sponsors of its own. Sponsors acquire the rights to use the USOC symbol which incorporates the five rings and also establishes Olympic identity.

Both Kodak Cameras and Fuji Film have signed up as sponsors of the U.S. Team. Anheuser-Busch is the official beer sponsor of the team, while Miller Brewing Company sponsors the Olympic training centers. The USOC is trying to fund an $80 million budget, $15 million of which is spent by national federations in developing each Olympic sport. The United States has the only major national Olympic committee which is independent of continuous government funding. In order to make its way in the free enterprise system, the USOC markets its symbols in the corporate world. It's a four-year opportunity to promote a company's image as a supporter of U.S. team preparation and the most direct form of assistance to the athletes.

THE PROGRAM

The events on each Olympic Games program are fixed by the IOC. Only sports played in at least fifty countries and on three continents may be included. In each Olympiad the IOC, in consultation with the international federations, may delete some events and add others.

There have been considerable changes in the Olympic program throughout eighty-eight years. Only six sports have been part of all Olympic games since 1896: athletics, swimming, cycling, rowing, gymnastics, and fencing. Until 1924, the events on the program fluctuated greatly, particularly due to the influence of the host organizers.

Among the events no longer on the Olympic program are:

Rugby

An official sport four times from 1896 to 1924.

Motorboat Race

Tried once in 1908 and discontinued. The only race in Olympic history in which mechanical power was used.

Cricket and Croquet

Each held once as official events in Paris (1900). Another form of croquet called Roque was contested in St. Louis in 1904.

Tug of War

A regular part of the athletics program from 1896 through 1920.

Throwing with Both Hands

In the shot, discus, and javelin events, the best right- and left-handed throws of each contestant were added together. This was tried only in 1912.

Polo

This sport was adopted five times in 1900, 1908, 1920, 1924, and 1936.

Twelve hour Cycling Race

This race was contested just once, on the 1896 program. It is the longest endurance event in Olympic history.

Golf

Introduced in 1900. Also included in the 1904 Games, then discontinued.

Swimming

An underwater swim was contested in 1900. In 1904, there was a plunge for distance.

DEMONSTRATION SPORTS: 1984

The demonstration of two sports not on the Olympic program can be conducted under the auspices of the host organizing committee, with the approval of the IOC. The last Olympics to have demonstration sports was Munich in 1972, where badminton and water skiing were contested. Los Angeles has chosen baseball and tennis demonstrations. No official Olympic medals are awarded in the demonstration sports.

Baseball

There have been six previous demonstrations of baseball, but the sport was never accepted to full Olympic status. This could finally occur in 1988. Six national teams have been selected for the 1984 tournament: United States, Korea, Cuba, Chinese Taipei, Nicaragua, and Italy.

Although baseball is considered the national pastime in the United States, it is Cuba that has the best amateur team in the world. They proved it again in the 1983 Pan Am Games, where Nicaragua beat the United States and finished second. Korea won the 1982 world championships in Seoul, an event Cuba decided not to attend.

The final 1984 Game is scheduled for August 7, at Dodger Stadium. The 56,000 capacity stadium is already sold out.

Tennis

Tennis was an official Olympic sport from 1896 to 1924, and is already accepted for Olympic competition in 1988.

Thirty-two players will compete in both men's and women's tournaments in 1984, held at the new UCLA tennis stadium. All must be twenty years or younger, with no regard to professional or amateur status. This innovative event marks an important step in the recognition that professionalism and the Olympic Games can coexist. As a result, some of the most highly ranked young tennis players will perform, including Andrea Jaeger of the United States and Mats Wilander of Sweden.

Among the official medal sports in Los Angeles, seventeen events have been added since the Moscow Games, bringing the total to 220 events in twenty-one official sports. The most significant additions are in women's events. They include three arduous events in track and field: 3,000 meters, marathon, and 400-meter hurdles. Women will get their first Olympic cycling event on the road. Rhythmic gymnastics will open the sport to greater artistic expression rather than risky acrobatics. Synchronized swimming is a new and popular addition to the aquatics program.

New events in the men's and mixed classes include a seventh yachting class, boardsailing; four new shooting events, three for women. Additionally, boxing, canoeing, and cycling have each grown by one event, and three former swimming events have been reinstated to Olympic stature.

OLYMPIC ARTS PROGRAM

In the ancient Olympic Games, there were competitions of art, music, and poetry. This tradition was resumed in Stockholm (1912) and continued until the 1948 London Olympics. Thereafter, numerous art forms have been exhibited in association with the Games, but the competitive format has been abandoned.

Beginning June 1, 1984, a variety of dance and theater performances, concerts, and exhibitions of art and film will be held under the Olympic banner. Over 200 events will be held in conjunction with the Los Angeles Games, featuring artists and performers on a worldwide scale as diverse as the Games themselves.

There will be an exhibition of French impressionistic paintings, a performance of London's Royal Opera, the Ballet Folklorico de Mexico, Kodo the demon drummers of Japan, and possibly Russia's Moiseyev dance company. The finale will be a pre-Olympic gala at the Hollywood Bowl featuring the Los Angeles Philharmonic Orchestra under the direction of Michael Tilson Thomas on July 27, the evening before the opening ceremony.

6

FASTER, HIGHER, STRONGER

— 6 —

"Citius, Altius, Fortius"; "Faster, Higher, Stronger." The Olympic motto expresses the desire which drives men and women to continually seek to redefine the boundaries of their athletic performances. This never-ending exploration of mankind's ultimate limits in speed, skill, strength, and endurance has resulted in his ability to run faster than 27 miles per hour, leap over 7 feet 9¾ inches, and lift 574 pounds.

Record books show an endless progression of improving performances throughout the eighty-eight years of Olympiads. There seems to be no end to the advance with no limits yet in sight. Undoubtedly, the competitors in Los Angeles will continue this quest, producing many Olympic and world records.

What are the limits? Common sense tells most of us there must be an ultimate performance beyond which man cannot go, but the pace of advancement has yet to slow. In the past, experts who attempted to predict ultimate performances found their prognostications quickly surpassed. The truly great athlete has no sense of limit, only the determined desire to better the last performance.

The Olympic athlete is an extremist. He explores every avenue in order to improve his performance and strain his physiology to the limit. The coach is only a scientific observer and motivator. He is not a participant in the Olympic adventure. Ultimately, it is the individual athlete who must decide the worth of the quest, the price he is willing to pay for success.

The years of training are not only for that one moment of glory and achievement. Along the way, the athlete achieves pleasure and renewed desire from those exquisite moments when a new advance in personal performance brings the awareness of growing strength and skill. These experiences are frequent rewards as the young athlete develops. Daily, he indulges in the joy of physical motion, an expression of the pure exuberance of youth.

Great champions relish the adventure. In Olympic competition, they condense the years of preparation into a final act of perfection, bringing all their intellectual and physical resources together in a symphony of powerful motion.

The pursuit of physical excellence is the most human of all instincts. It defines the species and assures survival. This is the essence of the Games. It is for this reason the Greeks created the Olympics and the modern world revived them. The athletes are pioneers, charting new frontiers of human capability. But, the price of excellence is very high.

In the early days of the Olympic movement, the athletes' approach toward training was casual. At one time, it was possible to train only three days a week and still achieve the skill level necessary to compete at the Olympic Games. In fact, it was considered "ungentlemanly" to push the body too hard.

When Harold Abrahams employed the services of a professional coach to improve his chances of winning the sprint championship in Paris (1924), the athletic world was aghast and his coach was barred from entering the stadium. Today, the training and preparation undertaken by a prospective Olympic medalist is unrelenting. And, as the athletes attempt to increase the training effort to a maximum, they reach a limit, the point at which the body begins to break down.

Gymnasts practice endless, repetitive exercise units, molding difficult movements into their routines. The hours spent are limited only by the constraints of muscle, joint, and ligament. There is a finite limit at which recurring injuries will retard progress. Gymnasts, competing for Olympic honors, will often be seen with their ankles or wrists taped, reflecting the demands imposed on these critical joints that are over-strained by the demands of the sport.

The modern marathon runner thrives on hard work and is only limited by the ability of the joints and tendons in his legs to endure the endless pounding against street and track. Running a hundred miles or more in training every week, year after year, takes a great toll. Many distance runners have scars from Achilles tendon surgery to prove it.

The sport of swimming provides another example where hard work and discipline are exploited to the maximum. Swimmers probably spend more time in training than any athlete. Since the swimmer is practically weightless in the pool, there is less risk of injury, although swimmers normally wear goggles to protect their eyes from chlorinated water. The limits, in this case, come from a swimmer's ability to endure hard work and the monotony of six hours a day in the pool. They swim more than 400 laps daily and perform various combinations to promote speed, technique, and endurance.

Decathlon athletes must deal with the stress of practicing and performing ten different events. Because of the endless absorption of shock and the resultant wear and tear on the joints, most decathletes must limit their training programs to less than three hours daily. Each sport or event has its inherent point of diminishing returns, when accumulative soreness and injury curtail the ability to train on successive days. It's possible a majority of Olympic decathlon competitors "call it quits" when recurring injuries finally cloud their futures.

Often, athletes are plagued by continuing minor injuries. Strains that would hardly be noticeable in every day circumstances prevent an athlete from operating at that 100 percent level required in Olympic competition. The athlete's body, composed of joints, ligaments, and tendons, seems to have a limited durability. Yet advancements in sports medicine and carefully structured rehabilitation programs allow each generation of athletes to get more out of themselves. These programs, combined with the bigger, stronger athletes of each generation, lead to continually improving performances.

Because of improved diets, individuals everywhere are stronger and taller than their recent ancestors. The world is better fed, since many nations have vastly increased the availability of protein in their diets. Japanese youngsters, for example, grow an average of five inches taller than their parents as a result of changes in dietary habits following World War II.

Worldwide, significant changes in human development are underway. The acceleration of growth is accompanied by a lengthening life span. Children mature faster. An average-sized British youth does not even fit into the suit of armor worn by medieval knights. The physiques of those champions of gallantry, at that time the finest examples of manhood, averaged little over five feet tall. The current generation of youth is the tallest and strongest in history.

Today's athletes work harder because the rewards for excellence are greater than ever. In many socialist countries, principally the USSR, Cuba, and China, as well as in Eastern European nations, Olympic sport is at the center of a vast governmental network of athletes, coaches, trainers, and bureaucrats.

Success within the system brings opportunity for advancement in all aspects of life. In these countries, sports are seen as the responsibility of the central government. Thus, sports schools, training facilities, and coaching systems are promoted and financed by the state, and the successful athletes are well rewarded. Eastern European athletes seem driven by a sense of duty instilled by the system, as well as by the benefits accrued from athletic achievement.

Perhaps the East Germans have developed the most notable example of governmental control of sport. Over the past thirty years, they have continued to regard fitness and sport as a national priority, making it an essential part of the educational system. It is said that over thirty-five percent of the population is involved in an active recreational program and fifty percent of all teenagers compete in organized sports.

In the West, the approach is less structured. In the United States, sport is part of the entertainment industry. The broad scale high school and college programs are the strength of the U.S. system. Until recently, graduation cast many Olympians out of their training systems, forcing them to rely on their own resources.

The United States Olympic Committee (USOC) has upgraded the development effort in many sports, allowing more athletes to continue in competition after graduation. But, much remains to be done. The stimulus for most athletes comes from their love of sport, the joy of physical activity, and the drive produced by competitive instinct. Few athletes translate Olympic gold into fame and wealth, but the ones who do inspire many more to train harder.

Only a small number of track and field athletes can make a decent living with incomes from races and endorsements. The vast majority of athletes get little or no support. For most athletes, preparing for Olympic competition is equivalent to being unemployed. But, this is just one of many sacrifices a dedicated athlete must be willing to make. The athlete's desire for improved performance may require other sacrifices as he pursues his Olympic dream.

In both eastern and western sports systems, the determination of athlete and coach to exploit all possible means of enhancing performance has led to widespread use of questionable pharmaceutical products by Olympic athletes.

Perhaps most common are anabolic steroids, which are used primarily to improve power and strength and to enhance work capacity during training. Initially, these compounds were only utilized by athletes in the heavier events, particularly weightlifting and the throwing events of track and field. Recently, however, steroid use has spread to other areas. While no research has proven the effectiveness of steroids, few athletes question their effectiveness and believe they improve performance. It is the use by young female athletes that most worries physicians, because steroids are synthetic derivatives of the male hormone testosterone.

Potential risks are linked to changes in secondary sexual characteristics: hairy chests, baldness, and changes in the tone of voice, in men as well as women. The long-term effects, the unknown risks, are yet to be documented, although steroids are tentatively linked to high blood pressure and heart disease.

It was at the Rome Olympics (1960) that rumors first surfaced in the West that Soviet athletes were using a substance to increase their strength. By the midsixties, the secret was out and steroid use among American weightlifters and throwers increased rapidly.

By the early seventies, some sprinters, jumpers, and decathletes were also using steroids. The International Olympic Committee (IOC) stepped up its drug testing, instituting spot checks after Olympic finals. In Los Angeles (1984), the top four finishers in each event and a number of participants, selected at random will be tested for drugs. In all, about fifteen percent of the athletes, more than 1,500, will be tested.

An athlete's refusal to submit to testing would lead to disqualification. Testing for steroids is a complex procedure and was not introduced officially until 1976, in time for the Montreal Olympic Games. At Montreal, seven weightlifters and one female discus thrower were disqualified when tests were found to be positive. Consequently, three weightlifting medals had to be returned to the IOC.

Such testing, however, has done little to discourage steroid use, even in the United States. The benefits can be accrued over a number of years, so an athlete can stop taking steroids several weeks before Olympic competition, purge his system of any trace, and still retain most of the beneficial effects of increased strength and power.

Testing procedures adopted by the International Amateur Athletic Federation (IAAF) in world-class competition quickly led to suspension of many of Europe's top women track and field athletes. The world's two top female middle distance

Slupianek GDR tested positive for steroids
in 1977, won Moscow shot title in 1980.

Ben Plucknett USA lost his world record
when suspended for steroids in 1981.

runners, Bulgaria's Totka Petrova and Romania's Natalia Marasescu, were caught in 1979 and suspended for eighteen months. This sentence was later reduced to allow both to compete in the Moscow Games. The leniency of the governing bodies in handing out such short suspensions seemed to show the IAAF recognizes abuse is widespread and those caught are just unlucky examples.

In 1981, Ben Plucknett of the United States was the finest discus thrower in the world. In May he had set a new world record at Modesto, California, with a throw of 233 feet 7 inches and throughout a successful summer European season, he reasserted his credential as the world's best. The man he replaced as the world record holder was Wolfgang Schmidt of East Germany. The two giants finally met in Stockholm in July. Plucknett produced the greatest discus throw ever, the implement finally coming to earth 237 feet 4 inches from the circle. "I think I can do even better in the future," Plucknett said. "I feel very strong, but I have to improve my technique."

But the future was not so bright. Just one week later, the IAAF announced Plucknett was banned for life, having tested positive for steroids after the Pan Pacific Games in New Zealand the previous January. As has been the case with other suspended athletes, Plucknett was reinstated after eighteen months and resumed his world leadership in the event in 1983. Plucknett was the twenty-fourth track and field athlete to be suspended for steroid use, the first from the United States.

Drug revelations jolted the sports world during the 1983 Pan Am Games in Caracas. Fifteen male athletes from the United States, Canada, Cuba, and Central and South America were disqualified when urinalysis, similar to the testing procedures planned for Los Angeles, revealed the presence of steroids or testosterone. One victim was Jeff Michels, the best U.S. Olympic weightlifting prospect, who returned three gold medals after tests proved positive. Later, Michaels and the other disqualified lifters were suspended for two years from the date of their indiscretions.

The Pan Am disqualifications raised hopes that the use of strength-enhancing drugs might be eradicated as a result of sophisticated testing, which is said to reveal traces of banned substances months after they have been ingested. There are claims, however, that high tech drugs exist that do not leave traces for as long, which can be consumed until just a few weeks before the Games.

A different drug-related incident involving an athlete from the United States was the case of Rick DeMont, a sixteen-year-old swimmer from San Rafael, California. He was the youngest member of the 1972 men's team. DeMont lost his gold medal in the 400-meter freestyle in Munich and was banned from competing in the 1,500 meters when tests revealed the presence of ephedrine. It turned out the drug had been prescribed for DeMont as treatment for asthma by his doctor. Many accusations followed. Why hadn't the Olympic committee made U.S. team doctors aware the drug had been banned? Why hadn't U.S. team doctors been aware? For the first time, it was clear many banned substances are contained in everyday patent drugs. DeMont was perhaps a victim of a complex set of rules and procedures which were poorly understood by athletes and coaches.

Amphetamines and other chemical stimulants have also been abused by Olympic athletes. One of the most tragic accidents was probably caused by the use of amphetamines by an athlete. The incident occurred in Rome (1960) on a blistering hot day. The cycling 100-kilometer team race was underway when, seven miles from the finish, twenty-three-year-old Danish cyclist Knud Jensen fell unconscious from his bicycle. He died four hours later from a fractured skull.

An autopsy revealed Jensen had stimulants in his blood which undoubtedly contributed to the tragedy. The stimulants had allowed him to push his body beyond the limits imposed by the heat and the race. Today, amphetamines are easily detected in tests, so the drug is rarely used by athletes in Olympic competition.

Although amphetamine use is no longer prevalent in the Olympics, another type of stimulant is used. For some time, Eastern European athletes have been known to take high doses of caffeine in tablet form, yielding a legal, yet stimulating effect. In order to close this loophole, the IOC has placed caffeine on its list of banned substances. However, the Los Angeles Olympic Organizing Committee (LAOOC) has announced it will not test for it. The LAOOC is concerned because many ordinary products contain caffeine and there has been no research indicating how much caffeine would constitute a stimulant.

The problem has gone far beyond a circumstance that can be contained by testing and suspension. Something profound is lost from sport if authorities are forced into a major policing effort. Yet, to compete against someone who has a chemical advantage is unfair. This dilemma was expressed repeatedly by Lord Killanin, former IOC president.

The center of the problem is attitude. Do we attach too much importance to winning? The benefits that are attributed to the Olympic movement, in terms of the healthy development of youth, must be questioned when health risks taken by top Olympic athletes in order to compete successfully are so extreme.

Sport can only survive when founded on an inviolate moral and ethical system. An ideal of fairness and religious sanctity were major themes of the ancient Games in classical times. It was this same spirit that Coubertin tried to revive in the modern Games. The Olympic ceremony and doctrine were intended to bond the participants to an idealized concept of competition. Coubertin stressed the importance of taking part to do one's best, whether or not that resulted in victory.

Drug use has had an important effect on performance and has caused a major crisis in the Olympic movement. However, we must remember that not every Olympian's performance is chemically altered. A majority still rely on their own resources of power. A more important cause of the vast improvement in athletic performance is the greater opportunity to train and compete. Worldwide, participation in Olympic sports is more available than ever. Each year more facilities are built and the event calendar expands.

In many sports, world-class competition can be found on a weekly basis "in season." Top athletes find themselves on an international circuit, jetting from continent to continent for meet after meet, many televised worldwide. Just as the railroad stimulated the beginning of many national sports activities in the last century, today air transportation and satellite television have had a considerable effect on international sports activity.

In recent years, the Olympic Games have widened their reach to every corner of the planet. The advent of serious African participation in the Olympic movement was symbolized clearly with the barefooted Abebe Bikila's initial marathon victory in Rome (1960).

Great runners from the high altitudes of East Africa have been prominent in distance running ever since. Still, even with such physical strength and skill in evidence, Africa has yet to make its full impact felt except in athletics and boxing, principally for economic reasons.

The USSR made its first Olympic appearance in 1952 and has spread its systematic approach to sport throughout its Eastern European satellites and to Cuba.

The 1984 Los Angeles Games mark perhaps the greatest expansion of the Olympic movement, with the inclusion of athletes representing the one billion people of mainland China. Chinese emphasis on sport has yielded desired national goals. China beat Japan in the overall medal count at the 1982 Asian Games and will vie seriously for gold in '84, especially in athletics, gymnastics, diving, and volleyball.

The tremendous involvement of women in sport is also a recent development. Women have discovered equal enjoyment in sports activity and competition. The time when their desire to compete was denied by cultural expectations is now history. Women were allowed to take part in Olympic swimming for the first time in Stockholm (1912) against the opposition of none other than Pierre de Coubertin. He viewed the introduction of three women's events as a step toward "an impractical, uninteresting, unaesthetic, and indecorous feminine Olympiad."

Today, the status of women is perhaps best symbolized by the addition of the marathon to the women's Olympic program. Joan Benoit's winning time of 2 hours, 22 minutes, 42 seconds in the 1983 Boston Marathon surpassed the performance of all male Olympic victors prior to 1960, including the performance of Emil Zatopek and the heralded marathon runners before him.

Human performance and Olympic records have also advanced greatly as a result of improved facilities and equipment. Tracks in the early Olympic Games were loose and soft, which certainly retarded running speed. Synthetic running tracks are considered much faster than the cinder tracks utilized until 1964. The surface of a modern track is polyurethane, which is fast and impervious to weather, and costs a half million dollars.

In the field events, the fiberglass pole and foam landing pits have enabled vaulters to increase their leaps an average of $3\frac{1}{2}$ feet in the twenty years since Don Bragg won the Rome pole vault event using a stiff aluminum pole. Today's fiberglass poles bend ninety degrees before elevating the pole vaulter over nineteen feet, as much as three feet above his hand hold.

Today's javelins utilize the latest in aerodynamic knowhow, providing stability in flight and range, while still meeting size and weight specifications.

Another innovation (introduced by Dick Fosbury at Mexico in 1968) has resulted in high jumpers, almost exclusively, employing a type of the "flop" technique, going over the bar backwards and landing on their shoulders in a soft foam pit. Earlier forms of jumping, first the scissors and cutoff styles, then the straddle, were developed as improving landing surfaces would allow.

In the first sixty years of modern Olympic history, pits advanced from flat sand to a built-up sawdust landing area. Anyone trying to use the flop in one of those pits would have wound up with a broken neck or back. Today, foam pits allow an almost uninhibited approach to the high jump bar.

The sophistication in the design of Olympic swimming pools is a factor that has also greatly enhanced performance. In the first three Olympic Games, swimming events were held in an ocean, a river, and a lake. It was not until the London Olympics (1908) that a pool was specially built for the Games. Today's heated pools are designed to eliminate backwash, provide as smooth a surface as possible, and are heated to an ideal temperature (72 degrees) to provide for optimum performance.

The development and proliferation of weight training apparatus over the last twenty years has had enormous influence on improving performances particularly in the power events. The majority of Olympic sports now incorporate progressive resistance weight training in the preparation of the athlete. Universal, Nautilus, and many other less expensive varieties of lifting apparatus are now found throughout the world and promote a stronger, more well conditioned athlete.

These are some of the tangible factors responsible for the ceaseless advance of performance in Olympic sports. Yet, in the constant assault on the record books, nothing is nearly as important as the human factor, the athletes themselves.

Creative spirit drives the physical adventurer to go where no one has gone before, to chart unexplored territory. The athlete's search for unlimited speed and strength is the fulfillment of an idea. The athlete holds in mind a vision of the future; the perfect performance that might yet be achieved. The record is a symbol of the past, something already accomplished, something to be exceeded.

7

OLYMPIC CEREMONY

— 7 —

On July 28, 1984, more than ten thousand athletes will assemble on the infield of Los Angeles Memorial Coliseum for the pageantry of the opening ceremony. The parade of athletes in their national costumes, the lighting of the Olympic flame, and the many colorful displays of Olympic tradition and symbolism are all part of the ritualistic opening of each Olympic festival.

The observance of the opening ceremony is the premium spectator event of the Games. The stadium will be packed. More than a billion people around the globe will witness the opening ceremony via television.

Pierre de Coubertin intended to make the Olympic Games a ceremonial affair. He envisioned the modern Games as an aesthetic and spiritual festival. In Coubertin's view, Olympism was a classical religion. As in ancient times, the modern athletes were to be bound together by a system of beliefs, a code of ethics that would ensure fair competition.

In the opening ceremony, the athletes honor the Olympic ideals and symbolically agree to follow the rules of Olympic competition. It is a solemn occasion and one of the world's most colorful and awe-inspiring human spectacles. It is an act of reverence to the spirit of Olympism, very pagan and classically Greek.

It took many Olympiads, however, for the symbolism to be developed and the ceremony to be choreographed. The Olympic rings are the symbol of the International Olympic Committee (IOC) and the Olympic movement. Five interlocking rings represent the linking together of the different peoples and cultures of the world's five continents. The design was found in 1913, carved on a rock at the site of the Pythian Games in Delphi, Greece. No one is certain what the rings represented in ancient times, but it is known that in ancient Greece, circles represented perfection and purity.

The rings were adopted by the IOC and first used on the flag that flew over the Antwerp Games of 1920. The Olympic flag is carried and raised majestically at the opening ceremony and flies dominantly over all Olympic venues.

The opening ceremony begins with a parade of athletes. All competing nations march into the arena, led by Greece, and concluding with the host country's team. Each team is preceded by a flag bearer carrying its national banner.

The president of the host city's organizing committee and the president of the IOC invite the host nation's chief of state to proclaim the Games open. In 1984, Peter Ueberroth of the Los Angeles Olympic Organizing Committed (LAOOC) and

John Monk enters the stadium to open the 1948 Games in London.

IOC President Juan Antonio Samaranch from Spain, plan to escort President Ronald Reagan. According to Olympic protocol, the chief of state, President Reagan will utter this simple phrase: "I declare open the Games of Los Angeles celebrating the twenty-third Olympiad of the modern era."

President Reagan's indication that he will open the 1984 Games ends a long and dismal record held by U.S. presidents. The five Olympic Games, two summer and three winter, that have been held in the United States have always been opened by a presidential surrogate. By contrast, the chief of state of the host nation has been on hand to declare the Games open, in practically every other country.

Vice-President Charles Curtis opened the Games of Los Angeles in 1932, and, in 1960, President Dwight Eisenhower appointed Vice-President Richard Nixon to open the Winter Olympic Games at Squaw Valley. President Jimmy Carter claimed that the troublesome international scene required him to stay in the White House. Therefore, Vice-President Walter Mondale attended the opening ceremony at Lake Placid in February, 1980.

After the Games are declared open, the Olympic hymn is played and the flag, with five colored interlocking rings on a white background, is slowly raised. This is followed by the arrival of the Olympic torch which culminates a relay begun in May, 1984 at the Temple of Hera, in Olympia, Greece. At Olympia, the torch is kindled with a mirror that focuses the rays of the midday sun.

In 1984, the torch and flame will be carried across the United Stated to Los Angeles, by a relay of thousands of runners. The last runner will enter the Coliseum, circle the track once, and climb the stairs that lead to a cauldron where the flame will burn continuously throughout the Olympic festival, until the closing ceremony on August 12, 1984.

The Olympic flame first burned in Amsterdam in 1928. In 1936, the flame was kindled at Olympia for the first time and carried by relay to arrive at the climax of the opening ceremonies at Berlin. This tradition, built through successive games, has become a central part of Olympic ceremony.

The lighting of the Olympic flame is perhaps the most dramatic moment of the ceremony. In Helsinki (1952), there was a thrilling roar as Paavo Nurmi entered the stadium and lit the flame with Hannes Kolehmainen. Together, the two greatest figures in Finland's legendary distance running tradition proclaimed the opening of the Games.

In Mexico City, Enriqueta Basilo became the first woman torchbearer. In Munich, torchbearer Gunter Zahn led distance runners Jim Ryun, Kip Keino, Derek Clayton, and Kenji Kimihara on the final circuit: five runners representing five continents.

In the 1980 opening ceremony, three-time triple jump champion Victor Saneev ran the last lap around the stadium, then handed the torch to basketball star Sergei Belov, who ascended the stairs and lit the flame in the bowl above Lenin Stadium.

The flame arrives in the Montreal Olympic stadium to open the 1976 Games.

More than six thousand athletes assembled for the Montreal opening ceremony.

Next, in the series of ceremonial traditions, an athlete from the host nation will take the Olympic oath on behalf of all participants in the Games. The athlete recites the traditional pledge:

"In the name of all the competitors, I promise that we shall take part in these Olympic Games, respecting and abiding by the rules which govern them, in the true spirit of sportsmanship, for the glory of sport and the honor of our teams."

This oath is symbolic of the vow taken by the athletes in the ancient Games at the Temple of Zeus, where they vowed they would follow the rules of the Games and they were worthy of competing. In modern times, Victor Boin, a Belgium fencer, took the first oath when it was introduced in Antwerp (1920).

The reciting of the oath is the last of the formal rituals of the opening ceremony as prescribed by the IOC. The host nation also contributes its own ideas and interpretation to the ceremony, adding to its character.

In 1984, in a host nation famed for half-time shows and Disneyland productions, the opening show at Los Angeles is expected to be among the most dramatic and festive ever. Robert Jani planned the ceremonies for the 1984 Games. He was formerly a creative director for Disney and produced half time shows for the 1977 and 1979 Super Bowl championships. However, Jani and the Disney organization subsequently withdrew as producers of the ceremonies when the LAOOC insisted the budget must be limited to $5 million. David Wolper was named as the new executive producer of the ceremonies. Adopting many of Jani's original plans, Wolper promises an opening that is "inspirational and majestic, with a traditional theme of world togetherness."

Many contend the opening parade marching and flag bearing carries militaristic overtones. The athletes themselves, facing strenuous competition, often complain there are just too many hours spent on their feet, but few decline the opportunity to be there.

THE VICTORY CEREMONY

Throughout the fifteen days of competition in Los Angeles, there will be 220 victory ceremonies, one for each Olympic event. Each time, the three medalists will climb the victory stand. After receiving their medals, they will watch as their countries' flags are raised to the top of the flagpoles, the gold-medalist's flag on the highest, central pole. The victor's national anthem is played while the flags are raised. It is another solemn occasion in keeping with Coubertin's vision that victory merited the highest moral reward.

The victory ceremony as we know it today was initiated in Los Angeles in 1932. At the previous Games in Amsterdam, all medals were awarded at one time during the closing ceremony. Queen Wilhelmina of Holland stood in the royal box and handed gold medals to the Olympic champions, lined up by nation.

Some people see the hoisting of national flags as a display of excessive nationalism. According to the IOC, the Games are for competition among individuals, not nations. No official medal count is taken. That is left to the media and is not recognized by the IOC.

Regardless, the athletes are representative of a nation's efforts to assemble a team and those efforts should be recognized at the time of an individual's victory. No real alternatives have been proposed and the medal ceremonies, despite their constant interruption of ongoing action, are deeply touching presentations, richly enjoyed by the spectators. For the medalists, it is a special celebration of their achievements, their moment of worldwide acclaim.

Medals

During the first modern Olympic Games in Athens, only the first and second finishers in each event received awards. The first place athlete received a silver medal and an olive wreath, the second place finisher a bronze medal and a wreath of laurel. The first event final in the 1896 program was the triple jump. Thus, the distinction of being the first modern Olympic medalist was earned by triple jumper James B. Connolly of the United States, who leaped almost 45 feet. It was an honor which may well have been overlooked at the time, the Games being in their infancy.

In the Paris Games, the medals awarded did not even mention the word "Olympic," although Pierre de Coubertin later sent all of the participants a commemorative medal to make it clear they had competed in an Olympics. Gold medals were awarded for the first time in London in 1908. In 1928, Giuseppe Cassioli of Italy designed a medal depicting victory. This design has since been incorporated in every Olympic medal.

The gold medal is actually made of silver, plated with at least six grams of gold. Although its material value is less than five hundred dollars, as a symbol of achievement, it is invaluable. The Olympic gold medal is the the highest honor that can be earned by an athlete.

CLOSING CEREMONY

The Olympic Games end with the emotionally-charged closing ceremony. Whereas the opening ceremony is based on formality, the closing moments are open and friendly. Athletes walk informally, without distinction of nationality, united as fellow Olympians.

The required ceremony is brief. Juan Samaranch will close the 1984 Games, as tradition demands, concluding with the words, "I call upon the youth of all countries to assemble four years from now at Seoul, South Korea, and there celebrate with us the Games of the twenty-fourth Olympiad." The Olympic flame flickers and is extinguished and, finally, the Olympic flag is slowly lowered.

In recent Olympics, the party and celebration of the athletes begin at this point. Before they exit, spontaneous and gleeful activity arises all over the arena. Some athletes concoct pranks, others dance, many wave joyously to the spectators.

This closing pageant strongly symbolizes the breaking down of national and racial barriers. It shows us the unity of spirit that is possible, but all too often missing among the world's nations. This spirit and unity, achieved throughout the competition and highlighted in the closing moments, is perhaps the most important objective and greatest accomplishment of the Olympic Games.

8

ARCHERY

— 8 —

1984 VENUE

The archery events will be held at El Dorado Park in Long Beach. Seating capacity is 4,000. Archers will face due north during the contest to avoid shooting into the sun. A crosswind from the left (west/northwest) averages 7 MPH on August afternoons.

EVENTS AND SCHEDULE

Men

2 X 36 arrows	August 8-11
(90, 70, 50, 30 meters)	

Women

2 X 36 arrows	August 8-11
(70, 60, 50, 30 meters)	

HISTORY OF ARCHERY

Cave paintings indicate the bow and arrow was used over 20,000 years ago, primarily for hunting. Archery improved early man's hunting success over spear and slingshot methods, assuring a greater food supply. In early civilizations, the bow and arrow was the principal instrument of warfare.

Archery competition is as old as the bow itself. Of all the world's existing sports events, the oldest is the Ancient Scorton Silver Arrow contest in Yorkshire, England. Contest records date from 1673, interrupted only by two world wars.

OLYMPIC HISTORY

Archery was a demonstration sport in the Games of 1900 and 1904, and was accorded full status at London in 1908. However, the sport was subsequently dropped after the 1920 Olympic Games.

The early problem with the sport and the reason archery was excluded from Olympic competition for over fifty years, was the lack of uniformity in international rules. This was solved with the growth of the international governing body, Federation Internationale de Tir á l'Arc (FITA). In 1957 the FITA introduced the present competitive format, the double FITA round, which prescribes the Olympic competition. Archery regained Olympic status in 1972 in Munich.

While Robin Hood remains the world's most famous archer, four Americans currently come closest to the ultimate mastery of the sport and to the domination of Olympic history. Since the reintroduction of archery to the Olympic program in 1972, the United States has won gold medals in all four Olympic archery events in which they have participated.

John Williams, an eighteen-year-old private in the U.S. Army, went to the Munich Olympics as the reigning world champion. He lived up to his billing by taking the lead in the competition on the first day and continuing to add to his lead throughout the four day tournament. His final total of 2,528 points was his best score by 73 points.

Another Munich medalist from the United States was Mrs. Doreen Wilber, a forty-two-year-old homemaker from Iowa. She was fourth at the halfway point of the women's competition, trailing well behind the favored Irena Szydlowska of Poland. On the final day, Mrs. Wilber overtook her rival, defeating the Polish markswoman by a mere 17 points.

In Montreal, nineteen-year-old Darrell Pace and his twenty-three-year-old female compatriot, Luann Ryon, continued the U.S. winning streak. Pace set an Olympic record for each of the four distances and recorded a total of 2,571 points, surpassing Williams' Olympic record by 43 points and winning by a comfortable margin over Hiroshi Michinaga of Japan.

Ryon had to survive a close struggle with two Soviet archers to collect her gold. After overcoming a shaky start caused by jumpy nerves, she went on in the second round to establish a world record of 1,282 points, for a winning total of 2,499. Valentina Korpan of the USSR set world records at 30 and 60 meters, but performed poorly at 50 meters and had to settle for the silver.

Olympic records established by Pace and Ryon in Montreal remained intact after the Moscow archery competition in 1980. Both will compete again for U.S. team berths in 1984 under the guidance of '72 champion John Williams, the '84 team coach.

RULES

A double FITA round of 288 arrows is shot over four days in both men's and women's Olympic championships. The purpose of each round is to hit the target. The men shoot two rounds of thirty-six arrows from 30, 50, 70, and 90 meters. The women also shoot two rounds of thirty-six arrows but the distances are 30, 50, 60, and 70 meters.

Darrell Pace USA Olympic champion in Montreal 1976.

Rick McKinney USA defeated Pace in 1983 world championship via tie-breaking procedures.

The target each is aiming at is a five-color target marked by ten concentric rings. A bull's-eye in the gold center scores ten points, a hit in the surrounding gold ring scores nine, and so on, down to one point for an arrow in the outermost white ring. A perfect score for each FITA round is 1,440 points; therefore 2,880 is the ultimate score for Olympic competition.

A large target is used for the two longest distances. The center "10-point" ring on the larger is 4.8 inches in diameter and just 3.2 inches on the smaller target. Each competitor is allowed 2½ minutes to shoot each group or "end" of three arrows.

THE BOW

There is no specified bow length. Longer bows are steadier in the hand, but shorter bows shoot a faster, more direct arrow, traveling at 150 MPH toward the target. Bows utilize stabilizing rods to limit the twisting of the bow upon release. A mechanical sight is permitted to aid in aiming. An archer may also use a leather device to allow a firmer grip on the string.

ARCHERY SKILLS

As in the story of William Tell, the center ring or the bull's-eye on the target is the size of an apple, only 4.8 inches in diameter. Olympic archers often hit the "apple" as many as eight of ten times from a distance of 90 meters, nearly 100 yards. They are capable of maintaining such accuracy for almost twenty hours of competition, while using 288 arrows.

Archery is the supreme test of the steadiest arm, the surest sight, the most focused mind. Competitors come in all ages, since there is little relationship between age and accuracy. It is hard work, however. A force of about 50 pounds is required to draw a man's bow. Counting the allowed twenty-four practice shots, the male archer will pull over seven tons during the four days of competition. The female archer will draw about five tons, since it takes an average force of about 35 pounds to draw a woman's bow.

1984 PROSPECTS

Montreal Olympic champions Darrell Pace and Luann Ryon are still going strong; however, they will have some stiff competition from U.S. teammates. Pace was narrowly out-scored by Rick McKinney of Arizona in the 1983 national championships, held on the Olympic range at El Dorado Park, Long Beach. But Pace reversed the placings, winning the Pan American Games.

The ongoing rivalry between the world's two finest male archers continued at the 1983 world championships also held at El Dorado Park. After four days of shooting, both men had scored a new championship record of 2617 points. Tie-breaking procedures gave the world title to McKinney, who had shot the most center bull's-eyes, 124 to Pace's 116.

Not to be dismissed is 1980 Olympic gold medalist Tomi Poikolainen of Finland, ninth in the world championships, yet his score of 2575 was impressive and indicated the high standard of the competition. Poikolainen will have to focus his efforts as a contender in order to upset U.S. domination of the sport.

Luann Ryon has plenty of competition from Nancy Myrick and Ruth Rowe, first and second place finishers in the 1983 U.S. Nationals, and she must also contend with stiff competition from the South Korean team. Four Korean women achieved individual scores higher than Myrick's in the open division at the National Archery Association.

The South Korean team gained a landslide win over West Germany and the United States in the 1983 World Championships. Leading her team to victory was Jin-Ho Kim, who secured a record 2616 total. Mi-Young Kim and Jea-Bong Jung are also excellent Korean archers, who should lead the close and exciting competition in Los Angeles.

South Korea is just one of the emerging archery powers that will be a strong contender in Los Angeles. The USSR has also been making rapid progress and archers from China are expected to do well. The United States has enjoyed almost complete dominance in the sport in recent years, but the rest of the world is catching up.

9

ATHLETICS
(TRACK AND FIELD)

— 9 —

1984 VENUE

At the opening ceremony on July 28, 1984, the Los Angeles Memorial Coliseum will become the only stadium in Olympic history to twice serve as the principal Games venue. The site of the athletics events, the Coliseum, will seat 92,604 spectators. When it was completed in May of 1923, at a cost of about $1 million, it was one of the world's greatest stadiums. Extensive refurbishments were required to prepare the track and field for the 1984 Games.

EVENTS AND SCHEDULE (Finals)

Men

100 meters	August 4
200 meters	August 8
400 meters	August 8
800 meters	August 6
1,500 meters	August 11
3,000-meter Steeplechase	August 10
5,000 meters	August 11
10,000 meters	August 6
Marathon	August 12
110-meter Hurdles	August 6
400-meter Hurdles	August 5
20-kilometer Walk	August 3
50-kilometer Walk	August 11
4 X 100-meter Relay	August 11
4 X 400-meter Relay	August 11
High Jump	August 11
Pole Vault	August 8
Long Jump	August 6
Triple Jump	August 4
Shot Put	August 11
Discus	August 10
Hammer	August 6
Javelin	August 5
Decathlon	August 8, 9

Women	
100 meters	August 5
200 meters	August 9
400 meters	August 6
800 meters	August 6
1,500 meters	August 11
3,000 meters	August 10
Marathon	August 5
100-meter Hurdles	August 10
400-meter Hurdles	August 8
4 X 100-meter Relay	August 11
4 X 400-meter Relay	August 11
High Jump	August 10
Long Jump	August 9
Shot Put	August 3
Discus	August 11
Javelin	August 6
Heptathlon	August 3, 4

HISTORY OF ATHLETICS

Track and field (athletics) is the keystone of the Olympic movement. It encompasses the truest tests of the most basic human motions. Running, jumping, and throwing are the building blocks of all sports activities. No other sport better symbolizes the Olympic motto, "Citius, Altius, Fortius" . . . "Faster, Higher, Stronger." The forty-one athletics events on the 1984 program are the most basic tests of speed, endurance, agility, and physical power.

The roots of track and field lie in man's natural interest in measuring his physical skill and concocting various challenges to test himself against others. He practices these motions and binds each test by a rigid set of rules. The sport measures the absolute speed man can run, the limits of his endurance, the height he can leap, and the distance he can throw basic implements.

Many of today's athletic events have a clear relationship to the ancient Olympic Games. In the ancient Games, the Stade race was the most popular and prestigious event. Athletes raced the length of the stadium to determine the fastest runner. Distance races of up to three miles were also run, but there was no marathon in the Ancient Games. The beginnings of discus and javelin throwing as well as jumping for distance were also firmly established at Olympia.

Another equally direct line of ancestry for modern athletics comes from the British Isles. Rural sports events linked to fairs took place early in the middle ages. It wasn't until the seventeenth century, however, before rules and records for the various events were kept.

Lewis wins world 100 meters title.

Carl Lewis USA won the 1983 world long jump.

Lewis enjoys another victory lap.

Carl Lewis anchors USA world champion 4 x 100-meter relay team setting a world record.

The famous Cotswold Games were well established by 1612. These games were held seventy miles northeast of London, only ten miles from Shakespeare's Stratford-on-Avon. The Cotswold Games were a spring festival in which show and pageantry were of great importance. The basic events, running, jumping, and throwing, were contested. Other Cotswold Games events included: bowling, wrestling, a free-for-all type of football, as well as music and dance competitions, and equestrian events.

It was the adoption of various events from the rural games by the British Universities in the midnineteenth century and the growth of the Highland Games in Scotland that provided the most direct influence on the program of the first modern Games in Athens. English public schools and universities instituted many of the events, much as we know them today. Soon the events and rules of the events were adopted by the universities and colleges on the East Coast of the United States.

This university athletic culture was eventually separated from the rural games, which had evolved into professional running matches that fostered gambling and attracted a "seedy," undesirable following.

There were some notable performances in professional athletics, however. The first international competition was staged in 1849. In 1862 Native American Louis "Deerfoot" Bennett was victorious in a series of races against the best English athletes. One epic duel was against Jack White, "The Gateshead Clipper," in which White ran 6 miles in under 30 minutes. It wasn't until Paavo Nurmi in the 1920's that these performance levels were again approached.

THE EVENTS

100 Meters

This race is a basic test of sheer speed. To the winner goes the title, "The World's Fastest Human." Competitors go through several qualifying rounds, advancing to an eight runner final. In one of the quietest moments in the Olympic stadium, the elite sprinters of the world take their marks, move to the set position, and wait for the gun. As the gun fires, there is an explosion of power as the sprinters propel themselves down the track, accelerating with powerful thrusting strides toward their maximum speeds. Sprinters reach speeds of about 27 MPH at the midpoint of the race.

As the athletes drive toward the finish line, the winner is the runner who can maintain speed and form, slowing down the least toward the end. In a tight finish, the racers lunge at the finish line, hoping to get their torso to the line first. Photo finish cameras and electronic timing devices precisely measure the outcome of this ultimate sprint race.

The sprint is a dichotomy; the runner must react powerfully and work as furiously as possible, yet there is a delicate balance at which the fastest speed is achieved only with control and relaxation. The Olympic champion may be the sprinter who doesn't tighten up during the most important ten seconds of his athletic career.

At the 1983 world championships in Helsinki, Carl Lewis of the United States proved he is one of those rare athletes who stand at a unique level of skill, possessing a natural ability beyond that of his rivals. Only an injury could threaten his firm grasp as the world's number one speedster.

At Helsinki, Lewis, often slow out of the blocks, trailed Emitt King by a yard at the halfway point. But in the next ten enormous, bounding strides, characteristic of Lewis in high gear, he surged a clear yard ahead of everyone. A broad smile came across his face, expressing the joy of his own ability. He finished in 10.07 seconds, ahead of the new world record holder Calvin Smith and collegiate champion Emitt King. It was a clean sweep for the United States. Britain's 1980 Olympic champion Allan Wells, in fourth, led the European sprinters.

Earlier, Calvin Smith had erased Jimmie Hines' long standing sprint record, achieved in the Mexico City Olympics. Running with the benefits of high altitude at the U.S. Air Force Academy, Colorado Springs (7,200 feet), Smith recorded 9.93 seconds. Lewis, who has run 9.97 seconds, the fastest at sea level, says he wants the record.

Marlies Gohr and Marita Koch of East Germany and Evelyn Ashford of the United States are currently the fastest women in the world, as they have been for several years. Ashford's difficult '83 season was marked by her world record performance of 10.79 seconds set also at the National Sports Festival, the same day as Calvin Smith's record. She raced Gohr twice during 1983. The first was over 100 meters on the Olympic track in the Coliseum, into a stiff breeze. Ashford simply could not match strides with Gohr, who won in a slow time.

When Evelyn ran a relaxed 10.99 in her semifinal at Helsinki, it seemed she had a good chance of turning the tables on her archrival. But as the eight fastest women got down in the blocks for the final, Evelyn knew she was hurt. She stayed in contention for nearly half the race, although she was veering to the right, favoring one leg. Suddenly, her right hamstring pulled and she fell to the track.

Gohr got to the line first in 10.97 and became world champion, barely ahead of Koch and Diane Williams of the United States. These sprinters will undoubtedly meet again in Los Angeles, where Evelyn may produce one of her bursts of speed, unequaled among women.

Of the rest, Chandra Cheeseborough of the United States has run very well, but has had less international experience. Merlene Ottey of Jamaica is better over 200 meters.

Marlies Gohr GDR (left) and Evelyn Ashford USA, the two fastest female sprinters.

Gohr wins this encounter in Los Angeles and later became the 1983 world champion.

200 Meters

A sustained sprint of half a lap requires a great sprinter with endurance, who can run around the turn, which at such speed is very tight. The start is crucial. The sprinters lean slightly into the turn as they accelerate. Most 200-meter specialists prefer the outside lanes where wide turns are thought to be faster than the tight inside lanes.

Calvin Smith USA, 1983 world champion 200 meters, world record holder 100 meters 9.93 sec.

The big question in 1984 will be whether Carl Lewis will compete in the 200 meters and try to emulate the four gold medal feat of Jesse Owens. His schedule will be tough, with two rounds of the 200 meters on the morning of the long jump final. His long jump performance may suffer, but he could choose to win the event by taking a couple of jumps and save something for the 200-meter final.

Lewis is immensely talented. In his first year of serious competition at the long sprint, he turned in the world's best time (19.75 seconds) and he will certainly be hard to beat. His chief 200-meter rival will be Calvin Smith of the United States, who blossomed suddenly to become world champion in 20.14 seconds, a race Lewis chose not to run.

Smith then went on to beat Lewis in 19.99 seconds in Berlin after Smith came into the homestretch two yards clear. Lewis, at 6 feet 3 inches and 182 pounds, bounded after Smith but couldn't catch him. Smith's size, 5 feet 9 inches and 140 pounds, is more conducive to fast running around the turn. World record holder (19.72 seconds) and Olympic champion Pietro Mennea of Italy was still running well in Helsinki, gaining the bronze. But Mennea will be thirty-two years old in Los Angeles, and may be too old to be a threat.

The 200 meters is Evelyn Ashford's best event and Marlies Gohr doesn't race at this distance. Evelyn, not a good starter, thrives at the longer sprint event and hasn't lost in five years. In 1981, she won her second consecutive World Cup title, defeating two time Olympic champion Barbel Wockel of East Germany.

Marita Koch's better event may be 400 meters, but she's the world champion in the 200. With Ashford injured, Koch held off the closing rush of Jamaican Merlene Ottey to win in 22.13 seconds. Ottey and Chandra Cheeseborough of the United States are both young, talented, and improving.

400 Meters

The race is one full lap of the track run on sheer willpower. Beginning from staggered starts, these sprinters attempt to run at speeds close to their maximum, but with an efficient, relaxed stride. The Olympic 400-meter champion must be close to 21 seconds as he passes the halfway point, but still cruising, conserving strength.

The third 100 meters is run hard around the turn. Shoulder to shoulder, competitors battle down the final straightaway, expending every ounce of strength and will. The stronger athlete can "hold on longer" and maintain rhythm, which takes tremendous physical conditioning.

Apart from Alberto Juantorena's performance (44.26 seconds) at the Montreal Games (1976), the world has not seen any greater one lap runners than the Tommie Smith, Lee Evans, and Larry James era of the late 60's. Lee Evans' world record in Mexico City (43.86 seconds) still stands.

It was a surprise that nobody could break 45 seconds in the Helsinki world championship final, won by Burt Cameron of Jamaica in 45.05 seconds. He has been the dominant 400-meter runner in the world for a number of years and would have pressed champion Victor Markin of the USSR had Jamaica competed in the Moscow Olympics. Cameron still has more speed than he has shown. He will need it all in Los Angeles.

Someone will emerge from the crowd with a new challenge of speed, intent on taking the gold. It could be young Michael Franks of the United States who, at nineteen years, collected the Helsinki silver. An even younger contender is seventeen-year-old Australian Darren Clarke, who set an age record of 45.05 seconds in London. But after three races in as many days, he was eliminated in the Helsinki semifinals.

One of the greatest showdowns of the Los Angeles Games will be the women's 400-meter confrontation between Jarmila Kratochvilova of Czechoslovakia and Marita Koch of East Germany. They will probably avoid each other until their August 6, 1984, appointment at the Olympics.

Kratochvilova's Helsinki performance was a shock to those who thought Koch's world record was safe. Having run three slow 400-meter heats, plus two heats and a final at 800 meters the night before, Jarmila ran the 400 meters all out, stopping the clocks at 47.99, an unbelievable world record. Only her teammate, Tatiana Kocembova, was close at 48.59. With little training, Koch restored her 400-meter threat with a 48.55 leg on the winning East German relay team.

800 Meters

The 800 is the metric half mile, just two strides less than 880 yards. The question has arisen whether this is a sprint or an endurance race, as recent champions of both 400 meters and 1,500 meters have both enjoyed Olympic success at 800 meters. Regardless, it is an "aerobic" event. The athlete must have a sprinter's speed, but also the strong heart and lungs of a middle distance runner who can replenish the body with oxygen and retard the onset of fatigue.

The race is staggered for two turns. It is 300 meters before the finalists merge and engage in a tactical battle in which a runner's position in the pack is vitally important. It takes more energy to run wide on the bends, yet one does not want to be "boxed" and unable to respond to the moves of the front runner.

The pack of runners is tightly bunched and fast. As a result, the 800 meters is a rough race, with bumping, pushing, and elbowing. To avoid this, a runner may try to steal the race from the front. More often, the strategic moves are made on the back straight of the last lap. The 800 meters has seen some epic struggles in the final 100-meter stretch. As they round the final turn, there will be a number of runners who can still win. Since 1948, the average time between gold and silver is only over two-tenths of a second, only one stride.

No one is very close to Sebastian Coe's world record of 1:41.73, set in 1981. Coe ran his races alone, unimpeded by the tactical problems of a competitive field. In Moscow, he showed the difficulty he has in dealing with the strategic Olympic final. Coe had a poor 1983 season, finally pulling out of the world championships because of illness.

The surprise winner at the world championship was Willi Wulbeck of West Germany, in a creditable 1:43.65, the best time of 1983. He chased down the young and brilliant Joaquim Cruz of Brazil, a freshman at the University of Oregon, who took off boldly at the gun. Cruz should improve greatly before the Olympic final and will be a factor in the race. Otherwise, Wulbeck's tactical skill might overcome Sebastian Coe's fleetness of foot.

Jarmila Kratochvilova of Czechoslovakia outran the women's field in Helsinki, recording a 1:54.68, more than a second slower than her world record. Yet it was remarkable, since the race was run only 35 minutes after she had won her semifinal heat at 400 meters. She is a dominant talent in both the 800 meters and the shorter race. The only apparent threat to her Olympic gold may be a decision to retire at age thirty-one, a threat she made before the world championship.

Robin Campbell finished fifth in Helsinki with a time just outside 2 minutes. She is the United States' best hope for a finalist but will need to improve dramatically in order to loosen the Eastern European grip on the medals.

1,500 Meters

This is the metric mile and every bit as prestigious. The contestants are the media superstars of track and field. It is four laps of the track, less one curve. It's 3½ minutes of captivating and tactical drama. The race requires a strong heart and lungs, economy of motion, efficiency of stride, and the will to endure. Athletes in this race must possess great speed and quantities of endurance. They must be able to run 400 meters in less than 50 seconds and also run competitively at distances as long as 10,000 meters.

The finalists average well under one minute per lap, maintaining an optimum tactical position, yet attempting to conserve strength. Often in an Olympic final, everyone is there to win and there may be no willing frontrunner to set the pace. But sooner or later, those without confidence in their finishing kick must make a move for home.

The 1983 world championship was such a slow and tactical race, with no runner willing to take the lead. The pack held back and was tightly clustered. But as the field accelerated on the final lap, no one could match strides with Steve Cram of Great Britain, who burst for home with 300 meters to go, covering the last lap in 52.2 seconds.

Steve Scott of the United States has enormous strength, but has often found himself in tactical difficulties as he did in Helsinki where he finished second. Allowing an athlete of Cram's ability to get more than a few yards ahead can be devastating. Cram is still young enough to improve in the Olympic year, but Scott, before a hometown crowd in Los Angeles, might run that inspired race everyone has awaited.

It is too soon to declare an end to the reign of Sebastian Coe and Steve Ovett. Coe, the 1980 Olympic champion, gave up on a frustrating 1983 season marked by injury and sickness. However, no one has yet to match his brilliant form of 1981 and he'll only be twenty-seven years old when he approaches the starting line in Los Angeles.

Steve Ovett made plenty of tactical mistakes in Helsinki, but finished fast for fourth place. In postworld championship competition, he lost his 1,500-meter world record to Sydney Maree, then regained it in Rieti, Italy, setting a new standard of 3:30.77.

Many people expected Mary Decker's world championship win at 3,000 meters, but few rated her as the world's best in the 1,500 meters until her surprising world championship victory. The manner in which she achieved it was impressive.

She led all the way and battled to stay ahead as the pack accelerated on the last lap with 200 meters to go. On the final curve, Zamira Zaitseva of the USSR

Steve Cram GBR in perfect striking position on back straight of Helsinki 1,500 meters.

Cram passes Aoita MOR and holds off Steve Scott USA to become 1983 world champion.

forced Mary to break stride and she lost 3 yards. It seemed her momentum may have been lost. Then, just as she had in the 3,000 meters, she dug deeply into her reserve on the final straightaway, and found a level of strength that no other female distance runner would match. She caught Zaitseva with 10 meters left. Soviet runners placed 2, 3, and 4 while Brit McRoberts from Canada was the only other non-European in the world championship final.

3,000-Meter Steeplechase

The original steeplechase was a cross-country run between village steeples in England and a common race in the last century. The event was placed within the confines of a 400-meter track and introduced into the Paris Olympics in 1900. The first Olympic races were over various distances, but from 1920, 3,000 meters was the standard.

The race takes place over 7½ laps of the 400-meter track and consists of twenty-eight, 3-foot barriers and seven water jumps. The water jump is a 3-foot barrier and a 12-foot expanse of water. The wide spacing between the obstacles is such that the essential skill of the steeplechaser remains his distance running ability.

The demands of strength and mobility in hurdle clearance do not change the physical character of the event. For this reason, Olympic champions and world record holders often come from the ranks of the great runners such as Amos Biwott, Ben Jipcho, and Kip Keino of Kenya and the current world record holder, Henry Rono, also of Kenya, who ran the distance in 8:05.4.

These great athletes relied upon their running between the barriers and modest hurdling technique. The event awaits a great distance runner who makes the commitment to become a skillful hurdler. Then the world record will drop to less than eight minutes.

Patriz Ilg of West Germany was easily the toughest of the Helsinki steeplechasers, bursting away from the pack over the last lap and becoming world champion with 8:15.06. Henry Marsh of the United States stayed out of trouble at the back of the pack, avoiding the risk of mass hurdling, moving up with 800 meters left. Marsh had closed to about 2 meters at the last hurdle, but took off too near to the barrier, hit it with his trail leg, and went down. He got back to his feet slowly and jogged home in eighth place. The way Ilg zipped home, he left little doubt he would have won anyway, and therefore is considered the world's premier steeplechaser.

Men's 5,000 Meters / Women's 3,000 Meters

A distance race of this length was run in the Ancient Olympics. The length of the dolichos varied between Olympiads, but usually was defined as 20 stades, about 3,800 meters. The 5,000 meters (3 miles, 176 yards) is 12½ laps around a modern track. The women's race is 7½ laps, which covers 3,000 meters or 1.86 miles.

Mary Decker USA leads Sly GBR and Kazankina USSR heading to 3,000 meters world title.

Eamonn Coghlan IRL bursts away from pack to become Helsinki 5,000 meters world champion.

The Olympic middle-distance runner is a superb athlete with a cardiovascular system that can transport and burn oxygen economically. Distance runners have strong hearts and lungs, smooth efficient strides, and the willpower to overcome their own doubts, to keep on going.

It is their strength of character, exhibited lap after lap as the race develops and expressed so fully in the final lap, that gives us so many distance running legends. The indomitable spirit of Finland's great runners Paavo Nurmi and Lasse Viren is shared by all distance greats.

Recent 5,000-meter championship races have tended to be tactical affairs. Running in a tight pack adds uncertainty, but it's tough to win from the front. The runners who played the tactical game, guarding their positions throughout the Helsinki world championship race, may have to change their plans for the Los Angeles Olympic contest because of Eamonn Coghlan of Ireland.

Coghlan's speed over the last two laps was unapproachable. The slow pace played into his hands. He zipped away from the field at will, covering the last 800 meters in 1:54.4 for an elapsed time of 13:28.53. Werner Schildhauer of East Germany was second, while Doug Padilla was the first non-European home, finishing fifth.

The only talent missing from Helsinki was Britain's world record holder Dave Moorecroft (13:00.42), who sat out 1983 with illness and injury. He might have the speed to respond to Coghlan's kick and the strength to win up front.

Mary Decker missed two Olympic Games because of injury and boycott and although she is the best U.S. middle-distance runner, she had never met the world's best until Helsinki. The 1983 world championship final was touted as a duel between Decker and history's greatest women distance runners, Soviets Svyetlana Ulmasova, the 3,000-meter record holder (8:26.78) and Tatyana Kazankina, a two-time Olympic champion and 1,500 meter record holder (3:52.47).

Decker led the final from start to finish. At first, the Soviet women let her do all the frontrunning, but at the bell, the challenge began. At each surge, Mary changed to a higher gear. On the final straight, Kazankina came up to Decker's shoulder. Then, gritting her teeth, Mary found yet another gear and won going away. Brigette Krause of West Germany outleaned the defeated Kazankina for the silver.

Undoubtedly, the Soviets will go back to the drawing board, intent on finding a solution to the one woman who singlehandedly broke their monopoly on women's distance running. Mary Decker faces two other threats to her Olympic aspirations; her propensity toward injury and the five races in four days that are required to repeat her 1,500 / 3,000 meters double.

10,000 Meters

This is the longest race on the track, consisting of twenty-five laps. The theory of middle and long distance tactics is that no runner can win a major championship from the front. The best times of the top runners are within a few seconds of each other. No one is superior enough to undertake the extra work of heading into the wind. United States record holder Alberto Salazar is a prime example of the determined frontrunner who has been out-kicked at the end of some of the world's fastest 10,000-meter races.

Everyone in an Olympic final is there to win. Given this tactical theory, as in most major races, the Olympics might be without a runner who goes to the front and pushes the pace. Such tactics result in a tightly-bunched leading group until the final stages of the race, which plays into the hands of the snappy kickers.

In a slow tactical race at the Helsinki world championship, Alberto Cova of Italy, not one of the fastest on a pure time basis, came sprinting through the last hundred meters, running the final lap in 53.9 seconds to defeat Werner Schildhauer in 28:01.4. Cova had done the same thing in the European championships the previous year. The first five finishers crossed the line within one second of one another. Thirteen of the eighteen finalists were still in contention after 9,000 meters. Many great distance runners were simply out-kicked or jostled into defeat, vainly trying to protect a strong position in the pack.

This outcome may have caused many runners to recalculate their strategy for the Olympic final in Los Angeles. The fact that world records have been run solo refutes the idea that the runner who drafts has a decisive advantage. Henry Rono's existing record of 27:22.5 was such a solo effort.

In 1972, Lasse Viren also demonstrated another of the great risks of pack running when he crashed to the track following a collision with another favorite, Mohamed Gammoudi of Tunisia, who was slower to get up, lost all hope, and quit.

Surely someone will emerge with the confidence to make an early bid from the front, a bold move that will exasperate the kickers. He must have the strength to lead and the belief that he can win while the best in the world breathe down his neck. Perhaps it will be one of the aging greats like Carlos Lopes of Portugal, who has the experience of a silver medalist (1976) and the endurance of a 2:08:39 marathoner, but lacks the last lap speed. Perhaps it will be one of the relatively unknown Ethiopians who have little international experience and rarely run in a crowd.

Marathon (26 miles 385 yards)

The ancient Greek historian, Herodotus, tells us how Pheidippides first ran from Athens to Sparta, 150 miles, in two days, to seek Spartan help for the Athenians in the Persian Wars. Later, at the cost of his life, he brought news to Athens of the victory over Persia at Marathon. According to legend, this Greek messenger was dispatched from the plains of Marathon, on foot, to carry the news of the victory to the people of Athens, 25 miles away. Upon arrival, he had only breath enough left to exclaim "Rejoice, we conquer," before dropping dead in the center of town.

Despite some doubt as to the authenticity of the legend of Pheidippides, the first Olympic marathon race in 1896 took place over the route he was reputed to

Henry Rono KENYA dual world record holder steeplechase 8:05.4 & 10,000 meters 27:22.5.

Alberto Cova ITA won 1983 world championship 10,000 meters with sizzling last lap kick.

have taken, from the battlefield of Marathon to the new Olympic Stadium, a distance of 42 kilometers, 24¾ miles.

Twenty-four competitors, seventeen from Greece, set out along the hot and dusty course from Marathon to the Averoff Stadium in central Athens. Such an endurance race had never before been held and none of the competitors were prepared for such an arduous task. The early leaders were Albin Lermusiaux of France and Edwin Flack of Australia, who had won the 800- and 1,500-meter races in the Olympic Stadium.

At the halfway point, Lermusiaux had such a commanding lead, that the villagers of Karvati attempted to crown him the victor with a laurel wreath. The Frenchman was astute enough to refuse, for shortly thereafter he suffered cramps and exhaustion and had to drop out. Edwin Flack then took the lead for awhile, but could not continue. Greek Spyridon Loues moved into the lead with 3 miles to go.

News of a possible Greek victory spread ahead of Loues. Sixty thousand people in the stadium heard the cheers of the Athenians outside in the streets as Loues approached. The crowd broke into a tumultuous roar as Loues trotted in, to become the first and only Greek victor in the Olympic athletic events. George and Constantine, the young princes, leaped from the Royal box and, dwarfing Loues, ran side by side with him to the finish line.

In his great moment of glory, he was offered anything he wanted by the gentry and businessmen of Athens. True to his heritage and background, he asked only for "a cart and a horse." Spyridon Loues was a shepherd. When he wasn't tending his goat herds, he hauled water and mail throughout the villages around Athens, running miles of trails daily, alongside his mules.

Loues' preparation for the endurance requirements of the marathon was far superior to his opponents' training. They were middle distance runners, unprepared for the demands of three hours of endurance running on trails between Marathon and Athens. Greek runners also finished second and third and only one of the seven foreign competitors finished the course.

Loues' moment of glory soon passed and he was back working the farms around his birthplace of Amaroussion, near Athens. He was seen again briefly during the opening ceremonies of the '36 Games in Berlin, where he was guest of honor of the Berlin Organizing Committee. He died at seventy-one while his country was occupied by the Nazis during World War II.

Compared with the heroic saga of Loues, the following two Olympic marathons were paltry affairs. Michel Theato, a Parisian baker, was awarded the Olympic victory of 1900. The 25-mile marathon course around the back streets of Paris was so confusing that twelve of the nineteen starters gave up in a mixture of confusion and fatigue. No one knew how Theato got to the front of the race and he was accused of taking shortcuts. The decision was clouded with allegations and counterallegations. It was twelve years before the IOC finally confirmed the Frenchman as the official winner.

In St. Louis (1904), English-born Thomas Hicks, representing the United States, won, but not until an imposter, Fred Lorz, had been crowned as the marathon champion. Having dropped out with severe cramps after nine miles, Lorz took an automobile ride towards the finish until the machine broke down four miles from the stadium. Feeling better, he trotted the remaining distance on foot and entered the stadium well ahead of Hicks.

Lorz did nothing to dispel the enthusiasm of the crowd, trapped in his deceit by the loud cheering and the picture taking with Alice Roosevelt, daughter of the President, who placed the laurel wreath on his brow. Eventually, the deception was uncovered in favor of Thomas Hicks, who must be judged as the victim of the biggest hoax in Olympic history. The occasion was perhaps more a testimony to the slipshod conduct of the St. Louis Olympic celebrations than it was to the deliberate deception of Fred Lorz, who the following year managed to win the national championship marathon event without any motorized assistance.

The 1908 London Olympic marathon brought the classic event to the forefront of public attention. It was also the year in which the present day marathon distance was established at 26 miles, 385 yards, the arbitrary distance required to finish the race in front of the royal box where Queen Alexandra was waiting to honor the winner. It was those few extra yards that proved to be the downfall of Dorando Pietri, the tiny moustached and balding Italian candymaker from the isle of Capri.

The typically wet London weather had consistently marred most of the Olympic events in London, but the day of the marathon dawned exceptionally hot. Fifty-six runners set out from Windsor Castle on their way to the new Olympic Stadium at White City. South African Charles Hefferon held a commanding four minute lead at 20 miles, but was fading rapidly when, with two miles to go, he was passed by the steadily trotting Pietri.

Pietri entered the stadium well ahead of Johnny Hayes, in second place. But something was wrong. First, he turned the wrong way onto the track. Once pointed in the right direction, he continued forward with a pathetic drunken stagger. Then, to both the excitement and horror of the capacity crowd, he fell. Four times Pietri collapsed to the track; three times he managed to get up. Finally, with the assistance of the British officials, Pietri was pulled to his feet and assisted across the finish line. The crowd was at first jubilant, but according to the rules, Pietri was disqualified.

Johnny Hayes of the United States finally entered the stadium and, with a rousing sprint, captured the Olympic championship. But it was Pietri and his incredible courage over the last lap within the stadium that captured the hearts of the sympathetic British public. While Hayes, the winner, faded to relative obscurity, Pietri was presented with a special gold cup and became one of the immortals of Olympic history.

The London marathon and all the attention it received triggered a great marathon boom which was to see both Dorando Pietri and Johnny Hayes turn professional and compete against Native-American Longboat and Alfred Schrubb in marathons throughout the world, including an indoor series at Madison Square Garden.

The event had gained new status when seventy competitors lined up at the start of the 1912 Olympic marathon in Stockholm. They were no longer the untrained optimists who had contested the first four Olympic marathons. Great interest in distance running was acknowledged by the addition of the 5,000- and 10,000-meter races to the Olympic program, both won in their inaugural year by Hannes Kolehmainen of Finland in world record times. Kenneth McArthur of South Africa had to overcome Tatu Kolehmainen, Hannes' brother, before he went on to win the marathon event, taking more than 18 minutes off the best time set by Hayes in the previous Games.

Eight years later, after the disruption of the First World War, Hannes Kolehmainen returned to Antwerp, making his first appearance in the classic marathon race and sprinting away from Yuri Lossman of Estonia to win in a record time of 2 hours, 32 minutes, 35.8 seconds, an Olympic record which would stand for twelve years.

In the intervening years, Finland's Paavo Nurmi had established himself as the world's greatest distance runner. Although he had never run in an Olympic Marathon, the thirty-five-year-old Nurmi came to Los Angeles in 1932 as the pre-Games favorite. But before the opening ceremony, he was declared ineligible, banned because he had accepted money to run and was, therefore, considered a professional. Nurmi could only watch the great marathon race that ensued. Argentina's Juan Zabala beat Britain's Sam Ferris in the tightest finish ever, the first four runners separated by only 400 yards. Zabala's gold medal performance of 2 hours, 31 minutes, 36 seconds eclipsed the Olympic record.

The world saw its first sub-two-and-a-half hour marathon at Berlin in 1936 when Kitei Son of Korea, running in the colors of Japan, established a new Olympic standard. It would stand until 1952 when the greatest marathon runner ever, Emil Zatopek, ran away from the field, concluding an historic sweep in the three long distance events on the Olympic program, a feat that has never been duplicated.

Modern marathon running began in Rome in 1960 when Abebe Bikila, running barefoot on the cobblestoned streets, established a standard for the event by running the distance in 2 hours, 15 minutes, 16.2 seconds. Bikila returned to Olympic marathon action in Tokyo four years later and, wearing shoes, ran away from the field, winning by over 4 minutes and setting a new record of 2 hours, 12 minutes, 11.2 seconds. He thus became the first marathon runner in Olympic history to retain the Olympic marathon title, an achievement even more remarkable considering that five weeks before the race in Tokyo, Bikila had undergone surgery for the removal of his appendix.

Bettine Jahn GDR streaking to a 1983 world championship in 100-meter hurdles.

Grete Waitz NOR '83 marathon title.

Rob de Castella AUS men's marathon.

Bikila returned to attempt his third Olympic marathon victory in 1968 in Mexico City. But a recurring leg injury forced him to retire after only 10 miles of the race. Mamo Wolde, also of Kenya, went on to win the race. At thirty-six, Wolde became the oldest Olympic marathon victor.

In 1972, the race went to a U.S. runner for the first time since 1908. Munich-born Frank Shorter broke away from the field after only nine miles and entered the Olympic stadium with a two-minute lead.

The fastest Olympic marathon was run in Montreal in 1976 by Waldemar Cierpinski (2:09:55). The East German, an ex-steeplechaser, ran through a drizzle with Lasse Viren, Frank Shorter, and Derek Clayton before making his move at 30 kilometers, pressing on to lower the Olympic record by more than two minutes.

In Moscow (1980), while many of the great marathon running nations stayed home, Cierpinski joined Abebe Bikila as history's second two-time marathon champion. In 1984, at thirty-four years of age, he will try for an unprecedented third marathon title.

The task is a difficult one, as the level of marathon-running has advanced greatly in recent years. Eight men have run faster than 2:09, with Alberto Salazar of the United States leading the all-time list at 2:08:13. Salazar faced the world's best in an financially attractive match in Rotterdam early in 1983. In finishing fifth, Salazar aggravated an old injury and missed the remainder of the season.

In Rotterdam, and again at the world championship, Rob de Castella of Australia proved to be the man to beat in 1984. He was in complete control of the Helsinki race and left the pack behind at 34 kilometers.

Kevede Balcha of Ethiopia stayed in contact until the final two miles when de Castella powered up a long hill, developing a twenty-second lead. He cruised into the stadium, waving to the crowd, finishing in 2:10:03, an excellent time for the hilly course. Balcha hung on for second while Cierpinski, finishing strongly in third, showed he will still be a serious factor in 1984. The only men missing an opportunity to confront de Castella in 1983 were Japan's Toshihiko Seko who had run 2:08.38 in Tokyo in February and Ron Dixon of New Zealand who won the New York City Marathon in October in a brilliant 2:08:58. When these ironmen come together in the heat of Los Angeles, the contest promises to be one of the classic marathons of all time.

Women will compete in their first Olympic marathon race in Los Angeles. The longest race on the women's program was previously 1,500 meters. The old belief that women were incapable of running greater distances has been completely demolished, not by argument, but by the amazing marathon performances of the women themselves. When Joan Benoit won the Boston Marathon in the record time of 2:22:43, she accomplished what no Olympic marathon champion had achieved prior to 1960, and that includes the performance of Emil Zatopek.

It is clear that women marathoners are nowhere near their limits, they're only beginning. The first women's three-hour time was achieved in 1971, but as soon as their participation in major races was encouraged, the record came tumbling down. Grete Waitz of Norway broke 2:30 for the first time, recording 2:27:33 in the 1979 New York marathon and 2:25:42 the following year.

Joan Benoit chose not to run in the world championships in Helsinki, waiting instead for the 1984 U.S. Olympic trials. Also missing from the field was Allison Roe of New Zealand who ran 2:25:29 in 1981. Thus, Grete Waitz won a comfortable victory, exactly 3 minutes ahead of Marianne Dickerson of the United States, running the marathon for only the third time. Dickerson obviously has room for improvement and joins Waitz, Benoit, and Julie Brown of the United States as serious Olympic contenders.

Men's 110 Meters / Women's 100 Meters

The essence of hurdling is fast sprinting over barriers, which is easier said than done. The men's hurdles are 3 feet, 6 inches high and ten yards apart. To make the optimum three strides between hurdles, it helps to be tall. Olympic finalists average around 6 feet, 2 inches in height. They are powerful sprinters capable of 10.5 seconds or less for 100 meters. Hurdling also requires great flexibility. The hurdler follows the lead leg, dipping toward the barrier, skimming over as low as possible. The trail leg is pulled through to the side and the knee is driven into the next running stride.

Greg Foster of the United States confirmed his world leadership in 1983 with the fastest time of 13.11 seconds and a world championship triumph in Helsinki (13.42), despite hitting the last three hurdles hard and just holding off Arto Bryggare of Finland. Foster is clearly the best bet for 1984, but he's still a stride short of Reynaldo Nehemiah, the world's fastest high hurdler ever at 12.93 seconds before he was lost to American professional football. Such was also the fate of Willie Gault who finished third at Helsinki.

Female hurdlers run over ten 3-foot barriers. Because of the lower height and closer spacings, making the three strides between hurdles does not require an especially tall woman. Hurdlers tend to be about the same size as the female sprinters and just as fast.

East Germany's Bettine Jahn held off teammate Kerstin Knabe for the world championship, recording 12.35, the fastest time ever. The record was disallowed, however, due to a following wind. Notably absent in Helsinki was Lucyna Kalek of Poland, the 1982 European champion in 12.45 seconds, and Yoldanka Donkova of Bulgaria.

Stephanie Hightower, the U.S. record holder (12.79), crashed in the U.S. trials and didn't make the Helsinki team. Benita Fitzgerald carried U.S. hopes in the final but finished eighth.

400-Meter Hurdles

One lap of the track over ten flights of 3-foot hurdles, this is one of the toughest events, demanding great endurance as well as natural speed. One of the most important skills is the athlete's ability to maintain a fast, long, and precise stride pattern between hurdles. Good intermediate hurdling disrupts the sprinting stride the least, the athlete seemingly running over the barrier.

Edwin Moses USA, world's champion 400-meter hurdler and record holder at 47.02 secs.

The stride length must be gauged accurately to avoid having to cut or stretch at a hurdle, thus retarding momentum. Most world-class male hurdlers will take thirteen strides between the hurdles, cutting back to fifteen as fatigue sets in. The hurdles are spaced 35 meters apart with a 45-meter approach to the first and a 40-meter run-in from the tenth barrier to the finish.

No athlete has dominated an event as much as Edwin Moses, the only hurdler to run thirteen strides all the way. Olympic champion in 1976 and undefeated since 1977, Moses finished the 1983 season with a world record 47.02 seconds in Koblenz, West Germany. It was his eighty-seventh consecutive victory. His eighty-first, twenty-two days earlier, was the coveted world championship at Helsinki. Moses, in the tight lane two, ran away from Harald Schmid of West Germany, winning by more than one second, in 47.50.

Andre Phillips of the United States, attempting thirteens for the full distance at Helsinki, came up short at the ninth hurdle and dropped to fifth place. In Koblenz, Phillips made his thirteens and came in with 47.78, the third fastest time in history behind Schmid's 47.38 in 1982. On the '84 horizon, these are the three to consider.

The women's event is a relative newcomer to international athletics and is being contested for the first time in the 1984 Olympics. It is an event which is evolving rapidly with the continual improvement by the Eastern European women.

The current record holder is Soviet Anna Ambrosene (54.02). Anna was beaten in a photo finish at Helsinki by teammate Yekaterina Fesenko in 54.14. Fesenko later said she would run 53 seconds as soon as she was strong enough to run fifteen strides between hurdles.

Ellen Fiedler of East Germany has run 54's each of the past four years and can't be discounted. Ann-Louise Skoglund of Sweden is the top Western hurdler. She ran 54.80 in Helsinki and led the world rankings in 1982 at the age of twenty.

20-Kilometer Walk / 50-Kilometer Walk

Walking is defined as a succession of steps during which contact with the ground is maintained at all times. With each stride, the advancing foot must strike the road or track before the rear foot leaves. Disqualification occurs if, in the opinion of three judges, a competitor's walking action breaks contact. He might at first be cautioned, but only once.

With this major constraint, race walkers have evolved a remarkably speedy technique that requires the flexibility of the hips, which gives walkers their familiar sway. Race walkers average over 9 MPH throughout the 20 kilometers (12.4 miles), while world-class times over 50 kilometers (31 miles) are equivalent to 3-hour marathon speeds. Walkers possess the same physiology as distance runners, usually being small of stature with a resting pulse rate in the low forties. With eight days between the two races on the Los Angeles schedule, many of the top walkers will double.

The '83 world championship results confirmed the status quo in the events, with a triumph for Mexico and East Germany. Young Ernesto Canto continued Mexico's great walking tradition in the 20 kilometer race, when he accelerated away from the field over the last 5 kilometers. Josef Pribilinec of Czechoslovakia, twenty-three years old and improving, stayed close and gained the silver while Spain's veteran '82 European champion, Jose Marin, faded to fourth. Moscow Olympic champion Maurizio Damilano of Italy stayed with the leaders for 15 kilometers, but failed to match speed with the medalists, finishing seventh.

In the 50 kilometers, Mexico's legendary walker, Raul Gonzales, ranked the world's number one walker several times since 1977, led the way for 35 kilometers. But as the Helsinki rain increased, Gonzales faded to fifth. Ronald Weigel of East Germany took over and increased the pace, moving away for a victory in 3:43:8, more than 3½ minutes ahead of Jose Marin. Finland's European champion, Reima Salonen, finished fourth.

Meanwhile, Marco Evoniuk put on a U.S. record performance of 3:56:57 for ninth place. Larry Young, with bronze medals in 1968 and 1972, is the only U.S. walking medalist in Olympic history.

4 X 100-Meter Relay

The sprint relay requires the passing of a 10½ inch-long baton among four teammates who are running at maximum speed. The exchange must be accomplished within a 20-meter passing zone, spaced at 100-meter intervals around the track. There is also a 10-meter acceleration zone which allows the outgoing runner to develop speed before reaching the passing zone.

As the baton carrier hits a check mark, the outgoing runner takes off. Once within the zone, accelerating toward full speed, the runner reaches back, holding his hand as steady as possible. If all goes well, the incoming runner, without slowing down, places the baton in his teammate's hand.

This relay event was first included in the Olympic program in Stockholm (1912), where the British team won in 42.4 seconds. Since then, the United States has been beaten only once. In 1960, Germany was declared the winner because the U.S. team was disqualified when Ray Norton received the baton 3 yards beyond the first passing zone.

The U.S. sprinting depth was well-demonstrated in the 100-meter sweep at the world championship in Helsinki with Carl Lewis, Calvin Smith, and Emmit King going 1–2–3. This speedy trio was joined by Willie Gault, who has since become a professional football player. As with many U.S. relay teams, they had little passing practice. While European national relay teams stay together longer and acquire more baton passing skill, the U.S. teams have always relied on natural speed.

In the Helsinki final, the smooth passing Soviets were only a stride back as Smith passed to Lewis on the anchor leg. Lewis, knowing he had the race won, grinned for a moment, then set out after the record with his bounding strides. The time of 37.86 eclipsed the world record time of 38.03 set by the U.S. squad in the 1977 World Cup.

The United States looked a solid favorite for 1984, but baton passing at such speeds is a risky business and there's no margin for error. The Helsinki final was the greatest relay ever run. The next four teams finished within seven-tenths of a second of the United States. Pietro Mennea's great anchor leg moved Italy into second place, while the USSR's baton skill won the bronze with runners who did not have enough speed to get beyond the quarterfinals of the 100 meters.

The sprint relay was among the first women's events, first appearing at Amsterdam in 1928. Historically, the United States has won the majority of gold, but no medal since 1968. The East Germans have taken over and will go for a fifth consecutive Olympic win in Los Angeles. With Marita Koch and Marlies Gohr, they are still the best, turning in a world record 41.53 in Berlin, followed by a 41.76 to become the 1983 world champions in Helsinki.

Without Evelyn Ashford, the United States world championship team was just a shadow of the inspired group that had beaten the East Germans in 41.63 at the Los Angeles Coliseum in July, 1983. The U.S. team fumbled every pass in the

Helsinki semifinal and didn't make the final. But the speed and determination exists for another challenge of the East Germans in 1984. Diane Williams and Chandra Cheeseborough continue to improve and that might make the difference.

4 X 400-Meter Relay

Whereas the shorter sprint relay depends greatly on baton passing skill, the 4 X 400 meters requires the speed of four great one lap runners. With plenty of depth at 400 meters, the United States has lost only four of the fourteen Olympic finals it has been involved in. U.S. relay teams have beaten three minutes six times, while Kenya is the only other team ever to have done so. The world record still belongs to the 1968 U.S. team at 2:56.16.

The first leg and first turn of the second leg are run in lanes. Thereafter, the runners break for the inside. Baton passing must occur within the 20-meter zone. As the incoming runner is tired and slowing unpredictably, the exchange is usually done visually, the outgoing runner looking back to grasp the baton.

In 1984, the United States will certainly have its usual quartet of 45-second speedsters, led by young Michael Franks, Sunder Nix, and the welcome addition of Edwin Moses to relay racing. The United States will be tough to beat, especially at home in Los Angeles. But the rest of the world has been catching up.

The world championships proved inconclusive when Willie Smith of the United States bumped the leading Soviet on the third leg and went down. Edwin Moses, running anchor, was deprived of a chance of seeing what he could do against 1980 Olympic champion, Viktor Markin, who went on for the Soviet victory in 3:00.79. The highly-touted West German team suffered when its European record holder, Erwin Skamrahl (44.50), lost 15 yards on the first leg to a brilliant run by Soviet Sergey Lovachev, a margin that remained intact throughout the race.

High Jump

The development of high jumping has risen in direct proportion to high jump landing areas. Valery Brumel of the USSR posted a world record 2.26 meters (7 ft. 5 in.) in 1962, rolling around the bar with the classic straddle technique, landing in a sawdust and sand pit.

With the advent of built-up foam rubber landing areas, the jumper has no reason to consider landing technique at all. Dick Fosbury surprised the world in the Mexico City Olympics (1968), unveiling his "Fosbury Flop," winning the gold medal with a back layout clearance of 7 feet 4¼ inches. The technique is now called the "Flop" and is employed by practically every jumper of world-class level.

The jumper approaches the bar with a curved run, plants the take-off foot powerfully, drives the leading knee, and while lifting the hips, lays back, curving the shoulders around the bar, bringing the legs and feet over last.

The big story of the Helsinki world championship was the appearance of China's Zhu Jianhua, who earlier in 1983 set a world record at 2.37 meters (7 ft. 9¼

Tamara Bykova USSR world high jump champion and record holder at 2.04 meters.

Sergey Bubka USSR 1983 world champion with a pole vault of 5.70 meters (18 ft 8 ¼in).

in.). He had never competed in a major international meet before the Helsinki world championships. He cleared every height through 2.26 meters (7 ft. 5 in.) with ease, then stalled after clearing 2.29 meters (7 ft. 6 in.) and settled for the bronze medal.

Tyke Peacock of the United States equaled the U.S. record at 2.32 meters (7 ft. 7¼ in.) on his third and final attempt, but unknown Soviet Gennadiy Avdeyenko went over on his first jump and won the championship. Prior to Helsinki, few had heard of this 6-foot 7-inch blond Ukrainian. At nineteen years of age, he was sent to Helsinki to gain experience. No one expected much. His ideal physical stature and youth suggests further room for improvement and mark him as the man to beat in '84. Perhaps Avdeyenko will be the one to provide the performance breakthrough that is expected when the top twelve jumpers on the '83 world list are separated by only two inches. Zhu Jianhua led all when, returning home from Helsinki, he improved his record to 2.38 meters (7 ft. 9¾ in.).

Tamara Bykova of the USSR is the best female jumper in the world and proved it with a 2.01 meter (6 ft. 7 in.) world championship victory over Ulrike Meyfarth of West Germany, the 1972 Olympic champion. Both women cleared a world record height of 2.03 meters (6 ft. 8 in.) in London two weeks after the Helsinki championship, before Bykova went 2.04 meters (6 ft. 8¼ in.) to claim sole possession.

U.S. jumpers are close. Louise Ritter cleared a national record 2.00 meters (6 ft. 6¾ in.) in the Coliseum, defeating East Germany's best. Coleen Reinstra-Sommer had injury problems in 1983, but has cleared 2 meters indoors and should be a factor in '84.

Pole Vault

In this discipline one finds the acrobats of track and field. The vault is a dramatic synthesis of speed, strength, and risk. Technically, the pole vault is perhaps the most complex of all track and field events.

The pole is a wrapped fiberglass tube at least 16 feet in length. The athlete utilizes an approach of at least 120 feet. As he sprints down the runway toward take-off, he builds speed. At the end of the approach, everything happens at once. Traveling at top speed, the vaulter plants the pole into the take-off box. Sounds simple, but it's the most critical move. Everything must be in line. The hand hold at the moment of the plant must be straight above the head. The take-off foot must be in the precise spot in line with the hands above. If the take-off foot is in front of this mark, the vaulter not only has a weak take-off position, but also puts severe strain on his arms and back.

Once off the ground, the vaulter must hold the pole away from his body. He pushes it toward the cross bar while beginning to invert, or turn upside down. When the pole returns from its bend, with his hips above his head, the vaulter pulls straight up with the inverted body. His top hand is guiding the catapulting action of

Wladyslaw Kozakiewicz POL vaulted a world record 5.78 meters to win Moscow Olympics.

the pole and pushing-off, clearing a bar three feet higher than his hand-hold. It happens quickly, but if watched in slow motion, the dynamics become perceptible.

After being introduced into the first Olympic Games in 1896, the U.S. men never lost a pole vault title until 1972, when Wolfgang Nordwig showed that the East Germans had learned to vault. Two Polish vaulters won the following two Olympics, Wladyslaw Kozakiewicz winning the gold in Moscow with 5.78 meters (18 ft. 11½ in.), a world record. Subsequently, two Frenchmen, first Thierry Vigneron and then Pierre Quinon, upped the record to 5.83 meters (19 ft. 1½ in.).

All of the top talent was assembled in Helsinki, including Billy Olson from Amarillo, Texas, who had cleared over 19 feet indoors. Unfortunately, the wind caused the downfall of many of the top vaulters in Helsinki. Pole vaulters dread head winds and blustery cross winds, which interfere with the approach and the accuracy of the pole plant. Europeans seem to do best at mastering difficult conditions, perhaps because they have more experience vaulting in less than ideal weather.

Olson and Quinon failed three times to clear their opening heights in Helsinki. They were out, along with five other vaulters. No vaulter came close to his best, except an unknown nineteen-year-old Soviet, Sergey Bubka, who easily cleared 5.70 meters (18 ft. 8¼ in.) on his first attempt. Soviet teammate Konstantin Volkov won the silver medal.

The outcome of the Olympic pole vault in 1984 could depend on wind conditions. Many of the world's best vaulters need the confidence provided by ideal conditions to vault close to their best. Bubka, who had nothing to lose in Helsinki, proved to have great competitive instincts for one so young. Afterward he said, "Now I want to better the world record at Los Angeles during the Olympic Games."

Long Jump

The feats of Jesse Owens in this event are legendary. His world record jump of 8.13 meters (26 ft. 8¼ in.) stood for twenty-five years.

If Owens was ahead of his time, how do we rate the 8.90 meters, (29 ft. 2½ in.) jump of Bob Beamon? In one instant in Mexico City (1968), the world record was advanced by 1 foot 9½ inches, more improvement than in the previous forty years. The effect of this magical performance was such that 1964 Olympic gold medalist Lynn Davis actually left the field in disgust and defeat after witnessing Beamon's enormous leap.

The best way to describe the character of the long jump is to analyze Bob Beamon's talents. The 6-foot 3-inch Beamon was world-class in the sprints. During pre-Olympic training at Lake Tahoe, California, he ran a 10.1 for 100 meters. Combine this raw speed with Beamon's jumping ability, developed through basketball, and you have the two basic requirements for the long jump.

Moments before his historic jump, dark clouds gathered and erratic winds announced an impending rain storm. With an assisting wind of two meters per second, the maximum allowable, Beamon sped down the runway and hit the take-off board perfectly. Then he seemed almost airborne. When he finally landed, Beamon had bypassed 28 feet and jumped close to ten yards. This was truly an incredible performance, one that seemed better suited to to the twenty-first century. Beamon broke the world record by 6.5 percent, the largest margin of improvement ever in a track and field event.

After the Beamon record, the long jump seemed to lose its luster. No athlete could even come close to the 29 foot 2½ inch mark. Athletes who could jump 27 feet were mere mortals, and the international competitions in this event seemed almost dull. Then, in 1982, a youngster from the University of Houston began to challenge the Beamon barrier. Carl Lewis was not intimidated by the record and has come close to joining the 29-foot club. His jump of 8.79 meters (28 ft. 10¾ in.) revived interest in the event and Lewis stands as the clear favorite for the 1984 Olympic Gold. Carl Lewis has sub-10 second, 100-meter speed and has his eyes set on becoming both the world's fastest runner and longest jumper.

Carl's sister, Carol Lewis, is the finest U.S. woman long jumper, who reached her best in placing third in the world championships. Heike Daute of East Germany won the Helsinki contest with a wind-aided 23 feet 10¼ inches, while just eighteen years old. She out-jumped Anisova Cusmir of Romania, the world record holder at 24 feet 4½ inches.

Triple Jump

The triple jump, like the long jump, requires good running speed on the approach to the take off board. During the "hop" phase, the triple-jumper tries to project himself more horizontally, covering as much distance as possible, yet preserving his momentum and control in order to execute the lengthy step and an effective jump, projected as far as possible into the pit.

The triple jump is a technical event in which the proper ratio of technique and effort must be made in each phase of the jump. When Joao de Oliviera of Brazil set the current world record in Mexico City (1975 Pan-Am Games), his hop measured 20 feet even, his step, 17 feet 7 inches, and his final jump, 21 feet 1 inch, giving him a total triple jump of 58 feet 8 inches.

A year later in Montreal, Oliviera could only manage the bronze medal. For the third straight Olympics the gold went to Victor Saneev of the USSR. Recent triple jump history has been dominated by East Europeans, especially the Soviets. Saneev came within inches of a fourth consecutive Olympic gold medal in Moscow, reluctantly yielding the championship to Jaak Uudmae, also from the USSR, with Oliviera again capturing the bronze.

Zdzislaw Hoffman of Poland surprised everyone, including himself, by winning the 1983 world championship with a leap of 17.42 meters (57 ft. 2 in.). The early leader, Willie Banks of the United States, placed second with the same distance as U.S. college student Ajayi Agbebaku of Nigeria. Banks received the silver based on the longer second-best jump. In the '84 final, it will most likely be these three and 1982 world leader Keith Connor of Great Britain contending for medals.

Shot Put

The men's shot is 8.257 kilograms (16 lb.), while the women's is 4 kilograms (8 lb. 13 oz.). The shot is thrown from the confines of a 7-foot concrete ring, encircled by a steel rim with a wooden stop-board at the front. The thrower attempts to use as much of the circle as possible in accelerating the shot from a static position to maximum velocity at the point of release.

Two techniques are most frequently employed. The O'Brien technique was devised by Parry O'Brien and helped him become the first thrower to break 60 feet and earn two Olympic gold medals in '52 and '56. The shot putter faces away from the throwing direction and hops backward in a direct glide across the circle. The feet are planted in the front of the ring where the lifting and rotating of the trunk create a torque effect. The shoulders, arm and wrist snap, accelerating the shot to the point of release over the stop-board, launching the implement on its parabolic flight.

The second method, the rotational technique, employs an action around the ring with footwork similar to that used by the discus thrower. The thrower arrives at the same throwing stance in the front of the ring as that yielded by the O'Brien method. However, if it can be mastered, there is more rotational energy to be applied to the shot.

Shot putters are big, fast, explosive athletes, trained as much in the weight room as they are in the throwing circle. Most world-class male shot putters weigh over 250 pounds, with enormous strength that some say is built with anabolic steroids.

In fear of sophisticated testing at the '84 Olympics, shot putters will have to stop steroid consumption at least two months before the event. This fear complicates the picture, because in projecting medalists, the question becomes, whose performance will drop off most?

Edward Sarul of Poland won the world championship with 21.40 meters (70 ft. 2 ¼ in.). The expected battle between Udo Beyer of East Germany and Dave Laut of the United States never materialized. Beyer, the '76 Olympic champion who had set a world record of 22.22 meters (72 ft. 10¾ in.) in the Coliseum just a month earlier, placed sixth and said he was injured. Laut, who had thrown almost 72 feet earlier, could do no better than 67 feet 7 inches for fourth. Regardless of their disappointments, Beyer and Laut are expected to be among the best shot putters in the world in 1984.

Discus Throw

The discus throw is one of the most ancient of events, often depicted in Greek art. The original discus was a flat stone of various weight. The modern discus weighs 2 kilograms (4.41 lb.). The women's discus is half as heavy at 1 kilogram (2.2 lb.). The discus is thrown from a concrete circle 2.50 meters (8 ft. 2½ in.) in diameter. It must land within a 45-degree sector. Each qualifier gets three throws, the best eight finishers advance for a final three throws.

The throwers use 1½ turns around the ring, endeavoring to generate rotational energy. Moving through a throwing position in the front of the ring, a final pull sends the discus along its flight path with maximum velocity. The discus rotates off the index finger, spinning through the air, creating some of its own aerodynamic lift. Throwers favor a moderate head wind.

It takes a good deal of strength to handle world-class technique, overcome the inert implement and toss the discus over 200 feet. Throwers are usually tall, have a wide arm span, and develop their explosive power through heavy weightlifting.

Appropriately for such a classical event, the modern history of the discus has had its classical, heroic figure. Al Oerter is the modern symbol of Olympic discus throwing, having held his Olympic title throughout four Olympiads. Oerter is also distinguished as the first man to throw over 200 feet, which he did in 1962, early in his career.

The world championship final was an all-European affair, with some notable disappointments. Mac Wilkins of the United States, 1976 Olympic champion and former record holder, failed to make the final rounds, finishing tenth. The world record holder, Yuriy Dumchev of the USSR at 71.86 meters (235 ft. 9 in.), threw only 193 feet in the qualifying round and progressed no further. Imrich Burger of Czechoslovakia produced the best throw of 67.72 meters (222 ft. 2 in.), winning by a foot over the muscular Cuban Luis Delis, the bronze medalist in Moscow (1980).

The most notable absentee from Helsinki was Ben Plucknett of the United States, who returned from a steroid suspension to throw 234 feet for second in the 1983 world rankings. He produced enough consistently long throws to become a serious factor in the '84 Olympics.

Hammer Throw

Today's hammer bears little resemblance to the wooden shafted sledgehammer thrown at the Scottish Highland Games a century ago. The modern hammer is a composite of a steel ball, cable, and handle, weighing 8.257 kilograms (16 lb.) and measuring 4 feet in length.

The thrower seeks to accelerate the hammer to maximum release velocity while remaining within the confines of a 7-foot diameter concrete circle. After a few preliminary swings, the first of three or four turns around the ring begins, the hammer being delivered with a final explosive pull. It must land within a 45-degree sector.

Tom Petranoff USA world record holder javelin.

Udo Beyer GDR Shot put gold 1976.

Yuri Sedykh USSR hammer gold 76/80.

The USSR has swept the last two Olympic championships. Both in Montreal and Moscow, the winner was Yuriy Syedikh, who retained his number one world ranking through 1982. His teammate, Sergey Litvinov, the silver medalist in Moscow, set a world record of 84.14 meters (276 ft.) earlier in 1983 and opened the Helsinki world championships with a winning throw of 82.68 meters (271 ft. 3 in.) in the first round. He also had two other throws in excess of Syedikh's silver medal throw of 80.94 meters (265 ft. 7 in.)

The United States has not provided a serious hammer contender since Hal Connolly won in 1956. None of the three U.S. throwers in Helsinki survived the qualifying round.

Javelin Throw

The men's javelin weighs 800 grams (1 lb. 12 oz.) and is a minimum of 2.60 meters (8 ft. 6¼ in.) long. The women throw an implement of 600 grams (1 lb. 5 oz.), which is 2.2 meters (7 ft. 2½ in.) in length.

The javelin thrower approaches the foul line with a run-up of approximately 100 feet. Through a series of cross-steps, the thrower brings the javelin back into a cocked position. The feet are planted and the javelin is pulled powerfully, with the maximum amount of energy being applied through the axis of the javelin, throwing through the point. The thrower executes a reverse step to avoid stepping over the scratch line and watches his javelin sail almost the length of a football field.

Slight headwinds favor the javelin thrower, giving the implement more lift. Blustery conditions, which may prevail in the Coliseum, could hinder some throwers and aid others. In track history, the Finns used to dominate the javelin. Not until 1953 did the Finns relinquish the world record. The Soviets took over with Janis Lusis becoming history's most accomplished javelin exponent, winning in Mexico City (1968) and falling just one centimeter short of Klaus Wolfermann in Munich (1972).

The current world leaders are Detlef Michel of East Germany and world record holder Tom Petranoff of the United States at 99.72 meters (327 ft. 2 in.). The two split the '83 season with Michel winning the all-important world championship from Petranoff on a cold, rainy night in Helsinki when everyone's distance was down. Petranoff won earlier in the '83 East Germany versus United States dual meet in the Coliseum. He sailed one throw out over 310 feet after Michel had applied the pressure of a 300-foot throw.

An inspired last round throw by Finland's Tiina Lillak brought the world championship to her javelin-crazed nation. The world record holder at 245 feet 3 inches, Lillak trailed Fatima Whitbread of Britain, who produced a first attempt of 69.14 meters (226 ft. 10 in.). As Lillak's final throw pierced the ground at 70.82 meters (232 ft. 4 in.), the Helsinki crowd roared its appreciation of Finland's only world championship victory. Whitbread won the silver medal, affirming her continued improvement. U.S. throwers Karin Smith and Kate Schmidt were far short of their previous world-class level.

Decathlon

The decathlon relates back to ancient Greece. The Greeks featured the pentathlon in the ancient Games and it consisted of long jump, discus, javelin, sprint, and wrestling.

America's first multi-event competition was held in 1884 when the AAU staged the all-around event, consisting of ten individual events. In the St. Louis Olympic Games (1904), there was an all-around event which consisted of the 100-yard dash, shot put, high jump, 880-yard walk, 16-pound hammer throw, pole vault, 120-yard hurdles, 56-pound weight, long jump, and mile run.

The modern version of the decathlon began in 1912 in Stockholm, with a U.S. victory in both the pentathlon and the decathlon by Jim Thorpe. Since then, the United States has won ten of a possible fourteen gold medals through 1980. Bob Mathias of the United States is the only man to repeat as a two-time gold medalist in the Olympic decathlon.

The United States is the only nation to win the event more than once. But the United States has suffered a recent slump and is waiting to discover an individual who can challenge the leaders in today's decathlon world: 1980 Olympic champion Daley Thompson of Great Britain, who also won the '83 world championship, and the current world record holder, Jurgen Hingsen of West Germany, who has scored 8777 points.

The two-day drama of the decathlon consists of ten events, five each day. On the first day, the events are the 100-meter sprint, long jump, shot put, high jump, and 400-meter run. The second day begins with the high hurdles, followed by the discus throw, pole vault, javelin throw, and the 1,500-meter race. The competitor's performance in each event is measured against a scoring table. An athlete does not have to win any event to be victorious overall; he simply has to have the highest cumulative score.

There have been five separate sets of scoring tables. The latest revision was adopted in 1962. The official tables are extremely detailed, giving the progressive performance required for each point. The following example indicates the relative performance at three levels.

The Olympic decathlon is an arduous event, requiring up to ten hours of competition each day. The decathlete approaches each trial with 100-percent effort as every stride, jump, and throw is a direct confrontation with the scoring table. The decathlon requires the ideal balance of physical qualities, speed, strength, agility, skill, and endurance. It is designed to measure the most well-developed athlete. To the Olympic decathlon champion goes the title, "World's Greatest Athlete."

Currently, the event is dominated by the two greatest decathlon exponents of all time, who have shared the last five world records. In two recent head-to-head contests, however, Britain's Daley Thompson has twice defeated West German Jurgen Hingsen.

DECATHLON SCORING GUIDE

Event	600 points	800 points	1000 points
100 m	12.0 sec	11.1 sec	10.3 sec
Long jump	5.98 m (19 ft 7½ in)	6.90 m (22 ft 7½ in)	7.90 m (25 ft 11 in)
Shot put	12.01 m (39 ft 4¾ in)	15.19 m (49 ft 10 in)	18.75 m (61 ft 6¼ in)
High jump	1.71 m (5 ft 7½ in)	1.93 m (6 ft 4 in)	2.17 m (7 ft 1½ in)
400 m	55.1 sec	50.2 sec	46.0 sec
110 m hurdles	17.8 sec	15.5 sec	13.7 sec
Discus	35.77 m (117 ft 4 in)	45.99 m (150 ft 10 in)	57.50 m (188 ft 7 in)
Pole vault	3.24 m (10 ft 7½ in)	3.97 m (13 ft 0¼ in)	4.78 m (15 ft 8 in)
Javelin	47.56 m (156 ft 1 in)	63.17 m (207 ft 3 in)	81.00 m (265 ft 9 in)
1500 m	4 min 28.4 sec	4 min 02.0 sec	3 min 40.2 sec

In 1982, Thompson came to the European championships in Athens having lost his world record to Hingsen. He proceeded not only to win, but regain the record as well. Doubt surrounded Thompson prior to the 1983 world championship due to groin and back injuries. But Thompson again proved to be the greater competitor, scoring 8666 points, more than 100 points ahead of Hingsen. It was an impressive total considering the rainy and windy conditions on the second day.

Their next meeting in Los Angeles will be eagerly awaited. Both athletes prepared throughout the winter in the friendly climate of Southern California, Thompson in Irvine and Hingsen in Santa Barbara. Thompson hopes to join Bob Mathias as the second two-time Olympic decathlon champion and is young enough to dream of a third gold in Seoul, Korea (1988).

Hingsen, who like Thompson will be twenty-six years old when the '84 decathlon gets underway, obviously has different plans. Almost 6 feet 7 inches tall and weighing 220 pounds, he is an awesome physical specimen with the powerful build ideal for a decathlete. He is the event's physical prototype, and has the mechanical advantages of an athlete who may one day break 9,000 points. Thompson at 6 feet 1 inch and 190 pounds will again rely on his speed and competitive tenacity against Hingsen.

If anyone can overcome the two it might be Hingsen's teammate, Siegfried Wentz, who improved to 8714 points in 1983. Mark Anderson is the best U.S. prospect having scored 8250, but his nonfinishing performance in Helsinki did little to improve his hopes for a medal in Los Angeles.

Heptathlon

In 1981, the heptathlon, a seven-event test of women's all-around ability, was introduced to replace the five-event pentathlon. New to the '84 Olympic program,

World champion Daley Thompson GBR & Jurgen Hingsen GER hurdle in 6th decathlon event.

Thompson and Hingsen in 1500 pack.

the heptathlon consists of the following events:
Day 1—100-meter hurdles, shotput, high jump, 200 meters.
Day 2—Long jump, javelin, 800 meters.

Many experts thought the addition of the 800 meters would change the physical character required for the heptathlon. However, the world's leading pentathletes easily made the adjustment.

Ramona Neubert of East Germany was twenty-two when she captured fourth place in the Moscow pentathlon (1980). Now she is the owner of the heptathlon world record at 6836 points and was winner of the Helsinki world championship with 6714 points. Her teammates, Sabine Paetz and young Anke Vater, pushed her all the way to sweep the event, and give Neubert her only real competition in the three-year history of the heptathlon, during which she has been unbeaten.

Jackie Joyner was the best of the U.S. heptathletes in Helsinki when she pulled out with an injury after the first day. U.S. record holder Jane Frederick (6457) failed to start the final event, the 800 meters, while in fourth place, adding to previous big meet disappointments.

A CHOICE OF CHAMPIONS

The fame of the Olympic festivals
Shines from afar among the racecourses . . .
The victor all his remaining days
Breathes a delicious and serene air
When he remembers the Games.
—Pindar

Featured herein are twenty of the great performers who illuminate Olympic history, athletes who peaked at the Games and thrived on the competition. Their moment of achievement stands fixed in time, preserved in memory and legend. They played their part on the Olympic stage to perfection.

Iolanda Balas (Romania. December 12, 1936)

Iolanda Balas dominated the high jump from 1958 to 1966, raised the world record fourteen times and won two Olympic titles. Her first world record came in July, 1956. She went to the Melbourne Olympics a few months later as one of the favorites, but cleared only 5 feet 5¾ inches, placing fifth. She also lost her world record to Mildred McDaniel, who cleared 1.76 meters (5 ft. 9¼ in.) to win the gold medal.

The tall, leggy blonde, 6 feet¾ inches tall, jumped her own height (1.85 m) and won her first Olympic championship in Rome (1960). She went on to achieve

Iolanda Balas ROM

1.91 meters (6 ft. 3¼ in.) in 1961, a world record that would last for a decade. In Tokyo (1964), she came within one centimeter of this record in winning her second consecutive Olympic title with 1.90 meters (6 ft. 2¾ in.).

Remarkably, as the most successful female high jumper, Balas employed a version of the old-fashioned scissors technique, considered to be extremely primitive. If she had utilized a modern flop technique, with her great talent, she may have set the record much higher.

Bob Beamon (USA. August 29, 1946)

Many people credit Bob Beamon with the single most-outstanding performance in track and field history in the Olympic Games. It was his 8.90 meter (29 ft. 2½ in.) long jump in Mexico City that added some 55 centimeters (21½ in.) to the world record.

It was on the afternoon of October 18, 1968 when darkening clouds were starting to envelop the Estadio Olympico. Bob Beamon, who had experienced difficulty qualifying that morning, stood at the head of the runway for his first jump in the finals. He was a talented sprinter and had jumped 27 feet 4 inches earlier in the year. Many thought he might win, but nobody in the Olympic world was expecting this jump.

He approached the take-off board at full speed, assisted by the altitude and a maximum allowable following wind. Beamon hit the board perfectly and was airborne. Upon landing, he knew immediately it was a great leap. The officials had to go for a measuring tape because he had jumped beyond the telescopic

Bob Beamon USA

measuring device. When the jump was measured, and the result announced, his legs became shaky. No one thought it was possible to jump so far, not even Beamon. The 1964 Olympic gold medalist from England, Lynn Davis, saw the jump, turned and left the stadium knowing he couldn't come close.

Bob Beamon took only one jump in the Olympic Games, competed one more season, but never again exceeded 27 feet. In one moment, he had achieved more than his ultimate goal. He had little incentive to continue jumping and retired.

Abebe Bikila (Ethiopia. August 7, 1932–October 25, 1973)

Abebe Bikila was the first man to win two Olympic marathon titles and the first of the great African distance runners. He was an unknown prior to the Rome Olympics (1960). No one realized his pre-Game performance of 2:21.23 was a very fast time, considering the altitude of Ethiopia.

The world became aware of Abebe Bikila when the barefoot runner with a beautifully regal stride pulled away from the marathon field along Rome's ancient Appian Way. Bikila reached the finish at the Arch of Constantine in 2 hours, 15 minutes, 16.2 seconds, the world's best time.

Four years later, he seemingly floated into the Tokyo stadium, four minutes ahead of the next Olympic marathon runner. With his magnificent stride, he crossed the finish line in 2 hours, 12 minutes, 11.2 seconds, another world record. Then, in his inexhaustible manner, having snapped the tape, he jogged to the infield to do some calisthenics, as if warming up for another race.

In Mexico City, Bikila returned as the favorite, but a leg injury kept him from continuing beyond 10 miles. Teammate Mamo Wolde maintained Ethiopia's string of victories.

The following year, Bikila was in a serious automobile accident, which damaged his spinal cord, leaving him paralyzed. He died in 1973 at forty-one, suffering a stroke as a result of compounded health problems related to his injury. Born a peasant, Abebe Bikila rose to become captain of his country's palace guard. He died a national hero and was buried with full military honors.

Fanny Blankers-Koen (Holland. April 26, 1918)

Fanny Blankers-Koen was unquestionably the greatest woman athlete of her era. Fanny was eighteen when she competed in the Berlin Olympics (1936) and finished sixth in the high jump. It would be twelve years and a war later before she would compete in the London Olympics (1948) as a thirty-year-old homemaker, mother of two and win four gold medals.

In the intervening years, when Germany occupied Holland, few athletics events were permitted. Fanny set world records in sprint events, hurdles, high jump, long jump, and the pentathlon.

In London, Fanny had a busy schedule. She ran in twelve races in nine days and won them all. Her four gold medal events were the 100 meters, 200 meters,

Abebe Bikila ETH

Fanny Blankers-Koen HOL

80-meter hurdles, and sprint relay. Had she had more time and energy she might have entered the jumping events and possibly won both.

As she raced around the Wembley track, so noticeable in her orange Dutch team shorts, she brought new respect for women's participation in Olympic sport. The appreciative crowd named her The Flying Dutchwoman.

Fanny Blankers-Koen won European titles in 1950 and competed in the Helsinki Olympics (1952) where, due to illness, she did not do well. After her retirement, she remained active in the administration of sport.

Valeri Borzov (USSR. October 20, 1949)

Although Valeri Borzov was not the first great athlete to win the Olympic sprint double, he was the first European and the only Soviet to accomplish this feat. But the superior style with which he achieved his Munich gold medals was indeed unique.

Borzov won the 100 meters and 200 meters in undisputed fashion. In the short run, the elegant sprinter glanced casually across at his opponents, his expression radiating self-confidence, his perfect stride widening his lead. His arms were held aloft in victory well before reaching the finish line in 10.17 seconds.

In the 200 meters, the field came out of the turn even, but the blond, elegant sprinter from the Ukraine was coming on with his powerful strides, driving quickly to a two-meter lead. When he knew his work was done, he again took a long look, threw up his arms, and eased across the finish line in a brilliant 20 seconds flat.

Valeri Borzov is said to have been built, almost machine-like, by the Soviet system. Athletically built, Borzov was reared in the weight room as well as on the track. The likable arrogance he demonstrated, however, is not the product of a laboratory. Such self-confidence and blazing speed is the mark of a gifted natural talent and the product of hard work.

Borzov performed again at the Montreal Olympics (1976). No male sprinter has ever achieved consecutive victories. Borzov, having lost an edge, worked hard all the way, leaned toward the finishing line to grab a bronze medal behind Hasely Crawford of Jamaica. He passed the 200 meters, but helped the USSR relay team to a bronze, adding to the relay silver Borzov had gained in Munich.

Borzov later married gymnastics star Ludmilla Turischeva.

Herb Elliott (Australia. February 25, 1938)

From the age of sixteen when he started serious training, until his retirement in 1961 at the age of twenty-two, Herb Elliott never lost a mile or a 1,500 meter race. In 1958, he ran his first four-minute mile before his twentieth birthday. Later that year, he set world records for the mile at 3:54.5 and 1,500 meters at 3:36.0.

In the Rome Olympics (1960), he won the 1,500 by a wide margin in a world record 3:35.6. With 700 meters remaining, he made his break, powering away from a discouraged field. His lead continued to increase to 20 yards at the tape, the most convincing victory ever.

Elliott was inspired watching the Olympic Games in Melbourne (1956), particularly by the performance of Vladimir Kuts. He began to train harder under the guidance of Percy Cerutty, whose nearby training camp at Portsea was set in the sand dunes. Elliott built his enormous strength racing around the trails, sprinting up the dunes, and lifting weights. His demanding training effort and self-confidence built a competitive spirit that was devastating on the track.

Alberto Juantorena (Cuba. November 21, 1950)

Many people believe Alberto Juantorena was the foremost athlete of the Montreal Olympics (1976). His unprecedented 400/800 meters double was accomplished with impressive raw strength and little tactical skill. The powerful, 6 foot 3 inch, 185-pound sprinter dwarfed his rivals, charging around the track, overpowering them with his elongated strides.

In the 800 meters, in which he had never competed seriously before 1976, Juantorena was always at the front of the pack, forcing a quick pace, resisting the challenges of Rick Wohlhuter of the United States and Ivo Van Damme of Belgium. He crossed the finish line in 1:43.5, a new world record.

Starting slowly in the 400 meters, Juantorena had to come from behind to win, catching and passing Fred Newhouse in a full power drive down the stretch. His 44.26 seconds was the best 400-meter performance ever achieved at sea level. Alberto Juantorena won Cuba's first track and field gold medals which he

Alberto Juantorena CUBA

enthusiastically dedicated to the Cuban revolution.

In 1977, Juantorena again won the 400 and 800 meters at the World Cup in Dusseldorf. He had his first Achilles tendon trouble the following year and, after surgery, was not fully recovered prior to the Moscow Olympics, where he ran fourth in the 400 meters.

He returned an aging warlord to contest the 1983 world championship in Helsinki, saying he was in great shape. After winning his first heat, he stepped on the curb of the track and severly tore ligaments in his ankle, requiring surgery. He was quick to point out that his career is not over and to expect him back in Los Angeles.

Tatyana Kazankina (USSR. December 17, 1950)

The diminutive Tatyana Kazankina, at 5 feet 3¾ inches tall and 106 pounds, must be one of the least imposing athletic legends ever. This tiny, frail looking economics graduate of Leningrad University came from nowhere to capture both women's middle distance titles in Montreal (1976) and, more than anyone, unfolded the real potential for women in these events.

The 800-meter event was revolutionized when three women set out on a 55.0-second first lap. Kazankina kicked coming off the last bend and took the lead 50 meters out, coming home in 1:54.94, which took more than a second off the world record.

Tatyana already held the record for the 1,500 meters, having run 3:55.0 just before the Games. In the Olympic final, the pace was very slow until the last lap. Kazankina hardly seemed to try until the final 80 meters when she sprinted ahead at will, winning in 4:05.48. Her last lap was covered in a sizzling 56.9 seconds.

Four years later, she contested only the 1,500 meters in Moscow and won her third Olympic gold with ease, finishing ten yards clear of the field in 3:56.58.

The final chapter in the Tatyana Kazankina saga still remains to be written. In 1984, at thirty-four years of age, she will try to capture her fourth gold medal at 3,000 meters.

Bob Mathias (USA. November 17, 1930)

In London (1948) Bob Mathias, a seventeen-year-old high school boy from Tulare, California, slogged through the mud and rain to win the most demanding of events, the decathlon. Four years later, with his world record of 7731 points in Helsinki, he became the only two-time Olympic decathlon winner in history.

Remarkably, Mathias had entered his first decathlon just two months before his London appearance. Before the 1948 season, he had never tried half of the ten tests of speed, skill, and stamina he would face in the Olympics under the most distressing conditions.

In 1950, having completed his freshman year at Stanford University in California, Mathias won the U.S. national championships with a world record 7453

Bob Mathias USA

points. In 1951, Mathias played football at Stanford and was part of a conference championship team.

In Helsinki (1952), Mathias won his second Olympic title at the ripe old age of twenty-one. His performances throughout the two-day competition were: 10.9 seconds 100 meters; 6.98 meters (22 ft. 11 in.) long jump; 15.30 meters(50 ft. 2½ in.) shot put; 1.90 meters (6 ft. 2¾ in.) high jump; 50.2 seconds 400 meters; 14.7 seconds hurdles; 46.89 meters (153 ft. 9¾ in.) discus throw; 4.00 meters (13 ft. 1½ in.) pole vault; 59.21 meters (194 ft. 2½ in.) javelin throw; and 4:50.8 1,500 meters. His total score was 7731 points, an improvement of almost 300 points over his old world record.

In 1953, Mathias acted in a movie about his life and was declared a professional. Reluctantly he retired, undefeated in all of his ten decathlons. After serving in the Marine Corps, Bob Mathias became a politician, was elected to the U.S. Congress and served for eight years. Subsequently, he was director of the U.S. Olympic Training Center in Colorado Springs, and in 1983, became the executive director of the National Fitness Foundation, based in Indianapolis.

Paavo Nurmi (Finland. June 13, 1897–October 2, 1973)

In twelve Olympic finals, Paavo Nurmi won nine gold medals and three silvers, the most track and field medals ever won by an individual in the Olympic Games. During his long career, he revolutionized middle and long distance running, setting twenty-two world records.

His career started with the influence of Hannes Kolehmainen who, in the 1912 Olympics, won four races and became both Nurmi's and Finland's hero. Running became Paavo's passion. He trained hard, carrying a stopwatch in his right hand, timing himself between the posts along the road, and learning pace judgment on the track.

Nurmi lost his first Olympic race at Antwerp (1920) over 5,000 meters to Joseph Guillemot. The tables were turned on the Frenchman in the 10,000 meters and Nurmi collected yet another gold medal, leading Finland to victory in the cross-country race.

It was at the Olympics in Paris (1924) that Nurmi's performance took on legendary proportions. Nurmi was an indomitable figure on the track. He lapped at exactly even pace and soon his opponents were strung out behind him as Paavo forged on, powered by his stoic will and determined stride.

His first gold medals came less than two hours apart. First, he easily won the 1,500 meters in 3:53.6, only a second off his own world record. Then he overcame teammate Ville Ritola in the 5,000 meters. Nurmi would beat Ritola again in the 10,000-meter cross-country and collect both individual and team golds.

He was upset that he hadn't been entered by Finland in the 10,000 meters on the track, which Ritola won. Legend has it that while the event was being run, Nurmi went to a training track and reeled off a superior time, just to satisfy himself.

Paavo Nurmi FIN

Four years later in Amsterdam (1928), Nurmi started out with a 10,000 meter victory, but slipped to second in the steeplechase and 5,000 meters.

He came to Los Angeles (1932) to run the marathon, but was banned a week before the Games opened for having taken a percentage of gate receipts for his races during the 1929 season. Nurmi was heartbroken.

Still considered an amateur in Finland and allowed to run the following year in domestic meets, Nurmi entered the national championship at 1,500 meters. To his great pleasure, he out-kicked countryman Lauri Lehtinen, the 1932 Olympic 5,000-meter champion.

Nurmi's last Olympic appearance was in 1952, when, to the delight of the Helsinki crowd, the heroic Nurmi entered the stadium carrying the Olympic torch, a fitting tribute to "Peerless Paavo," the greatest prewar distance runner.

Al Oerter (USA. September 19, 1936)

No one has won as many successive Olympic gold medals as Al Oerter. The twenty-year-old youngster from Floral Park, New York, first entered the Olympic arena in Melbourne (1956). Producing a personal best on his very first throw of 56.36 meters (184 ft. 11 in.), he upset a number of established discus throwers, including three-time Olympian Fortune Gordien. No one realized this was to be the first in an unprecedented series of Olympic golds.

Four years later, he went to Rome and exceeded his winning distance in Melbourne by more than ten feet. Oerter trailed Rink Babka until the fifth round, when he gathered his composure, stepped into the throwing circle, and unleashed his longest discus throw, another gold medal winner at 59.18 meters (194 ft. 2 in.).

Tokyo, Japan (1964), was the scene of Oerter's third Olympiad and he was hurt so severely he had to have his lower ribcage wrapped heavily and iced before throwing. Nevertheless, he had prescribed for himself a competitive intensity for the Olympic Games which no injury could diminish. But the champion was still having trouble and was only in fourth place at the start of the penultimate round. Oerter, drawing on his wealth of experience, went back to basics. He slowed down his turn and arrived at the front of the ring in a more powerful, cocked position. An explosive pull sent the discus out to 61.00 meters (200 ft. 1½ in.) and brought his third gold.

In 1968, Oerter finished third in the U.S. Olympic Trials, behind world record holder, Jay Silvester. It rained during the discus final in Mexico City, but Oerter was able to adjust his technique to the conditions and on his third throw had a full hit. The platter spun out to 64.78 meters (212 ft. 6 in.), almost five feet farther than he had thrown before. He had garnered his fourth gold medal.

Remarkably, Oerter achieved his best throw in 1980 while preparing for the boycotted Moscow Olympics. He improved again in 1981 to 225 feet 7 inches. In 1984, he will still be throwing at forty-eight years of age.

Al Oerter USA

Jesse Owens (USA. September 12, 1913–March 31, 1980)

In a short, brilliant career, culminating with four gold medals in Berlin (1936), Jesse Owens became what sportswriters have often described as the greatest track and field athlete of all time.

In 1933, as a high school senior in Cleveland, Ohio, Owens set national records in the long jump, 100 yards, and 220 yards. He selected Ohio State University from among twenty-eight college scholarship offers.

In the Big Ten Championships at Ann Arbor, Michigan, on May 25, 1935, Owens produced the most amazing one hour of athletics in history. He opened by equaling the world 100-yard record in 9.4 seconds. Ten minutes later, he sprinted down the long jump runway and launched himself to a world record 8.13 meters (26 ft. 8¼ in.), a record that would last for twenty-five years.

Moving on to the 220 final, Owens zipped down the long straight with rapid, fluid strides recording 20.3 seconds, a world record for both the 220 yards and the slightly shorter 200 meters. To conclude his afternoon's work, Owens skimmed over the 220-low hurdles in 22.6 seconds, which together with the 200-meter distance, brought two more records. In one hour, Jesse Owens had posted six entries in the world record book.

A month later, Owens would win these same four individual events at the NCAA championships. He would duplicate this feat in 1936, performing the world's first 10.2 second 100-meter clocking.

In the Berlin Olympics (1936), Owens was again unbeatable. He won the 100 and 200 meters convincingly, achieving a world record in the latter. In the long jump qualifying, Owens opened with two fouls, took off two feet behind the board on this third and final attempt, yet still qualified by a fraction of an inch. In the final, he settled down, although Lutz Long of Germany pressed him by equaling Owens' best leap of 7.86 meters (25 ft. 9¾ in.) in the fifth round. Owens then put it out of reach with his final two jumps spanning 8.06 meters (26 ft. 5¼ in.) on his final leap, an Olympic record which would stand until Ralph Boston's winning leap in 1960.

Jesse Owens won his fourth gold medal in the 4 X 100-meter relay, contributing to a U.S. world record of 39.8 seconds. He was clearly the most dominant athlete of the '36 Games. His performance clearly made him a devastating opponent for Nazi racial beliefs, which Hitler had hoped would be substantiated by Aryan supremacy on the track.

Owens retired to pursue some lucrative offers that were very slow to materialize. Eventually, he became a professional spokesperson for many causes and commercial products and put in many years as an accomplished motivational speaker on the banquet circuit.

In 1950, a panel of sports experts for the Associated Press voted Owens the greatest track and field performer of the first half of the century, ahead of Jim Thorpe and Paavo Nurmi. Owens died in 1980 of lung cancer.

Jesse Owens USA

JESSE OWENS

— 100 METERS —

August 2	1st round	10.3	equals Olympic record
August 2	quarter-final	10.2	wind aided
August 3	semifinal	10.4	
August 3	FINAL	10.3	

— 200 METERS —

August 4	1st round	21.1	Olympic record
August 4	2nd round	21.1	

— LONG JUMP —

August 4	qualifying		
August 4	FINAL	26 ft. 5¼ in.	wind aided

— 200 METERS —

August 5	semifinal	21.3	
August 5	FINAL	20.7	Olympic record

— 4 X 100-METER RELAY —

August 8	heat	40.0	equals world record
August 9	FINAL	39.8	world record

Wilma Rudolph (USA. June 23, 1940)

Wilma Rudolph was the star woman athlete of the Rome Olympics (1960). She won the sprint double by the most convincing margins ever and anchored the U.S. relay team to a world record.

Wilma was the seventeenth of nineteen children. At four years of age, she contracted polio which left her partially paralyzed. She wore a leg brace until she was eleven. As a high school sprinter, she never lost a race. She earned a place on the 1956 U.S. relay team, winning a bronze medal in the Melbourne Olympics.

In Rome, Wilma, then a student at Tennessee State University, proved to be the fastest woman ever. Her long legs, (she was 5 feet, 11 inches tall), strode to a world record equaling 11.3 seconds in the 100-meter semifinal. Then in the final, she powered to an unbelievable 11.0 seconds, with a wind assistance slightly over the allowable limit. She won the 200 meters by a wide 5-yard margin and overcame a serious deficit to win her third gold medal in the relay.

Two months before Rome, Wilma set a world record of 22.9 for 200 meters and in the summer of 1961, she recorded the first ever 11.2 for 100 meters.

Viktor Saneev (USSR. October 3, 1945)

Viktor Saneev's three straight triple jump Olympic golds has been equaled only by John Flanagan in the hammer event in 1900, 1904, and 1908, and surpassed only by Al Oerter's four discus golds. Throwers tend to last a lot longer and can maintain

Victor Saneev USSR

their shoulder strength more easily, while Saneev is unique in retaining his triple jumping skill, agility, and competitive drive for so long.

It all began in Mexico City (1968), during an amazing Olympic triple jump, when the world record was improved upon five times. Saneev, the last jumper in the contest, needed a world record to win. He produced 17.39 meters (57 ft. ¾ in.), by passing Brazil's Nelson Prudencio with a distance more than a foot better than the pre-Games world record.

Saneev retained his Olympic title in Munich with a wind aided 17.35 meters (56 ft. 11 in.). A month later, in his hometown of Sukhumi on the Black Sea, he improved the world record to 17.44 meters (57 ft. 2 ¾ in.).

He made it three straight in Montreal (1976), again coming from behind with a fifth round leap of 17.29 meters (56 ft. 8 ¾ in.). Viktor Saneev almost pulled off a fourth gold in Moscow (1980) jumping 17.24 meters (56 ft. 6 ¾ in.) only to lose to countryman Jaak Uudmae by less than five inches.

Peter Snell (New Zealand. December 17, 1938)

Peter Snell went to the 1960 Rome Olympics as an unknown 800-meter runner. His best time before the Games was 1:49.2. Only Snell knew he was much stronger than before, the result of extreme endurance training in far-away New Zealand.

Snell romped through his first heat in 1:48.1, a New Zealand record, then ran 1:48.5 in the second round the same afternoon. When he ran 1:47.2 in the semifinal, people started to realize he had a chance.

Roger Moens, the world record holder from Belgium, was still expected to win the final. Snell ran in the leading pack but remained boxed in. Moens had a perfect striking position as the field hit the homestretch. Moens moved out to get a clear lane and suddenly Snell had an opening which he seized with a stunning burst of speed. The upstart Snell came flying past the surprised Moens on the inside to win by a yard in 1:46.3.

New Zealand had won its first track gold since Jack Lovelock in Berlin (1936). While Snell was awaiting the victory ceremony, Murray Halberg stole the 5,000 meters, a second gold for the South Pacific isle. Halberg was Snell's training partner and a member of Arthur Lydiard's school of long mileage-oriented distance runners.

Early in 1962, Snell clipped a tenth from Herb Elliott's mile record with 3:54.5, followed a week later by world records for 880 yards of 1:45.1 and 1:44.3 for 800 meters, which he passed on the way to the finish line.

During the winter of 1964, Snell trained harder than ever for the Tokyo Games. In one period of endurance work, he ran more than 100 miles a week for ten weeks.

Both Olympic finals were exhibitions of his middle distance supremacy. In the 800 meters, he ran casually in the pack until he broke into the open with an unapproachable burst of speed and maintained a four-yard margin to the tape, recording a fast 1:45.1. The 1,500 meters saw Snell utilize the same tactical approach. Snell moved through the pack and must have looked like a black vested blur as he flashed past the leaders with 300 meters to go. He opened up a 5-meter gap that he extended to 12 meters at the finish, accomplishing a last lap of 52.7 and a final time of 3:38.1.

A month later, in Auckland, he lowered the mile record to 3:54.1. He ran a closing series of races in the United States, then retired. Although Snell had a perfect competitive record and had earned three gold medals, many feel he never realized his immense potential. His bursting speed was without equal among his peers.

Snell, who had left school when he was sixteen, enrolled in a U.S. college when he was thirty-five and eventually earned his doctorate degree in exercise physiology. He now resides in Dallas, Texas.

Irena Szewinska-Kirszenstein (Poland. May 24, 1946)

During four Olympiads, Irena Szewinska won seven Olympic medals in five different events. A shy eighteen-year-old in Tokyo, she won Olympic silver medals in the 200 meters and long jump before helping Poland's sprint relay team to a victory in a world record 43.6 seconds.

In Mexico City (1968), she won the gold medal at 200 meters in 22.5 seconds, setting another world record, and finished third in the 100 meters. In Munich (1972), having just given birth to her first child, Irena was not fully trained, but still captured the bronze medal in the 200 meters.

Switching to the longer distance in 1974, Szewinska became the first woman to run 400 meters in under 50 seconds. In the Montreal Olympics (1976), the thirty-year-old homemaker won the 400 meters in convincing style. Entering the homestretch, leading by just two yards, she sprinted away from the field to snap the tape twelve yards clear in a world record 49.29 seconds.

All three of Irena Szewinska's gold medals were won with world record performances.

Jim Thorpe (USA. May 28, 1888–March 28, 1953)

An incredibly gifted natural athlete, Native American Jim Thorpe was a football, baseball, and track star while attending Carlisle Indian School in Pennsylvania. In 1912, Thorpe won the Olympic decathlon event by nearly 700 points. He also won the pentathlon, finishing first in four of the five events. King Gustav acclaimed Thorpe on the Stockholm victory stand saying, "You, sir, are the greatest athlete in the world."

The following year, he was disqualified for violating the amateur status regulations, having played minor league baseball for two years before the Games. He returned his gold medals and his name was removed from the official record books.

Lasse Viren FINLAND

Irena Szewinska-Kirszenstein POL

Peter Snell NZL

Jim Thorpe USA

In 1913, Thorpe played professional baseball as a National League outfielder for the New York Giants and in 1915 he returned to his first love, football. Thorpe was the star player in the league that would soon become the National Football League (NFL).

A 1950 Associated Press poll voted Jim Thorpe the greatest American athlete of the half century.

In 1983, twenty years after his death, Thorpe was reinstated as winner of the decathlon and pentathlon. His heirs were presented with original 1912 gold medals and Thorpe now appears in the record books as co-winner with Hugo Wieslander (decathlon) and Ferdinand Bie (pentathlon).

Wyomia Tyus (USA. August 29, 1945)

Speed is an elusive quality. The fastest sprinters rarely maintain an edge of superiority for long. The only sprinter, male or female, to win Olympic championships in successive Games is Wyomia Tyus.

Young Wyomia emerged suddenly in the Olympic year of 1964, running at first in the wake of Edith McGuire, but proving to be the very best when she arrived in Tokyo for the Olympics. She equaled Wilma Rudolph's 100-meter world record of 11.2 seconds in her heat and, running into a breeze, won the final by two meters in 11.4. She gained a silver when the U.S. sprint relay team ran second to Poland.

In Mexico City (1968), Wyomia set a world record of 11.0 to become the first two-time sprint champion. She went on to finish sixth in the 200 meters, then anchored the victorious 4 X 100-meter relay team, which set a new world record of 42.8 seconds, and brought Wyomia Tyus her third gold medal.

Lasse Viren (Finland. July 22, 1949)

His father was quoted as saying: "We never had to encourage Lasse to train or to run. He always did things by himself and would tell us afterward."

Lasse Viren was virtually unknown to the world until two weeks before the Munich Games (1972) when he announced himself with a brilliant world record of 8:14.0, crushing a great field in Stockholm. Suddenly, he was an Olympic favorite.

In his first Munich race at 10,000 meters, Viren fell before the halfway point, the result of a collision in the pack. Instantly, he was back on his feet, having lost only 20 yards. He quickly caught up with the leaders. In a sustained kick, covering the final 800 meters in 1:56.4, the smooth-striding Finn danced away from Emiel Puttemans of Belgium and Miruts Yifter of Ethiopia, setting a world record of 27:38.4. It was the first track victory for Finland since World War II had interrupted his country's dominance of distance running events.

The 5,000-meter final was slow until Steve Prefontaine of the United States began his drive with four laps to go. But Viren outkicked a number of speedsters, covering the last mile in a phenomenal 4:01.2, recording 13:26.4 for the race.

In achieving his distance double, his style and competitive instincts were impeccable. The bearded Viren explained afterward, "The important thing is a strong will and ambition, coupled with clear objectives."

In the weeks after the Games, Viren ran a number of great races, including a world record 13:16.4 for 5,000 meters. After a series of poor races the following season, he doubled brilliantly in the European championships, then faded into obscurity.

"The key is knowing how to peak," he said, and in Montreal for the 1976 Olympics, Viren renewed his dual ownership in distance running events.

After a slow start in the 10,000 meters, Carlos Lopes of Portugal began a strong surge, breaking the pack one by one. Only Viren remained, floating along with his unchanging stride. Suddenly, with a lap to go, he struck with ease and was gone, opening up a five-second lead and coasting home in 27:40.38.

The racing began in the 5,000 meters with two laps to go. Into the final 100 meters, five men were even, but Viren easily won the dash for the tape in 13:24.76. He had done what no one had done before, a second successive distance double.

The next day, Lasse Viren lined up for the start of his first marathon. He must have been very sore as he faced forty-five miles of racing in one week. Viren echoed Emil Zatopek, "All I want is to finish honorably." He finished a very honorable fifth in 2:13:10.8, the fastest first marathon ever run.

A repeat of Zatopek's distance triple was thought impossible, since distance races had become so much more competitive since Zatopek's era. Viren's successive doubles, as well, may never be repeated.

Emil Zatopek (Czechoslovakia. September 19, 1922)

The 60,000 spectators who saw Zatopek make his Olympic debut over 10,000 meters in London (1948) were astonished that he seemed to be running in pain, each lap looking as if would be his last. But all the flailing of arms and his agonized expression disguised the heart and strength of a great champion. Zatopek burst from the pack at the halfway point and continued to extend his lead over Alain Mimoun of France to almost 300 yards at the finish, recording an Olympic record of 29:59.6.

Three days later, Zatopek led the 5,000 meters, taking the brunt of wind and rain until Gaston Reiff moved past him with four laps remaining and opened the lead to 30 yards at the bell. Then, Zatopek started a courageous charge, gaining on the fading Reiff with every stride but coming up just a yard short at the tape.

The following year (1949), Emil Zatopek made his first entry in the world record book and lowered the 10,000-meter record in 1950, to 29:02.6. Only six men had ever beaten 30 minutes for the distance. On September 29, 1951, Zatopek ran faster over twice the distance, setting a phenomenal world record for 20,000 meters with 59:51.8.

Emil Zatopek CZE

Zatopek had established himself as the world's greatest distance runner. He brought to the sport a new level of hard training. He built his stamina and disciplined his iron will with interval running on the track.

Zatopek went to the Helsinki Olympics to perform before the Finns, who perhaps appreciated his art the most. Early in the 10,000 meters, his sustained drive soon left everyone strung out around the track. Zatopek pushed on to his second Olympic gold, recording 29:17.0.

The 5,000 meters was a classic. Down the backstretch of the final lap, Zatopek was fourth. The hysterical crowd was on its feet when he made his bid with 200 meters to go, charging in the third lane past Herbert Schade, Chris Chataway of Britain, and Alain Mimoun. Zatopek pulled away with an agonized, raging sprint to win his third Olympic gold in 14:06.6. Later that afternoon, his wife Dana added to the family gold medal collection with a surprise win in the javelin.

Two days later, Zatopek set out on his most courageous exploit, his first marathon. He had never raced even half the distance before, and said, "I only want to perform honorably."

The first half of the race he ran patiently with the leaders. Then, with 10 miles remaining, Zatopek made his break, pushing hard over two hills. Now he was alone, running at unexplored levels of fatigue. Pushing on, he reached the outskirts of Helsinki with a lead of over two minutes. Now he knew he would win. Inside the stadium spectators from every nation chanted together "Za-to-pek, Za-to-pek," lifting the weary runner to the finish line. At 2:23:3.2, he finished one of the fastest marathons ever run. It was a fitting climax to the greatest distance running performance, the Olympic triple, an unprecedented feat unlikely to be repeated.

Within two days, Zatopek broke Gunder Hagg's twelve-year-old 5,000-meter record in 13:57.2, and then became the first man to better 29 minutes for 10,000 meters, recording a 28:54.2. He now held every distance running record from five to thirty kilometers.

Emil Zatopek went on to his third Olympics in Melbourne (1956) and finished sixth in the marathon. Following his retirement, he continued to coach and attended subsequent Olympic celebrations. In Mexico City, he showed up despite official censure, having lost his army rank of colonel for speaking out on behalf of the Dubcek government against the 1968 Soviet incursion into his country.

10

BASKETBALL

— *10* —

1984 VENUE

The basketball finals will be held at the Forum, in Inglewood, which has a seating capacity of 17,505. One of the world's largest and most beautiful basketball arenas, the Forum is also home of the Los Angeles Lakers, National Basketball Association world champions in 1972, 1980, and 1982. Built in 1966, the Forum has played host to the NBA's professional championships six times.

EVENTS AND SCHEDULE (Finals)

Men

Team Championship   August 10

Women

Team Championship   August 7

HISTORY OF BASKETBALL

Basketball is one of the world's most popular spectator sports and is part of the fabric of life in North America. The game is unique among Olympic sports in that it has distinctly American roots. The 1984 Olympic competition will attract particular interest in the host nation where there are millions of people with a great appreciation of the sport and the skills involved.

The game was invented in 1891 at the Springfield, Massachusetts, YMCA. Dr. James A. Naismith set out to create a game suited for indoor play during the winter in the many gymnasiums along the Eastern seaboard. Naismith wanted a noncontact sport and initially the ball could be advanced only by passing. Running with the ball constituted a foul and dribbling was not introduced until later.

"For goals, I wanted two boxes, eighteen inches square," Dr. Naismith recalled, "but Mr. Stebbins, the janitor, couldn't find any. He did, however, locate two peach baskets in the storeroom."

The bottoms were cut from the baskets, which were nailed to opposite ends of the gymnasium. The game was called "basketball," but might just as well been called "boxball." Interest in the game developed rapidly, particularly in the colleges and schools throughout the United States.

OLYMPIC HISTORY

Only thirteen years after its invention, basketball was included as a demonstration sport in the 1904 St. Louis Olympics. It was also included as a demonstration sport in Amsterdam (1928). In Los Angeles (1932), basketball was replaced by demonstrations of lacrosse and American football.

The formation of the Federation Internationale de Basketball Amateur (FIBA) did much to advance the final adoption of basketball as an Olympic sport in Berlin (1936). The FIBA translated the rules into thirty languages and basketball enthusiasts quickly sprung up throughout the world. Remarkably, the rules initially set forth by Naismith remained almost intact.

Twelve of Naismith's thirteen basic rules still govern today's game. Naismith wanted the basket to be placed high enough to ensure that players could not just slam the ball through. Obviously, he did not envision the power, agility, and enormous physical stature of today's great players, and the resulting advent of the "slam-dunk."

Dr. Naismith was in Berlin for the ceremonies inaugurating basketball as an Olympic sport and threw-up the first jump-ball. At that point, his enthusiasm at seeing his invention adopted as an Olympic sport, with twenty-three nations entered at Berlin must have been extremely high. But, what was about to transpire was a definite setback.

Without an appropriate indoor facility, the tournament was played on outdoor clay courts. When the rains came, disaster struck. The courts were virtually unplayable. For the championship game between the United States and Canada, more than an inch of water sat on the playing surface. The players skidded and slid and there was no way the ball could be dribbled.

One of the star U.S. players, Sam Balter, remembered: "To show you how bad things were, we led 15-4 at the half. After that, things got even worse and neither team was able to score more than 4 points in the second half."

The Olympic basketball tournament found an indoor home in London for the 1948 Games, where the superior skill of the United States team was again evident. The United States completely outplayed France in the championship game, winning 65-21.

In the 1952 Olympics, Brazil gave the United States a tough time in an intense semifinal game featuring aggressive defense. The U.S. held off the Brazilian challenge, 26-24. Inevitably, the USSR adopted the Brazilian defensive strategy when the Soviets met the United States in the final. Although it was close, the United States was not really threatened and drew away in the second half to win, 36-25. The stalling tactics employed in this game led to FIBA's adoption of the

Inaugural basketball tournament in Berlin 1936. Clay courts became mired when it rained.

30-second clock.

In Melbourne in 1956, and in Rome in 1960, the United States maintained its domination of the game. This is perhaps because some of the greatest players in the history of the sport came together on the U.S. Olympic team during those years. In Melbourne, the team was built around Bill Russell and K.C. Jones, both members of the University of San Francisco's collegiate championship team.

The 1960 Olympic team was perhaps the finest in Olympic history, with the likes of Jerry West, Jerry Lucas, Oscar Robertson, and Walt Bellamy. The team averaged more than 101 points per game.

The 1964 Tokyo final once again saw a match-up of the undefeated U.S. team and the Soviets. And, again, the U.S. won, 73-59. But, in the 1968 final in Mexico City, things were different. For the first time, the United States was not a clear favorite to win, having lost to both the USSR and Yugoslavia in pre-Olympic competition. Also, for the first time, the Soviets were taller than their American counterparts.

But, the USSR and the United States never met. Yugoslavia took care of the Soviets in the semifinals before losing to the United States, 65-50 in the finals. The scene was now set for one of the most dramatic basketball games in Olympic history.

The Munich final in 1972 was between the Soviet Union, still searching for its first Olympic victory and a young and somewhat inexperienced U.S. team. The Soviets played well enough to win and the Americans poor enough to lose. With five minutes to play, the Soviets were ahead by an almost insurmountable 44-36. The United States then mounted a dramatic comeback, led by two field goals by Kevin Joyce.

The Soviets, still ahead by a point, slowed down the tempo. Then Doug Collins stole the ball and, while driving the length of the court for a final shot, was fouled. He stepped to the foul line and, under the most intense pressure imaginable, dropped them both through the hoop.

The Soviets called time out, with the clock set at 3 seconds. They had just one chance. The in-bounds pass was a ninety foot desperation lob towards the other end of the court. Alexander Belov was waiting for the ball, but the buzzer sounded before the ball arrived. The American team, sure it had won the championship, 50-49, started its celebration.

But now there was a protest. The Soviets claimed they had been given only one second before the buzzer sounded and not the full 3 seconds. Dr. William Jones, Secretary General of the FIBA, told the timekeeper to reset the clock at three seconds. Thus, the Soviets were given another chance—and another 3 seconds.

Another ninety-foot pass was lobbed towards Belov. An instant later, Belov was under the basket with the ball in his hands and the Americans, Jim Forbes and Kevin Joyce could do nothing but watch helplessly as the 7-foot 4-inch Soviet giant dropped the ball in, unopposed.

Basketball shot.

Now it was time for another victory celebration, this time on the Soviet side. The controversy raged on throughout the night and it was not until the following day that the medals were finally presented. Meanwhile, at a team meeting, the United States team decided not to accept the silver medals and the Soviets were awarded the gold alone.

Any anticipation of a grudge match between the USSR and the United Stated in Montreal (1976) was dispelled when Russia drew Yugoslavia in one semifinal. Yugoslavia had beaten the Soviets five straight times in non-Olympic games since Munich. They did it again, surging to a 17-4 lead early in the game, and hanging on for an 89-84 victory.

The United States had a scare early in the tournament when the Puerto Rican team, led by U.S. collegiate players, came within a point. After that, the United States overcame Yugoslavia for the first time, 112-93, and sent them to face the Soviets in one semifinal. The United States went on to end the hopes of upstart Canada in the other.

In the final, the United States jumped out to a 44-22 lead over the Yugoslavs and went on to a 95-72 victory behind Adrian Dantley's 30 points.

Without the United States, the Moscow (1980) basketball finals lost much of its significance. Again, Yugoslavia was to be the USSR's nemesis. In the semifinal, the teams played to an 81-81 tie in regulation time before the Yugoslav's quickly ran up a ten point margin for an overtime victory. They went on to beat Italy in the championship game, 86-77.

Women's basketball was first included in the Olympic program in Montreal (1976). It proved to be more of a basketball demonstration than a competition, as the Soviets, who had not lost a single international tournament in the previous eight years, easily won the gold.

The Soviet women were led by 7-foot, 280-pound Iuliana Semenova who was, predictably, one of the leading scorers of the Olympic tournament. The U.S. team, led by Lucy Harris and Nancy Dunkle, won the silver, losing, 112-77, in the final. At the Moscow Olympics, Semenova led her team to a second consecutive Olympic victory, this time beating Bulgaria, 104-73.

RULES

Some of the basic rules of Olympic basketball competition are:

1. The basket is 3.05 meters (10 feet) above the floor.
2. A 30-second clock, identical to the one used by the National Basketball Association, limits the offensive team's freedom and prevents offensive stalling.
3. Play consists of two, 20-minute halves, separated by a 10-minute halftime interval, much like the U.S. College game.

4.   Five personal fouls result in disqualification of a player.

It is generally accepted that international referees permit more contact than American collegiate officials. The FIBA's rules defining personal fouls are listed below.

A PERSONAL FOUL is a player foul which involves contact with an opponent.

BLOCKING is personal contact which impedes the progress of an opponent who is not in possession of the ball.

HOLDING is personal contact with an opponent that interferes with his freedom of movement.

GUARDING FROM THE REAR which results in personal contact is a personal foul. Officials should give special attention to this type of infraction. The mere fact that the defensive player is attempting to play the ball does not justify his making contact with the player in possession of the ball.

A PLAYER SHALL NOT hold, push, charge, trip, impede progress of an opponent by: extending his arm, shoulder, hip, or knee, or by bending his body into other than normal positions, nor use any rough tactics.

A DRIBBLER SHALL NOT CHARGE into nor contact an opponent in his path, nor attempt a dribble between two opponents or between an opponent and a boundary line, unless the space is such as to provide a reasonable chance for him to go through without contact.

1984 PROSPECTS MEN

The United States expects to have the number one men's basketball team. They invented the game and have sent coaches throughout the world to teach it. The nation pays adulation to the game in secondary school and college gymnasiums.

The United States still has the best talent and plays the finest game of basketball in the world, but the world is catching up. The problem is that U.S. teams never stay together very long, before the lure of professional ball attracts the best talent. Teams in other countries work together throughout a number of Olympiads, have time to develop a team concept, acquire great experience, and create intricate team strategies.

The United States trailed Mexico, 20-4, in its first Pan Am win in Caracas in 1983, unable, at first, to cope with Mexico's ingenious screens. In the next game, against Brazil, the United States trailed most of the game. The U.S. players could not deal with Brazil's incessant sharpshooting from the outside until the final minute, when they pulled out a 72-69 win.

But, the U.S. players learned fast. With Michael Jordan flying around the court and Wayman Tisdale working under the basket, the United States got going. The U.S. didn't have much trouble in the remaining six games, wrapping up another

Cheryl Miller dynamic star of powerful USA women's basketball squad.

Cheryl Miller

Cheryl Miller

Pan Am title in front of a generally hostile crowd in Venezuela.

U.S. Olympic coach Bobby Knight has the nucleus of a great team for Los Angeles and the motivation to keep a team together. The stars will have more to gain in demonstrating their skills at the Olympics, rather than rushing into an National Basketball Association (NBA) contract.

The United States will have to play superlative basketball to counter the Eastern Europeans, Italians, and Brazilians who all continue to improve. The Soviets play with the kind of team unity that comes only with years of experience. The young U.S. collegians will be relative strangers.

1984 PROSPECTS WOMEN

The Los Angeles Games will give the Soviet women a chance for a third successive gold medal, but U.S. stars such as Cheryl Miller and Janice Lawrence will lead a talented, and dedicated U.S. team. In the summer of 1983, the U.S. team beat the Soviet Union, 76-70 in Kansas City as Miller led the scoring with 18 points. This victory repeated the upset of the previous year when, in an international tournament in Hungary, the United States handed the Soviet team, including Iuliana Semenova, its first defeat in twenty years of international competition.

The Soviet women later resumed their long string of international tournament victories, scoring in the closing seconds of the '83 world championship final at Sao Paulo, Brazil, to edge the U.S., 84-82. The United States led at halftime and throughout much of the second half until Semenova, playing with four fouls, rallied her team.

The U.S. women are young and still improving. Cheryl Miller will be a mere nineteen years old at the time of the Olympic final. But already her energy, leadership, and great ability have proven to be just what the United States needs to challenge the Soviet Olympic monopoly.

In the National Collegiate Athletic Association final against Louisiana Tech, Cheryl put on a one-woman show, leading the University of Southern California to a 69-67 victory. In addition to her rebounding, stealing, and blocking shots, Cheryl also scored 27 points in the win.

Miller's high school and college teams have won 164 games and lost only 6 with her in the lineup. Cheryl's exciting, scrappy style of play and sheer exuberance on the court have brought a new following to women's basketball.

Played just a few miles from the USC campus, at the Forum, the 1984 women's Olympic basketball tournament will be one of the most exciting contests of the Games.

11

BOXING

— 11 —

1984 VENUE

The boxing events will be held at the Los Angeles Memorial Sports Arena which seats over 16,000 spectators. The Sports Arena was completed in 1959 and is part of the Exposition Park Complex, next door to the Coliseum. The Sports Arena was used as a set in the series of *Rocky* motion pictures.

EVENTS AND SCHEDULE (Finals)

Weight Classes	Maximum Bodyweight	
Light Flyweight	Up to 48 kg—105.8 lbs.	August 11
Flyweight	51 kg—112.4 lbs.	August 11
Bantamweight	54 kg—119.1 lbs.	August 11
Featherweight	57 kg—125.7 lbs.	August 11
Lightweight	60 kg—132.3 lbs.	August 11
Light-Welterweight	63.5 kg—140.0 lbs.	August 11
Welterweight	67 kg—147.7 lbs.	August 11
Light-Middleweight	71 kg—156.5 lbs.	August 11
Middleweight	75 kg—165.4 lbs.	August 11
Light-Heavyweight	81 kg—178.6 lbs.	August 11
Heavyweight	91 kg—200.6 lbs.	August 11
Super Heavyweight	Over 91 kg—200.6 lbs.	August 11

HISTORY OF BOXING

Boxing measures man's skill and instinct for personal defense and his capability to overcome a foe. Organized contests resembling modern boxing occurred in Egypt more than 3,000 years ago. The sport crossed the Mediterranean and was introduced into the ancient Olympics in 686 B.C.

Ancient Olympic contestants wore headgear and leather wrappings around their hands. Boxing was called "pugilism," derived from the same base as the Latin words for fist and to be of a fighting nature or "pugnacious." As the sport developed, it became exceedingly brutal and, in time, the only restricted actions were biting and eye-gouging. The Romans further brutalized the sport with the introduction of studded gauntlets, and boxing thus became a forerunner of future gladiator battles.

Boxing, as we know it today, appeared early in the eighteenth century when James Figg, a self-declared English champion, opened a school for boxing in London where he taught the art of fencing and "fisticuffs." Jack Broughton, another fisticuffs teacher, compiled seven rules which gradually evolved into the sport we recognize today.

In 1747, Broughton introduced padded gloves to replace the bare fist. World championship fights, however, remained bare-knuckled until 1892 when gloves and three-minute rounds were first used in the championship fight in which "Gentleman Jim" Corbett defeated the great John L. Sullivan in twenty-one rounds.

OLYMPIC HISTORY

Boxing was left off the first Olympic program in Athens in 1896 because it was thought an ungentlemanly sport for professionals, and one which attracted betting and the lower elements of society.

Olympic boxing appeared for the first time in St. Louis (1904), with competitions in seven weight categories. The finalists were all American. There were only a few entries and several boxers fought in more than one weight division. The most successful was O. L. Kirk of St. Louis, who won the bantamweight and featherweight divisions. He remains the only man ever to win two weight divisions at the same Olympic boxing tournament.

Five weight divisions were contested in London in 1908, and all were won by British fighters. It was an equally unrepresentative tournament, just as the one in St. Louis four years earlier. Boxing was removed from the Olympic program in Stockholm in 1912 because the sport was prohibited by Swedish law.

When boxing returned to the Olympics in Antwerp in 1920, there were eight weight divisions on the program, attracting athletes from more nations than ever before. The tournament was marred by arguments which resulted from lack of clear international standards of scoring. Eddie Eagan earned one of the three U.S. gold medals, becoming the light-heavyweight champion.

Eagan returned to Olympic boxing in 1924, but was eliminated in a first round bout. Eight years later, he became an Olympic legend of sorts while riding on the winning U.S. four-man bobsled team at Lake Placid. Eagan thus became the only individual to ever win gold medals at both winter and summer Olympic Games.

The 1924 Olympic boxing events in Paris also suffered from problems with judging. An official British report said, "The boxing tournament provided several incidents of a most regrettable nature, completely destroying the pleasure of all those who understand the true meaning of the word 'sportsmanship'."

The featherweight final brought together two Americans, Jackie Fields and Joe Salas. They went to school together in Los Angeles, were the best of friends, boxed for the same club, and were coached by the same man. Fields won and was hugged by his friend at the conclusion of the fight. At this point, it was decided that each country should restrict the entries and only one boxer per weight division was allowed in subsequent Olympic Games.

Despite the problems with judging, the overall caliber of boxing in Paris had advanced greatly. A total of 252 boxers from twenty-nine countries competed, and for the first time, they were some of the best fighters in the world. Three members of the United States team, Fields, Fidel La Barba, and Pete Sarron, later became professional world champions.

The new restriction on entries reduced the number of boxers entered at Amsterdam (1928) to 146. The United States failed to win a single championship and the honors were divided among other competing nations. Italy won the most gold medals with three, followed closely by the surprising Argentine boxers who won the light-heavyweight and heavyweight divisions.

Because of the expense involved in travel to Los Angeles, only thirty-five boxers representing eighteen countries competed for 1932 Olympic titles. For a change, the official Games report proudly pointed out that there was "no dispute of consequence over decisions."

At Berlin in 1936, thirty-two nations sent 183 boxers. European nations won most of the medals, with Argentina proving to be the strongest representative from the western hemisphere.

Before the start of the 1948 Games in London, the Association Internationale de Boxe Amateur (AIBA) was formed. This new governing body eliminated inferior judges and almost eradicated the doubts about decisions that had plagued the Olympic sport until that time.

In London, Laszlo Papp won his first gold medal in the middleweight division. A Hungarian southpaw with a hard right jab and a tearing left hook, Papp out-pointed British seaman Johnny Wright, and started his string of three Olympic championships. He won a second gold medal in the light-middleweight division in Helsinki (1952) and a third in Melbourne (1956).

Colonel Don Hull, President of AIBA, and a keen observer of every Olympic boxing tournament since 1932, regards Papp as the greatest Olympic boxer of all-time.

"Papp had the style of Marciano, with short arms and vicious hard punches that hurt his opponents, wherever he hit them," recalls Hull. "In 1952, he met Ellsworth 'Spider' Webb of the U.S, one of the world's better boxers, in the first round of the tournament. Webb was doing all right until Papp simply moved in and started chopping him down with repeated hard punches to the belly, which folded Spider up."

"In Melbourne," Hull continued, "Papp out-pointed Jose Torres, who later became a professional lightweight champion. Both Webb and Torres were formidable boxers and Papp, through the years, beat all of the very best. That is the mark of a good champion—to be around for a long time and to beat all of the best competitors."

Papp, in an unusual move for an iron curtain boxer, also turned professional. He was undefeated in twenty-nine consecutive fights, with two draws. He retired as reigning European middleweight champion and became, and remains, a very successful coach of Hungarian Olympic boxers.

Another London Olympic titlist who went on to a great professional career was Argentine flyweight Pascual Perez. The Olympic Games have been the springboard for many world professional champions.

In Helsinki (1952), Floyd Patterson, a middleweight boxer, was one of five United States Olympic champions. Later, as a professional, he became the world's youngest heavyweight champion. Interestingly, Ingemar Johansson of Sweden, who went on to become one of Patterson's most formidable professional foes, and who exchanged the championship with him, was the loser of the Helsinki heavyweight final. He was disqualified for an excessively defensive fight and, in an unprecedented decision, was also deprived of the silver medal. This act was reversed in 1981 when the IOC asked Colonel Hull to award Johansson his Olympic medal.

Soviet fighters made a promising Olympic debut in 1952, winning six medals, none gold. In Melbourne (1956), this promise was realized with three Soviet championships.

British fighters, who had not won a medal since 1928, captured two gold medals in Melbourne. They were led by Dick McTaggart, who won the Val Barker Cup, an award given to the athlete judged the best Olympic boxer, regardless of weight.

To the joy of the home crowd, six Italians made the finals in Rome (1960) and half of them won the gold. Of the three winners, the welterweight victory of Giovanni Benvenuti, who later won the world professional middleweight title, was most popular.

In Rome, light-heavyweight Cassius Clay, an eighteen-year-old from Louisville, Kentucky, seemed unintimidated by experienced European and Polish champion Zbigniew Pietrzykowski, with 240 fights to his credit. Clay's defensive, dancing artistry had been well established. During the final, his dodging style rendered the Pole's attack ineffective. Clay sensed that his lead on points was not enough and in the third round he released a torrent of rapid blows onto his opponent. Only the final bell released the Pole from his bewilderment.

Clay changed his name to Muhammad Ali, a name consistent with his Moslem beliefs. Soon, as a professional, he thrilled and charmed his audiences with his speed, physical cunning, and quick wit. He overcame challengers with a flurry of blows in a round which he had previously predicted.

In his prime, as one of the most dominant heavyweight champions ever, Ali was prosecuted for refusing to serve in the military, which he said was against his

Muhammad Ali USA began his career as Cassius Clay, winning Light-Heavyweight in Rome 1960.

Howard Davis USA was voted as the outstanding boxer of the Montreal tournament.

religious principles. Stripped of his title and his career, he fought a long battle in the courts to gain reinstatement. He then fought a long battle to regain his world championship, which he did in 1974, defeating George Foreman in Zaire.

Muhammad Ali has an international audience which he boldly entertains and educates with poetic puns. With his proud attitude and terrific energy, he speaks for himself and for black people. Ali has become one of the greatest legends in boxing history.

The 1964 boxing tournament at the Tokyo Games proved to be a bonanza for Soviet boxers. There were seven Soviet finalists in the ten divisions, three of whom won. In the heavyweight division, Joe Frazier won the gold for the United States, another Olympic champion on his way to a distinguished professional career. Frazier later became the first man ever to beat Muhammad Ali to gain the coveted world heavyweight title.

Ricardo Delgado, a flyweight and Antonio Roldan, a featherweight, achieved Mexico's first Olympic boxing golds before the home crowd in Mexico City (1968). For the United States, George Foreman punched his way to an impressive victory in the heavyweight championship. A few years later, he won the professional world championship from Joe Frazier, before losing it to Muhammad Ali.

The United States won two golds in Mexico City. Only the USSR won more championships. Middleweight Boris Lagutin's win was among the most notable. Against strong opposition, Lagutin retained the middleweight title he had won at Tokyo in 1964.

The sensation of the 1972 boxing tournament in Munich was the sudden and brilliant appearance of the Cubans, who struck gold in three weight divisions. The heavyweight contest introduced the world to Cuban Teofilo Stevenson, who won the final when his Romanian opponent withdrew because of injury. In the third round of his semifinal bout, Stevenson flattened the highly-rated Duane Bobick of the United States. Bobick had beaten Stevenson in the 1971 Pan Am Games. Lightweight Ray Seales was the only U.S. gold medalist in Munich.

The total number of medals won by U.S. boxers in Montreal (1976) was unprecedented. The first Olympic champion boxing brothers, Leon and Michael Spinks, both stopped their opponents in the third round of their finals. Eighteen-year-old Leo Randolph won the flyweight division in a close decision over Cuban Ramon Duvalon.

Howard Davis won a unanimous decision over Cutov of Romania, a two-time European champion, a veteran of more than 200 bouts. The performance of Davis throughout the Montreal tournament is considered one of the best in Olympic history. Davis was inspired and fought with incredible speed and determination. Before the final, many regarded Cutov one of the best European boxers in years, yet Davis completely outclassed him. Davis was awarded the Val Barker trophy as the tournament's outstanding boxer.

Sugar Ray Leonard won the light-welterweight title despite sore hands. He had fought the preliminary rounds without attempting to land hard blows, saving his strength instead to overpower Cuban Andres Aldano in the final.

Leonard talked of retiring shortly after the Montreal fight, and enrolled in the University of Maryland. He was finally lured into the professional ranks by a lucrative offer. His competitive instincts brought $40 million in a six-year pro career. His welterweight showdown with Thomas Hearns at Caesar's Palace in Las Vegas brought him the title and $15 million. It was one of the richest fights in history.

Teofilo Stevenson again led the Cubans to three golds in Montreal. He dropped John Tate of the United States after only one-and-a-half minutes in his semifinal bout. With his win over Mircea Simon of Romania in the final, Stevenson became the first heavyweight ever to win back-to-back golds.

Experts began debating what Stevenson would do in the ring against Muhammad Ali. A plan for a series of three exhibition bouts of five, two-minute rounds, fought under amateur rules, almost came to fruition. The Cuban boxing federation was to make $1 million and Ali $3 million.

The AIBA assured the Cuban federation, and Castro personally, that Stevenson would not lose his amateur status and would be eligible to compete in Moscow if the exhibitions went ahead. Under AIBA rules, Stevenson would receive none of the money. The money was not the goal of Stevenson or Cuba. His Olympic renown had brought great credit to Cuba, promoting the country throughout the world. In the end, it was Ali, then well past his prime, who pulled out of the deal.

Cuba dominated the boxing events in Moscow (1980), winning six of eleven gold medals. One of the most eagerly anticipated fights was the middleweight final in which Jose Gomez, an aggressive brawler from Cuba, easily outpointed Viktor Savchenko of the USSR.

Teofilo Stevenson collected his third consecutive gold, joining Laszlo Papp of Hungary as the only man in history to do so. This time the Soviets had entered Pyotr Zaev, not their best heavyweight, but one whose crouching, closed style was calculated to upset Stevenson. It was a close final. Zaev exposed Stevenson's weakness. If Stevenson is crowded, he becomes less effective. Stevenson prefers to operate at a distance, using his long reach and size to his best advantage. The final decision 4–1 in favor of the Cuban, was greeted by "boos" from the Soviet crowd.

THE FIGHT—BASIC RULES

1. Olympic boxing consists of three, 3-minute rounds with a 1-minute break between rounds.
2. The ring is six meters (over nineteen feet) square and no more than four feet above the ground.

3. The weight registered by a boxer at the official weigh-in the first day determines the weight class of the boxer for the entire competition.

4. One boxer per nation may be entered in each category and no boxer under seventeen years of age is allowed to compete.

5. Each glove must weigh a minimum of 8 ounces, a maximum of 4 ounces for the leather covering, and a minimum of 4 ounces for the padding.

OLYMPIC VERSUS PROFESSIONAL BOXING

To understand and appreciate the Olympic contest, one must first recognize the difference between amateur Olympic boxing and professional boxing. The most obvious difference is the length of the fight. Professional championships are contested for up to fifteen rounds, while Olympic bouts last only three rounds. Because of this, professional fights can be arduous affairs, and boxers can perform only a few times each year.

Olympic boxers, on the other hand, have to fight five or six bouts as they progress to the final, usually on alternate days. Unlike professional fighters, who will pace themselves throughout the early rounds, Olympic boxers tend to go all-out throughout the entire nine minute contest.

Since severe fatigue reaches dangerous proportions in professional boxing, the fight can be far more punishing, with severe injuries more likely to occur. The shorter duration of Olympic fights also tends to place more emphasis on athletic ability rather than rewarding the one who can take the most punishment.

In eighty years of Olympic boxing, there has never been a serious injury. There have been some serious injuries in amateur boxing, but usually they are bouts fought in some backwoods area, refereed without the amateur philosophy.

Professional-oriented referees allow too much punishment and tend to let the bouts go on too long. In the Olympics, referees are repeatedly briefed on the philosophy of Olympic boxing. Its purpose is to show which boxer is the more clever and which has the tactical ability to score on the other man. There is no premium for punishment.

JUDGING THE CONTEST

Each boxer attempts to hit his opponent on his target area, which is the front part of the head and the body to the waistline. The arms are not included in the target area. The important scoring elements are the part of the glove used in making contact, and the part of the body hit by the glove. The judges also assess accuracy of punches and power with which they are delivered.

Five judges, selected from countries other than those of the competitors, decide the winner. Scoring is on a twenty point-must system, whereby the best

"Sugar" Ray Leonard was Light-Welterweight champion in Montreal 1976.

boxer is awarded twenty points per round. The other boxer is awarded a proportionally lower number of points based upon relative performance.

The referee officiates in the ring and controls the contest, while a jury from AIBA monitors conduct of the events. When a boxer is knocked to the canvas, the referee starts to count from one to ten seconds, while the other boxer retires to a neutral corner. If the fallen boxer fails to continue before the count of ten, or if he is not ready to defend himself, he is "knocked-out."

The referee may also stop the fight if he decides a boxer is out-classed or unable to defend himself. A boxer may also fail to answer the bell for the start of a round. These are known as "technical knockouts."

A fighter who is knocked down during a round may still be able to get up and win that round if he makes more scoring blows than his opponent and if he is thought to deserve the win. The referee may call a standing eight-count if he sees a boxer has been hurt, yet has not fallen to the canvas. During the count, the referee decides whether or not the boxer can continue without incurring serious injury.

1984 PROSPECTS

Teofilo Stevenson, at thirty-two, promises to be in Los Angeles for a fourth Olympic appearance. Any doubts that Stevenson had lost any of his legendary boxing skill was dispelled in November, 1982, with his win over Tyrell Biggs in Reno. Biggs had won the world championship in Munich earlier that year, a tournament in which Stevenson lost his semifinal to the husky Italian, Francisco Damiani, who then lost to Biggs in the final. Although he has tremendous experience, Stevenson can be beaten by a man his own size or by an inside, aggressive brawler.

The 1982 world championship otherwise confirmed the status quo in international boxing, with Cuba again winning the team championship over the United States and the USSR.

In the United States, there has been a dramatic reconstruction of team strength which was tragically extinguished in a 1980 plane crash in Poland, which killed the twenty-two member U.S boxing team.

The leading hopeful for '84 is Mark Breland, a 6-foot 2-inch welterweight (147 pounds). He was named outstanding boxer at the world championship tournament, after a convincing victory over Serik Onakbaev of the USSR. Breland has resisted enormous pressures and lucrative offers to turn professional. He said recently, "I only have one goal now, that is to win a gold medal at the Olympics." Breland is a great talent, but his road to Olympic gold will be a rough one. His weight category is filled with great boxers, especially Cuba's Candelario Duvergel.

Another top U.S. prospect is Pernell Whitaker (132 pounds). Whitaker posted a unanimous decision over Cuba's Olympic and 1982 world champion, Angel Herrera, acquiring the world championship under a new challenge format. Whitaker, a southpaw, completely overwhelmed his renowned opponent, keeping the Cuban continually off balance with unceasing left jabs. Other 1984 hopefuls are Floyd Favors, a bantamweight who was world champion in '82 and '83, and Paul Gonzales, a tough 106-pounder from East Los Angeles.

The USSR sent its best team to fight in a series of three dual meets against the United States in the spring of 1983, and won two. The Soviets' only reigning Olympic champion, Shamil Sabirov, won his first bout over Ricky Romero, then lost to Paul Gonzales.

One of the interesting features of the Los Angeles Games will be the formal entry of China into the boxing tournament. It is a symbolic gesture as no Chinese boxers are expected to compete. In China there are three million shadow boxers who are judged by a scoring system similar to that of gymnastics. Until now, no contact boxing has been allowed in China. The Chinese are quickly converting some of their best shadow boxers to the contact sport. None will be ready by 1984, but one suspects that, with such resources, they will be a factor in Seoul, South Korea, in 1988.

The Cubans should be the team to beat in Los Angeles. Their strength was exhibited with a 12-0 defeat of the United States in a dual meet in Havana in April, 1983. The Cubans systematically went through the U.S. lineup, which, admittedly, was not their best team.

Many Cubans made fast work of their opponents. The fastest was Ernesto Luis DeLis who, at the outset, unloaded a flurry of blows on Lupe Gutirrez of the United States. DeLis finished the fight with a hard right after just one minute, forty-eight seconds. World champion and Moscow silver medalist Adolfo Horta also had an easy time, stopping his opponent five seconds before the end of the first round.

The fact that neither Breland nor Whitaker, the United States' top prospects, fought in Havana, gives the United States some confidence for a gold strike in Los Angeles. Cuba is still expected to be the best in the world, but the United States may be able to catch up with the USSR by 1984. Interest in Olympic boxing is growing in the United States and the athletes are gaining more support and performing with increasing determination and self-confidence.

12

CANOEING

— *12* —

1984 VENUE

Canoeing and kayaking events will be held at Lake Casitas, 80 miles north of Los Angeles, near Ojai. The last time these Olympic events were held on a natural lake was 1960. Lake Casitas is known for strong winds which buffet its surface, so all races are scheduled to be held early morning, the calmest part of the day. There will be seating for approximately 10,000 spectators.

EVENTS AND SCHEDULE (Finals)

Men

500-meter Kayak singles (K-1)	August 10
1,000-meter Kayak singles (K-1)	August 11
500-meter Kayak pairs (K-2)	August 10
1,000-meter Kayak pairs (K-2)	August 11
1,000-meter Kayak fours (K-4)	August 11
500-meter Canadian singles (C-1)	August 10
1,000-meter Canadian singles (C-1)	August 11
500-meter Canadian pairs (C-2)	August 10
1,000-meter Canadian pairs (C-2)	August 11

Women

500-meter Kayak singles (K-1)	August 10
500-meter Kayak pairs (K-2)	August 10
500-meter Kayak fours (K-4)	August 10

HISTORY OF CANOEING

For thousands of years, narrow canoe-style boats have been used for transportation by natives throughout the world. These include reed canoes of the Peruvian Indians in South America, wood canoes of the American Indians, and sealskin and whalebone canoes of the Eskimos in North America. Although steamboats and barges replaced the canoe as a transport vessel, the canoe remains a popular craft for competition and recreation.

Englishman John MacGregor built a canoe he called the "Rob Roy," modeled after the Eskimo kayak. In 1865, MacGregor journeyed by canoe through the rivers and lakes of Europe. He then returned to England and wrote a book about his adventures.

MacGregor's book inspired a great deal of enthusiasm throughout Britain. Canoeing clubs began springing up all over England. These clubs organized both touring and competitive events and, by 1868, boasted over 300 members. Competitive canoeing continued to spread rapidly throughout the world, first through France and Western Europe, then to the United States and Canada.

OLYMPIC HISTORY

Although canoeing was enormously popular in Europe in the early 1900's, it took years of appeals by various national canoeing associations before it was finally included in the Olympic Games in 1936. Nineteen nations participated in the Berlin canoeing events and in the opinion of most competitors and spectators, it was a tremendous success. Ironically, most of the medals were not won by North Americans, whose ancestors first invented the canoe, but rather, by Central Europeans.

In London (1948), when the next Olympic canoeing events were held, separate events were held for kayak and canoe and a single women's event was also included. Scandinavian canoeists displayed for the first time a domination of the sport which they were to retain for many years. Karen Hoff of Denmark won the women's 500-meter kayak singles, while the men were led by Gert Fredriksson of Sweden, who won the 1,000-meter and 10,000-meter individual kayak events. Over the next three Olympic Games, Fredriksson collected a total of six gold medals, five for individual events and one for pairs as well as numerous individual silver and bronze medals.

As the interest and number of teams competing in Olympic canoeing increased, the power and dominance began to shift from Scandinavian nations to Eastern European nations. In Rome (1960), on Lake Albano, Soviets won three of the seven canoeing events, including the two women's events. Race distances finally became somewhat standardized and the 10,000-meter event was permanently dropped from the Olympic schedule.

The sport proved to be a tremendous success, with every Olympic canoeing and kayaking record shattered. But, world records are no longer maintained for these events because wind plays such a major part in determining performance, especially on open lakes where most Olympic races are held. Headwinds can add twenty seconds or more to a 1,000-meter time and crosswinds can slow times by requiring the athlete to put more effort into keeping his craft in line.

Munich provided a big boost to the sport by adding several canoeing events. For the first time, slalom or "white-water" canoeing was included. Building a slalom course is quite expensive, so, despite the popularity at the Munich Games, slalom events were not included in Montreal or Moscow.

Kayak Pairs (K-2).

Eastern Europeans dominated canoeing in Munich, winning sixteen of twenty-one medals. East Germany managed to win all four of the new slalom events, the only time they would occur on the Olympic program. In Montreal, the Soviets were led by Vladimir Parfenovich, who won three golds in three kayaking events, the 500-meter individual and doubles, and the 1,000-meter doubles. The East Germans were led by Rudiger Helm, the 1,000-meter individual kayak winner in Montreal, who repeated the feat again in Moscow (1980).

It is not unusual to see canoeists and kayakers like Rudiger Helm and Gert Fredriksson, remain in world-class competition through several Olympics. Although these events require strength and power, athletes suffer relatively few traumatic injuries. Like swimmers, the top athletes train up to eight hours per day and include weightlifting, running, and cycling as part of their training regimen.

RULES

Although the sport is commonly referred to as canoeing, it actually includes both canoeing and kayaking events. The canoes or "canadians," are narrow, rudderless boats propelled with a single-bladed paddle. The canoeist kneels in the boat, using his arm and body motion both to steer and propel his craft forward.

By contrast, the kayak is propelled from a sitting position, with a double-bladed paddle. Kayakers have foot-controlled rudders for steering the craft, allowing them to concentrate all of their arm motion to power the craft forward. Thus, kayaks are slightly faster over the water than canoes.

Each stroke demands absolute efficiency, since one bad pull can make the difference between winning and losing. In fact, the winner is often determined according to which athlete makes the least bad pulls.

The flatwater canoes and kayaks are both designed to ride on the surface of the water as much as possible, to minimize drag. However, the less hull below the surface, the less stability. So, canoeists and kayakers must make a tradeoff between a stable craft with increased water resistance and a less stable, but higher riding craft.

Canoes and kayaks used in slalom events are shorter and more maneuverable than flatwater or racing vessels, since slalom courses require greater maneuverability through the rapids and gates. Canoes and kayaks differ in width and weight. Both are roughly equal in length (about 17 feet). The singles canoe is slightly heavier and wider, weighing 35.3 pounds and measuring 29.5 inches across, while a kayak weighs only 26 pounds and has a width of only 20 inches.

EVENTS

Singles and doubles canoeing events are designated C-1 and C-2 respectively, while corresponding kayaking events are designated K-1, K-2, and K-4. Paddlers start from a standstill and must travel the entire length of the race within a 9-meter wide lane. A team may be disqualified for interfering with its competitors, colliding with another boat, or for capsizing. Each nation is permitted to enter one participant or team of participants per event.

1984 PROSPECTS

The Soviets and East Germans are certain to provide some very tough competition in Los Angeles. Best hope for the United States is flatwater kayaker Terry White. White was the 1982 national 500 and 1,000-meter champion and proved his versatility in international competition by winning the 1982 whitewater world championships. Also representing the United States will be Ann Turner and Theresa Haught, national K-2 (double kayak) champions and seventh place finishers in the 1981 world championships.

Another strong candidate for '84 gold is Australia's Grant Kinney, who races singles kayak. Kinney is most famous for his achievements as Australia's oceanic ironman champion, a competition which includes surfing, kayaking, and various other ocean skills.

13

CYCLING

— *13* —

1984 VENUE

The new cycling velodrome was recently built on the campus of California State University, Dominguez Hills, under a sponsorship agreement with the Southland Corporation. The oval track is the only world-class cycling facility in the western United States. It measures 333.33 meters around and is seven meters wide. (Three laps are equivalent to one kilometer.) The turns are banked thirty-three degrees. Permanent seating exists for 2,000 spectators and 6,000 temporary seats will be added for the Games.

EVENTS AND SCHEDULE (Finals)

Men

1,000-meter sprint	August 3
1,000-meter time trial	July 30
4,000-meter individual pursuit	August 1
4,000-meter team pursuit	August 3
Individual road race	July 29
Road team time trial	August 5
Individual points race	August 3

Women

Individual road race	July 29

HISTORY OF CYCLING

The first bicycle-type conveyance was designed in 1790 when Frenchman Count de Sivrac first attached two wheels to a crossbar and propelled himself with his feet. In 1839, Kirkpatrick MacMillan, a Scottish blacksmith, invented a method of powering the cycle by means of cranks and also improved the steering mechanism. John Dunlop introduced the first air-filled tire, which allowed a much more comfortable ride and a lighter vehicle.

These men and many other ingenious mechanics, mostly from England and France, developed what eventually would become one of the most viable and inexpensive forms of mass transportation in the world. Late in the last century, as a form of personal transportation and recreation, cycling caught the fancy of the world.

Bicycle racing was firmly established by 1870. The first world championship event took place in Chicago in 1893, three years before the first modern Olympic Games included cycling on its program of nine sports.

OLYMPIC HISTORY

Six cycling events were included at the first Games in Athens. Among them was the twelve-hour race, the longest Olympic cycling race ever held. Adolf Schmal of Austria covered 314 kilometers (196.8 miles) to win by a margin of just 300 meters over a British competitor.

There was only one cycling event on the Paris (1900) program. Details of the race other than the results are sketchy, reflecting the haphazard conduct of the second Olympic Games. Seven track races were conducted at St. Louis (1904). All were won by American professional cyclists; there were no foreign entries.

The London Games were a step forward in terms of organization. Track events were held on the new, banked, 500-meter oval inside the main Olympic stadium. Unfortunately, the weather was terrible and many racers were hampered by the wet, slippery surface. British cyclists swept the board, with the exception of the successful French team which won the 2,000-meter tandem race.

The early Olympic Games were plagued by the question, What is an amateur? Professional cycling was well established, while its Olympic sister failed to attract interest because disputes over eligibility limited the entry of the best cyclists. Even today, one rarely hears of the same cyclists competing from one Olympics to the next. The rich rewards offered to professional cyclists in famous road races such as the Tour de France appear to be a better motivator than the prospect of an Olympic medal.

European nations provided the best riders in the early Olympic Games, especially Great Britain, France, and Holland. The United States worked hard to field the best possible teams. French bicycles were custom-made for 1924 team members, who took two-hour training sessions aboard the S.S. President Roosevelt on the trip across the Atlantic to France for the 1928 Olympics.

Yet, not one U.S. cyclist has won a medal since 1908. This may be due to the increased status of the sport in Europe, where it has a storied history and enthusiastic spectator support. However, cycling is currently experiencing a phenomenal jump in popularity and participation in the United States.

Paradoxically, cycling's popularity in Western European countries has undermined its Olympic success for those nations. With such rich rewards on the professional circuits, few outstanding cyclists choose to remain amateur and retain the right to compete in the Olympics. As a result, while all the best riders in the world are from Western Europe, more and more Olympic medals are being won by Eastern Europeans. In 1960, Viktor Kapitanov won the first cycling gold medal for the USSR in the 175 kilometer road race, the only cycling event at the Rome Games not won by an Italian.

In Tokyo (1964), outstanding cyclist Eddy Merckx (France) competed in his first and only Olympic Games. After leading the individual road race throughout, he suffered a fall less than one mile from the finish line. The pack was so bunched, he could only manage twelfth place, although he was only 11/100 of a second behind the winner, Mario Zanin of Italy. Merckx subsequently became a professional, dominating European road racing for many years, winning the Tour de France five times and becoming one of the most famous cyclists of all time.

Another outstanding Frenchman is Daniel Morelon, who won his first Olympic medal, a bronze, in 1964, in the 1,000-meter sprint at the age of twenty. He returned in Mexico City (1968), where he took the gold in the same event and an additional gold in the 2,000-meter tandem event.

In Munich, Morelon repeated his 1,000-meter sprint victory, the first cyclist ever to win an event in back-to-back Games. Finally, in Montreal, at the age of thirty-two, a relatively advanced age for a competitive cyclist, Morelon attempted a third straight sprint victory, but had to settle for a silver.

THE EVENTS

The exciting action and careful strategies employed on both the track and roads might appear confusing to the uninitiated. Once the purposes of these movements are understood, however, cycling transforms into a fascinating and exciting sport. The following summarizes some of the objectives, rules, and strategies of each of the Olympic cycling events.

Sprints

Sprint events take place on the velodrome track, where two or more riders compete in highly strategic confrontations of wits and speed. The sprints are contested in an elimination tournament, where individual riders progress through a series of heats to establish themselves as quarterfinalists. The winning eight sprint cyclists are then paired and race in a best of three sprint series. The winner of each race progresses to the final round to determine the gold medalist.

The sprint race takes place over 1,000 meters, three laps of the track. The rider who has drawn the inside position must lead for the first lap, so the other rider has the benefit of reduced wind resistance and can better judge when to vie for the lead.

After the first lap, the battle of wits begins. Riders compete fiercely for the strategic trailing position. At times the riders hardly move, standing on their machines, practically motionless, in an attempt to force the other rider into the lead.

At some point, usually on the last lap, one rider will decide to strike. His rival must respond quickly, using the beneficial effects of drafting, to catch up and take the lead before crossing the finish line.

Only the last 200 meters of the sprint race is timed, since the first 800 meters are more a test of strategy and control than speed. This final head-to-head duel provides some of the most dramatic moments in the sport. The sprinters are the gladiators of cycling, powerfully built athletes who can power a bicycle at close to 45 MPH.

1,000-Meter Time Trial

This sprint event is easier to understand. It is an individual, all out effort against the clock over three laps of the track. Contestants begin on the cycle in a standing position, the bicycle held stationary by an official who, when the gun sounds, is careful not to assist the competitor by pushing the cycle.

A vital factor in this race is the ability of the cyclist to accelerate immediately and quickly reach maximum speed. Then, without any benefit from drafting, he races alone at nearly 60 KPH. This event is a clear test of speed and endurance.

4,000-Meter Individual Pursuit

Two riders start at opposite sides of the track, and right from the start, each attempts to overtake the other. If one is successful, the race is over. If neither succeeds in overtaking the other, the winner is the one with the fastest time over the 4,000-meter course, twelve laps of the track.

Qualification trials are held to determine the sixteen finalists, who will pursue one another in paired competitions throughout the twelve-lap pursuit event. In the early qualification trials, each cyclist rides alone, simply racing against time. Like the time trial, this event is a test of speed and endurance.

4,000-Meter Team Pursuit

The team pursuit is the same type of event as the individual pursuit. Elimination rounds against the clock determine which teams will compete in the final rounds. Each team consists of four riders, who alternate leading the group, thereby splitting the load of reducing the wind. Lead cyclists split the wind for the remainder of the team, then pull aside to let the second member move into the lead to take the brunt of the wind resistance. The winning team's time is determined when the third member of the team crosses the finish line.

Success requires smooth teamwork, particularly during the crucial moments when the riders change positions. Teams can gain approximately 20 seconds over the best individual efforts over the twelve laps. The team rides as a single unit in motion, working to maximize the benefits of drafting and thus to preserve their strength and speed.

Individual Points race, an event new to the 1984 Olympic cycling program.

USA 4,000-meter pursuit team.

Sprinters maneuver for position.

Individual Points Race

This event is new to the Olympic program and consists of a 30-kilometer race, ninety laps, during which riders sprint for points after every five laps. Points are distributed among the first four riders in each of eighteen sprints that are staged during the course of the event. Points are doubled at the halfway mark of 15 kilometers and at the finish. The overall winner is the rider with the most points, not necessarily the rider with the fastest overall time.

Individual Road Race

The men's road race in Los Angeles will cover 189 kilometers (117.2 miles), thirteen laps of a 15-kilometer circuit over highways and roads. The women will race 70 kilometers (43 miles) over a course in Mission Viejo in Orange County.

Although it is basically an individual event, there is plenty of cooperation between national team members. Teams determine strategies which will help one or more individuals in their bid for a medal. They will pace each other, draft one another against the wind, exchange drinks, and assist with equipment needs.

Teamwork is crucial in a breakaway in which a group of cyclists from the same team or in a temporary partnership with their competitors, attempt to break away from the pack. They may accomplish this by waiting until the other cyclists are not concentrating or are blocked and not ready to chase. When the breakaway has been completed, the remaining cyclists continue to vie for position.

100-meter Road Team Time Trial

This is a race against the clock by national teams consisting of four cyclists. Each team rides as a group, with groups starting at two-minute intervals. Cooperation between team members, with each member taking turns at splitting the wind while others draft, is crucial. When one team passes another, the passed team is obliged to drop back a minimum of 25 meters. The overall time is gauged by the third rider crossing the finish line.

EQUIPMENT

Track bicycles are equipped with a single-speed fixed gear. They cannot spin or coast and they have no brakes. The thin, hard tires are inflated to pressures of 200 pounds, which reduces friction. The cyclists wear cleats with double straps so pedals can be powered by both pushing and pulling. The typical road bike is more familiar to nonracers. It is lighter in weight, has ten or twelve speeds, a free wheel, and two brakes.

1984 PROSPECTS

The prestigious Olympic sprint championship once again shapes up as a struggle between the Eastern Europeans. Moscow Olympic Champion Lutz Hesslich of East Germany had an impressive series of victories on the Olympic track at Dominguez

Hills during 1983. His greatest challenger will probably be Soviet sprinter Sergey Kopylov, who won the world championship in '81 and '82.

Mark Gorski of La Jolla, California, gained valuable experience, meeting both Hesslich and Kopylov several times during 1983. He says confidently, "I'm getting closer." Indeed, Gorski is the first world-class U.S. sprinter and has an outside chance of winning the first U.S. men's cycling medal since 1912.

Twenty-seven-year-old Leonard Nitz is probably the United States' best hope to challenge the consistently strong European contingent. Nitz began cycling in 1973 and was immediately successful in national competition. It was not until 1979 though, that he finally overcame the stigma that a United States cyclist would never amount to much in world competition and began to challenge the Europeans.

Nitz is a track specialist. His best event is the individual points race, in which he challenged the Europeans at the World Cycling Championship of 1981 in Czechoslovakia, finishing second. Nitz has also made progress in the 4,000-meter individual pursuit in which he retained his national title and lowered the national record to 4:48.20. This performance, however, did not remain in the record books, as David Grylls improved the mark significantly with 4:43.90 at the Pan Am Games.

The new women's Olympic road race will feature U.S. entrants Rebecca Twigg and Connie Carpenter. Carpenter, twenty-seven years old, has won the national championship twelve times and has several years of experience over the twenty-one-year-old Twigg, but Twigg has several recent wins over Carpenter to her credit.

Twigg was the 1982 world pursuit champion, Carpenter was second. The road race, commonly considered a team event, should provide some interesting action. Carpenter and Twigg have a fierce rivalry since they are among the world's best female cyclists, and both have set their sights on Olympic gold.

Road racing teams, each consisting of three members, usually work together, with some members sacrificing themselves to help the strongest individual. These sacrifices take the form of breaking the wind, blocking rival cyclists, or even giving up tires and tubes if the strong cyclist has an equipment failure. With such an intense rivalry between these women, one wonders whether the team concept and team sacrifices will prevail.

14

EQUESTRIAN

— *14* —

1984 VENUE

Most of the 1984 Olympic equestrian events will be held at Santa Anita Park in Arcadia. The track, normally used for horse racing, was opened in 1934. The grandstand currently seats 25,000, but with temporary stands, Santa Anita will accommodate more than 40,000 people during the Games. Its thirty-three acres include sweeping lawns, elegant gardens, and thousands of flowers, a fitting setting for the "Sport of Kings."

While the show jumping, dressage, and the first and third days of the three-day event will be held at Santa Anita Park, the second day, consisting of speed and endurance tests, will be held 100 miles south of Los Angeles at Fairbanks Ranch, near San Diego.

EVENTS AND SCHEDULE (Finals)

Three-day Event

Individual	July 29, 30 (Dressage)
Team Competition	August 1 (Endurance)
	August 3 (Jumping)

Grand Prix Jumping

Individual	August 12
Team Competition	August 7

Dressage

Individual	August 10
Team Competition	August 8, 9

BACKGROUND

The teaming of man and horse goes back more than 4,000 years to the Bronze Age. Earlier, horses had been hunted as wild game, but during this age, horses were domesticated and used for hunting and war. Equestrian competitions in the form of horse and chariot racing existed in Greece at the time of the Ancient Games in 776 B.C., although it wasn't until the twenty-fifth Olympiad in 680 B.C., that chariot racing was added to the official Olympic program.

Chariot racing was undoubtedly one of the most exciting sports, with teams of horses racing two to three miles around a track similar in size and shape to that used in modern footraces. Because of the sharp, narrow turns, there were many crashes and upsets to thrill the crowd. More controlled mounted races were introduced in 648 B.C.

In the sixteenth through nineteenth centuries, horses were widely used in cavalries, making new skills and maneuvers valuable. Contests were set up to test these skills. The dressage event, which tests movement, execution, and horse and rider communication, evolved from medieval tournaments and the military parade ground. Jumping events stemmed from fox-hunting, a sport enjoyed by the aristocracy.

Finally, the three-day event, which combines all equestrian skills, was derived from the military skills of cross-country riding, jumping, and endurance. The influence of the military on the sport has greatly diminished just as the use of the horse for transportation has become obsolete in much of the world.

OLYMPIC HISTORY

With equestrian events such an integral part of the ancient Olympic Games, and horses an essential mode of transportation, it was only natural they be included in the Modern Games, although it wasn't until Stockholm (1912) that the three modern equestrian events became standard Olympic events. Sweden and Holland set the standards for the sport between 1912 and 1932, with *Marcroix* and Lieutenant Pahud de Mortanges of Holland earning four gold and two silver medals in the Games between 1924 and 1932.

Riders in these early Olympic Games were usually military officers. At the time, horses were important to military operations and the cavalry was well stocked with excellent riders and horses. In the 1936 Olympic Games, only one civilian was entered in the entire equestrian tournament.

Polo was introduced to the Games in 1924 as an exhibition sport and again in 1936. Since each competing nation required between thirty and forty horses for the series of polo games, the expenses of maintenance and transportation prevented polo's inclusion as a regular equestrian event.

After the 1948 Games, women were allowed to compete in the Olympic dressage event, earning their first medals in Helsinki in 1952. Lis Hartel of Denmark won an individual silver in the dressage event and Baroness Ida von Nagel won a bronze in the team competition. In 1956, women were declared eligible for jumping, but could not enter the Olympic three-day event until 1964.

The 1956 Olympic equestrian events were held in Stockholm rather than Melbourne, where the other competitions were held, because of strict Australian quarantine laws. For many athletes and spectators, these isolated Games were one of the most enjoyable series of Olympic equestrian events, with horses and riders from twenty-nine nations traveling to Sweden, a nation known for its enthusiastic support of the sport.

One of the stars of the competition was *Halla* whose rider, Hans Winkler of Germany, had injured himself in the first round of Grand Prix jumping. While Winkler "tried not to interfere" and just managed to stay astride, *Halla* completed a perfect second round, winning the individual competition and helping to win the team competition. *Halla* and Winkler again led Germany to the team jumping title in Rome (1960). Also competing in Rome was Major Henri St. Cyr of Sweden, appearing in his fifth and final Olympics. He collected a total of four golds in five Games between 1936 and 1960.

Women riders again made their presence felt in 1956 as Lis Hartel earned her second silver medal in the individual dressage and Liselott Linsenhoff of Germany won the bronze. At this time, the military presence and influence on the sport was beginning to wane, partly due to the decreased use of horses by the armed forces and the consequent restructuring of international equestrian sport.

Because the horse suffers most of the wear and tear of competition and ages relatively quickly, it rarely stays in competitive form long enough to make it to more than two Olympics. Riders are generally not subjected to such abuse and may compete at relatively advanced ages. This was evident in Mexico City (1968), where gold medal winners from the '52, '56, '60, and '64 Games were all competing.

The three-day event in Mexico City took place in Avandaro, about a two-hour drive from Mexico City. The event turned out to be a disaster, heavy rains and floods making the already difficult course nearly impossible. One horse drowned and two had to be destroyed due to broken legs. Many riders were injured, none seriously. Competitors from Great Britain proved best under the miserable conditions, winning the team competition. Jean Guyon of France won the individual gold.

Bill Steinkraus of the United States won an individual gold in Grand Prix jumping in Mexico City, having won a bronze in the team event in Helsinki (1952) and a silver in the team event in Rome (1960). He won another silver in Munich (1972). Steinkraus retired following his fifth Olympics. Today, he continues to use his vast experience as Chairman of the U.S. Equestrian Team, Inc., which carries the responsibility of financing, selecting, and training the current U.S. team.

One of the standouts of the 1972 equestrian competition was the team of *Piaff* and German millionairess, Liselott Linsenhoff. Competing in their second Olympics, they managed a nearly perfect dressage round and won the gold.

Many equestrian athletes have won medals in several Olympics, including Richard Meade. Competing in his third Olympics, he won Britain's first individual gold as he and *Laurieston* captured the Munich three-day event and led his team to the gold as well.

In Montreal (1976), durable Hans Winkler surpassed them all by competing in his sixth Games and winning his sixth Olympic medal in the team competition.

Another outstanding competitor in Montreal was Alwin Schockemoehle of West Germany on *Warwick Rex*. They jumped two perfect rounds, winning the individual Grand Prix jumping and leading West Germany to a team silver. Distinguished equestrienne Princess Anne of Great Britain finished the demanding three-day event, but placed only twenty-fourth after a hard fall. Edmund Coffin, astride *Bally Cor,* won the individual gold for the three-day event, leading the United States to the team championship.

The rider adds the quality of skill and judgment to the rider-horse pairing. As a rider's youth and agility declines, his judgment may grow. A younger rider may do best in the three-day event which requires great stamina and a certain youthful vigor. The same rider might specialize in show jumping as he matures and, as he grows older, may turn to dressage, the event that requires the most patience and knowledge.

THE EVENTS

Equestrian sports are unusual among Olympic sports in several respects. First, a horse and rider compete as a paired team. Secondly, it is one of the few sports in which men and women compete together.

There are three separate equestrian disciplines, with individual and team competitions in each. These are dressage, show jumping, and the three-day event.

Dressage

Each nation may enter one team consisting of three rider-horse pairs in the dressage event. Dressage is a test of a horse's obedience and responsiveness as the horse and rider perform a complex series of classical maneuvers entirely from memory. Judges rate this performance on a ten-point scale, basing their decision on the quality of excellence of the movements, accuracy, and communication between horse and rider. Scores for the three rider-horse pairs are combined to determine the overall winner of the team event. The best ten riders in the team event then ride off in a different test, the Grand Prix Special, for the individual titles.

Show Jumping

In Grand Prix jumping, horses and riders must twice complete an obstacle course they have never seen before, jumping over high barriers, multiple fences, and a water jump. Their score is based on the number of faults incurred, with the team incurring the fewest becoming the winner of the Prix des Nations. The individual winner must jump two different courses in a separate competition, also based on faults. Ties are broken with jump-offs over a shorter course, with elapsed time counting if there are equal faults.

Each nation may enter one team composed of four rider-horse pairs in the jumping event, with the top three scores added together to determine the team

Grand Prix jumping.

Three-day event, Richel Bayliss on "Gurgle the Greek" in cross-country endurance trials.

championship. To illustrate the difficulty of the jumping course, in the 1932 Olympics, when no nation managed to produce a full team of three finishers in the event, no team medals were given.

Three-Day Event

The three-day event combines dressage, endurance tests, and show jumping. Dressage, which is held on the first day, is less demanding than the Grand Prix dressage, containing fewer maneuvers and being scored on a smaller, six-point scale.

The endurance test, held on the second day, is a grueling test for both horse and rider. They must complete a five-phase, twenty-two mile course which combines jumping, endurance, and speed trials. Each phase tests a different aspect of the horse and rider's ability. Scoring is based on the number of penalty points accumulated throughout the entire ride. The endurance portion is responsible for eliminating the most horses and riders in a competition.

On the third and final day, a similar, but less severe course than the one used in the Prix des Nations jumping must be completed. It is scored in the same fashion as the Prix des Nations. Finally, the total scores for the three-day event are determined by adding up faults and penalty points accumulated throughout the three days of the competition. The horse and rider with the lowest total win the individual gold. Team scores are composites of scores from the top three of the four horse-rider pairs.

THE HORSES

While not necessarily the "better half" of the horse-rider pair, the horse is just as important as its human counterpart in Olympic equestrian competition. Very few horses have the potential to become world-class and those that do require extensive training to refine it. The training adds expense to the already prohibitive costs of breeding or purchasing, maintaining, and transporting Olympic horses. For most events, this cost is multiplied several times, since Grand Prix jumping and three-day event competitors require several back-up horses for training. Only in the dressage event can competitors get by with just one horse.

Unlike riders, horses rarely remain in competition for many years. One notable exception is the champion jumper *Jet Run*. Although *Jet Run* has yet to win an Olympic medal, he has won the Grand Prix jumping event in two successive Pan American Games. Born and bred in the United States, he represented Mexico in 1975, where he was ridden by Fernando Senderos, a member of a wealthy Mexican banking family.

Jet Run returned to the U.S. equestrian team for the 1979 Pan American Games, where he and rider Michael Matz captured the gold. *Jet Run's* new owner was F. Eugene Dixon, then owner of the Philadelphia 76ers professional basketball team. Dixon in reputed to have paid $250,000 to bring the horse back to the U.S. stable. Following the Moscow boycott, *Jet Run* reaffirmed his value with a win in the 1981 World Cup Finals.

Equestrian competition is often limited to the very wealthy or very well-sponsored riders. Some owners of Olympic-caliber horses loan them to the U.S. Equestrian Team in return for the publicity and/or satisfaction that the horse's success will bring them. However, such sponsors are relatively rare and it seems inevitable that equestrian sport will remain as it began, the "Sport of Kings."

Those who can afford the sport include corporations, which own many of the horses that compete on Europe's professional show jumping circuit. The growth of professional riding has placed even more of a strain on the economics of Olympic equestrianism as the prices of the best horses have escalated.

1984 PROSPECTS

Equestrian competition is among the most difficult of Olympic sports to forecast. There are many variables in the horse-rider combination and every course is different. Seldom do a horse and rider maintain a long winning streak. More experienced riders usually bring knowledge and finesse to the competition, but on any given day there are a dozen or so who could win.

Once again, the traditional equestrian powers are favored to win medals in 1984. West Germany is always strong, reflecting the stature of the sport in that country. The Germans breed more horses, train more riders, and regard the sport very highly. Their rivals, as before, should come from England, France, Italy, and the United States. As in the Moscow Games, the USSR should continue to be the strongest of the Eastern European countries.

An outstanding U.S. prospect for the Los Angeles Games is Melanie Smith, who should be riding *Calypso* in the Grand Prix jumping event, just as she did when winning the 1982 World Cup jumping event in Gothenburg, Sweden. Because of that victory, Smith was named the top woman rider in the world by the international federation. Smith found *Calypso* in Holland in 1978 and paid a bargain $40,000. Their unprecedented string of Grand Prix wins has established *Calypso* as the top jumper in the world, valued at $1.2 million.

15

FENCING

— *15* —

1984 VENUE

The 1984 Olympic Fencing competition will be held at the Long Beach Convention Center, located next to the Long Beach Shoreline Marina. The trials will take place in the Exhibition Hall which has a seating capacity of 6,000. The fencing finals, however, will be held at the 3,000-seat Terrace Theater adjacent to the Exhibition Hall.

EVENTS AND SCHEDULE (Finals)

Men

Foil:	
Individual	August 2
Team	August 5
Epee:	
Individual	August 8
Team	August 11
Sabre:	
Individual	August 4
Team	August 9

Women

Foil:	
Individual	August 3
Team	August 7

HISTORY OF FENCING

The ancient and once practical art of swordsmanship is now an exciting, complex, and physically demanding international sport. Participants experience the thrill of hand-to-hand combat, without the need to pulverize opponents. The three different weapons used in fencing are mere toys, play swords designed not to harm an opponent. Yet, the sense of battle is the same, the duel equally heroic. Modern fencing requires courage and skill and has evolved throughout many centuries of tradition.

The origin of fencing goes back at least 3,000 years. An Egyptian temple constructed in 1190 B.C. depicts fencers using weapons with safety tips. It also shows spectators and judges, confirming an early interest in fencing as pure sport, not necessarily an act of warfare. The disciplined practice of fencing technique was firmly established by the fifteenth century. A 1599 English treatise by George Silver claimed many benefits of the sport:

"The exercising of weapons puts away aches, griefs, and diseases. It increases strength and sharpens the wits. It gives perfect judgment. It dispels melancholy, anger, and evil conceits. It keeps a man in breath, perfect health, and long life."

By the end of the nineteenth century, fencing was practiced throughout Europe. Many nations claimed to be the birthplace of the sport, among them Hungary, France, Spain, and Italy, as well as several Oriental countries.

OLYMPIC HISTORY

Baron Pierre de Coubertin, founder of the Games, was an active swordsman so it is no surprise that fencing was included in the first Olympic Games (1896). What is surprising, however, is that fencing masters, as professionals, were allowed to compete with their students in the first two Olympic fencing tournaments.

The French and Italians provided most of the outstanding fencers in early Olympic competitions. Later, due to their organized approach to the sport, it was nations with state-supported programs for fencers that developed the top athletes. Strong military nations, such as those in Eastern Europe, currently produce many of the best fencers.

Ramon Fonst, a Cuban who lived and trained in France, was one of the earliest fencing masters. He won the epee event in Paris (1900) and returned in St. Louis (1904), to try for a second epee gold. He won the foil and sword competitions as well. One of his foremost successors was Lucien Gaudin of France, who earned a total of four golds and two silvers in an Olympic career which spanned five Games and ended at age forty-two.

The first women's fencing event was introduced in 1924 when Ellen Osiier of Denmark took the gold. Her successor was Helene Mayer of Germany, who won the foil event in 1928 and was runner-up to Ilona Elek in 1936. Mayer, of Jewish heritage, immigrated to the United States before she was asked to fence for Germany in Berlin. Later, she won the U.S. national championship eight times in twelve years. Although she became a U.S. citizen, Mayer was prohibited from competing on the U.S. Olympic team by an eligibility rule that prevented anyone who had competed in the Olympics for one nation from later representing another. Mayer instead went into coaching.

The 1948 London Games saw a record twenty-two nations represented in fencing events. They also saw the first Olympic appearance of future greats Christian d'Oriola of France and Rudolf Karpati of Hungary. In the 1948 foil competition, d'Oriola was narrowly defeated, but avenged his loss by winning the gold in 1952 and again in 1956.

Karpati, the sabre champion of Hungary, led his countrymen to sabre team championships in '48, '52, '56, and '60, and captured the '56 and '60 individual titles as well. Also competing in London was Karpati's compatriot, forty-one-year-old Ilona Elek, a testament to the phenomenal durability of competitive fencers. Here, Elek took a second foil gold medal, her previous gold having been won in 1936, when she defeated Helene Mayer.

The most notable fencer during the era spanning 1936 to 1960 was Edoardo Mangiarotti. The left-handed epee and foil expert began his twenty-four year Olympic winning streak in Berlin (1936) where, at the age of seventeen, he won his first gold medal in the epee team competition. Mangiarotti, with his Italian teammates, continued until 1960 to capture three more epee titles and one foil title. Mangiarotti even acquired a gold for his individual epee expertise in 1952. Besides his collection of six gold medals, he also amassed five silver and two bronze, totaling an astounding thirteen medals, clearly epitomizing the Italian fencing tradition and their passion for the sport.

In Rome (1960), fencing began to feel the influence of a new force, the Eastern Europeans. Here, with athletes from forty-three nations competing, the USSR dominated the foil events and showed it had at last reached a competitive level equal to that of such historically strong nations as Italy, France, and Hungary. The long-standing domination of fencing by these three nations finally began to slip.

In Tokyo (1964), for the first time in thirty-six years, Italy relinquished its dominance in the epee event to a Soviet. In Mexico City, Poland's Jerzy Pawlowski won the sabre event, the first time in forty-eight years the event was won by a non-Hungarian.

Montreal (1976) saw continued success for Soviet fencers, who had introduced strength and athleticism into a sport which had traditionally favored finesse and technique. The big upset of the competition was a win by nineteen-year-old Fabio del Zotto of Italy in the foil event. Due to the technical requirements of the sport, most fencers require many years of training to reach such a finely-tuned level of skill.

Another upset, although in a negative sense, was the discovery that Soviet pentathlete, Boris Onishenko, used a rigged epee which recorded hits whether or not they were actually made. This unsportsmanlike incident, although occurring in a pentathlon competition, blackened fencing's historically pristine image, but alerted officials to guard against future violations. A far more stringent series of weapons checks has since been adopted.

In Moscow (1980), the star of the women's competition was Pascale Trinquet of France, who won golds in the individual and team foil events. Soviet sabre fencer Viktor Krovopuskov added two medals to his 1976 sabre gold, repeating his individual sabre victory and leading his team to the team sabre gold as well. This team included previous sabre medalists Vladimir Nazlymov and Viktor Sidiak who have helped to develop the Soviets' long tradition of outstanding sabre athletes.

Franco Riccardi ITA scores a hit on Campbell GBR on his way to the individual epee gold.

In direct contrast, the United States has little history of outstanding Olympic fencers. Many of the athletes who have done well in U.S. national competition were not always native Americans, such as Helene Mayer and Leo Nunes, who emigrated from Italy and subsequently went on to win sixteen foil, epee, and sabre national championships between 1917 and 1932. Like Mayer, Nunes was not permitted to compete with the U.S. Olympic team. Among outstanding fencers born, raised, and trained in the United States, Joe Levis won the silver medal in 1932, and Albert Axelrod, a bronze in 1960. Janice Lee Romary, the 1984 Olympic fencing commissioner, just missed a medal, finishing fourth in 1952.

RULES

The sport of fencing utilizes three different types of weapons. They are the foil, the epee, and the sabre. Each weapon requires a different style and its own individual competition. All fencing competitions share the same goal, to score a touch on the opponent's valid target area. The various body part targets are different for each of the three weapons.

The command "On Guard, Ready, Fence!" initiates the action. The objective of the bout is to score five hits on an opponent. If this does not occur, the winner is the fencer who achieves the most hits during the six minutes allotted for both men's and women's bouts.

The essence of fencing is speed and finesse rather than pure physical strength. Success is based upon keen perception and fast reaction time, combined with dexterity and agility. The influence of the East European and Soviet fencers since the 1960 Olympics in Rome has had a definite effect on style. They have introduced more aggression and a completely athletic approach to fencing that now makes strength and conditioning a prerequisite to championship stature.

Because of the incredible speed and quickness of fencing action, the uninitiated viewer finds it a difficult sport to observe. Even the judging relies upon electronic devices to determine the scoring in the epee and foil events. As the observer becomes accustomed to the speed of the combat, he may begin to follow the tactics of each fencer.

Fencers try to maintain a safe distance until one commits to an attack. The attack may be parried by the defensive fencer, who may then counter-attack in a movement called riposte, the quick thrust after the parry. Each combative encounter consists of attack, parry, riposte, and counter riposte. The particular combination leading to a hit is referred to as a "phrase." Each fencer searches for an opening, an inefficient motion of his opponent, an instant where a precision response and skillful action can produce a hit.

Success is marked by flashing lights, rather than flowing blood. Foil and epee fencers turn instantly after a touch to see what story the electric current tells. Sabre fighters turn to study the faces of four judges and a director, ever prepared to argue their case.

THE WEAPONS

Foil

The foil is the modern version of what was once known as the dueling rapier. The foil was developed in 1635 as a practice implement for the epee, which is more than a third heavier; the maximum weight for the foil is 500 grams compared to 770 grams for the epee. The foil is a thrust weapon, which means hits may be made only with the point of the weapon and must land on the torso, including the area above the groin lines on the front and to the waist on the back. Arms and masks are off target.

Electronic scoring equipment was introduced to the foil event in 1954. The target area is covered with a metallic vest. To score a hit, the blade must touch the vest to complete an electrical circuit. When a touch occurs, a buzzer sounds and a colored light goes on, indicating which fencer has scored the hit.

If the lights indicate that both fencers have made hits, the director decides who scored first, determining which fencer has the right of way and which is the attacker. Only the attacker is allowed to initiate the next combative encounter.

Epee

The epee, also a thrust weapon, was developed at the start of the sixteenth century. Again, one can score only with the point. The electronic scoring system used in fencing was used initially for the epee event as early as 1933. At first it was felt that the electronic wiring was interfering with the balance of the competitors. After some improvements it is now considered to be of no hindrance to the fencer and is considered essential to the accurate scoring of the event.

In epee, there is no right-of-way and fencers can score simultaneously. If hits occur within 0.25 of a second, a "double-hit" is recorded and the hit is counted against both fencers. In epee events, the valid taget is the entire body, anywhere blood could be drawn with a real weapon.

Sabre

The sabre is a cut and thrust weapon with a straight, light blade. Whereas the thrust weapons, the foil and epee, were popular in Western Europe, the sabre had its origin and growth in Central and Eastern Europe. The sabre is the modern version of the slashing, swinging, cavalry sword. The target area is the upper body above the waist, the arms, and the head. Hits can be scored with the point, the front edge of the blade, and one-third of the back edge. The blade is flexible and triangular in shape.

There is currently no approved electronic scoring system; therefore, the hits are decided by a jury made up of a director and four judges. Each judge has one vote and the director has 1½ votes. As two judges watch each fencer, the director can essentially overrule a split decision.

1984 PROSPECTS

Prospects for the '84 U.S. team are not especially bright against the traditionally strong Europeans, as seen in Vienna at the '83 world championships. West Germany won five medals while the powerful Italians walked away with a total of seven medals, two gold. Surprisingly, Cuba made an excellent showing by placing third overall after beating Italy for entry into the team finals, and then defeating Hungary, another strong fencing nation.

Another surprise at the world championships was the poor showing of the Soviet team. Two-time foil team title winners in the men's competition ('81 and '82), the Soviets took home only two golds through the performances of the Soviet sabre team and Alexander Romankov, who added a fifth men's individual foil championship to his collection.

Looking ahead to '84, Peter Westbrook possesses the best chance for the United States in the sabre competition, while Jane Angelakis in the women's foil and Michael Marx in the men's foil may help produce the best U.S. Olympic showing in many years. However, with less experience, compared to that of the Europeans, the United States team cannot realistically hope for a medal in '84.

16

FOOTBALL (SOCCER)

— *16* —

1984 VENUE

The Rose Bowl, located in Pasadena, has a seating capacity of 105,000. Completed in 1922 with an original seating capacity of 57,000, the Rose Bowl was the site of the cycling events in the 1932 Olympics. Since then, expansion has brought the stadium to its present size.

Preliminary games in the 1984 tournament will also take place at Harvard Stadium, Massachusetts; Navy-Marine Corps Stadium, Annapolis, Maryland; and Stanford University Stadium, Stanford, California.

EVENTS AND SCHEDULE (Finals)

Men

Team Championship   August 11

HISTORY OF FOOTBALL

In terms of participation and spectator interest, football, or soccer as it's known in the United States, is the world's most popular sport. It is estimated that 100 million people actually play the game. In 1950, 200,000 people packed Rio De Janeiro's Maracana stadium to watch the World Cup final between Brazil and Uruguay. It was the biggest crowd ever for an international sports event. The World Cup, played every four years, attracts a worldwide audience and is rivaled in size only by the Olympic Games.

The direct lineage of modern football can be traced to the ball games played in the British Isles over the last thousand years. All modern football-type games: soccer, rugby, American football, Canadian football, Gaelic football, and Australian football, evolved from this common ancestry.

An even more ancient origin, however, is far more difficult to discern, since many ancient cultures played games that have some relationship to football. As early as 600 B.C., the Japanese played a game called Kemari. Our only knowledge of the game comes from woodcuts, which indicate that kicking a ball into a goal was one of the game's primary objectives. In pre-Columbian cultures throughout South and Central America and extending as far north as Arizona in the United States, ball games were considered an essential component of religious ceremonies. It is not clear what part kicking skills played in these early games.

Perhaps a more direct ancestry is found in ball-juggling exercises, using thighs and feet, which were practiced by the Romans, Egyptians, and Greeks. The first football game probably evolved from the concept of combining these juggling skills with the passing skills common to several games.

The first known literary reference to football dates back to 1175 and was followed by many more writings. Of these references, the most remarkable describe the game of mass football, which was played during Christian holidays. Hordes of players, representing different factions, attempted to move the ball toward their opponent's goal line. There seemed to be no limit to the size of each of the teams and one can easily imagine the din as most of the barking dogs in the town joined the chase.

This version of the game soon became a chaotic and violent contest in which entire towns and villages competed, driving toward goals, which were sometimes miles apart. There were really no rules, the only objective, to move the ball toward the opponents' goal.

By the fourteenth century, football action had become a popular recreation and created frequent mob scenes in the streets. Edward II prohibited the sport in 1314 and this ban was followed by a succession of royal decrees prohibiting such unruly scenes. In spite of such decrees, interest and enjoyment continued to expand and, as it grew, rules were added.

Football was played by small groups of students at Cambridge University where a degree of gentlemanly conduct was expected. These unwritten rules were passed on to other public schools in England and in the early part of the nineteenth century, dozens of other colleges adopted the game. The game as we know it today was first codified at Cambridge in 1848, and the creation of the Football Association in 1863 marked the beginning of the organized football we now know.

OLYMPIC HISTORY

Football first joined the Olympic program in Paris in 1900. This event, and the one that followed in St. Louis in 1904, was a tournament involving club teams, rather than a national team competition. The first international Olympic tournament was held in 1908 in London. Utilizing the services of professional players, the British team won the first of two successive gold medals. The second tournament in Stockholm attracted eleven nations, but the sport was still new to many and, once again, British victory was virtually uncontested.

The 1920 Olympic tournament at Antwerp was won by Belgium, but only after Czechoslovakia walked off the field following a disputed goal. By 1924 in Paris, the football tournament had become worldwide in scope. The United States entered for the first time and there were teams from Egypt, Turkey, and Uruguay.

Britain claimed her players were now all amateurs, whereas other team players were receiving expenses from their national associations. It was over this issue that Britain abandoned the Federation Internationale de Football Association (FIFA) and withdrew from Olympic competition. In the 1924 final, Uruguay impressed the world with their speed and agility and easily defeated Switzerland.

Uruguay brought virtually the same team to Amsterdam in 1928 to retain its Olympic title. It was a South American final, Argentina playing Uruguay to a 1–1 draw in the first game, before losing the replay, 2–1. In 1926, the issue of amateurism, which was coming to plague Olympic football, was addressed with the introduction of the World Cup for professionals. Remarkably, the same Olympic team from Uruguay again proved good enough to win the first World Cup (1930).

The World Cup brings together national teams of professional players. There are professional teams in the majority of the 145 nations who are members of FIFA, the governing body for both World Cup and Olympic competition.

The debate of payments to football players continued, resulting in football being deleted from the Los Angeles Games (1932). The declining status of Olympic football was further worsened by the shoddy tournament in Berlin, where Peruvian spectators invaded the pitch during a game with Austria and the match was abandoned with Peru leading, 4–2. Austria protested and the IOC ordered a replay, for which Peru failed to show up. Austria thereby progressed to the final, only to lose to Italy 2–1 in overtime.

The start of the Eastern European monopoly in Olympic football occurred in 1952 with the victory by Hungary. The team was comprised mostly of Army personnel who, supported by the state, trained together continuously. The Hungarians introduced a national team concept to a sport in which most players had come from clubs and played more as individuals. They developed tactics and discipline as a team unit, an approach that proved so successful that the same Hungarian team went all the way to the final of the World Cup in 1954 before losing to West Germany.

Since 1952, countries which have no professional sports have dominated Olympic football, whereas countries with the strongest football traditions, have had no success in the Olympics. Eastern European nations draw from the entire pool of talent, while the other countries have their most skilled players drawn into the professional ranks.

In the countries of Eastern Europe, state-sponsored teams are considered nonprofessional and eligible for Olympic competition. Not since 1928 in Amsterdam, when Uruguay's extraordinary Olympic team was considered the world's best, have the leading football nations of Europe and South America brought their best football talent to the Olympic arena. Today, the best young players are quickly lured by the rewards of professional football.

The Hungarian team won the championship in Tokyo (1964) and retained it in Mexico City. Entering the 1972 final in Munich, the Hungarians were unbeaten and so was Poland. On a heavy, rain- soaked pitch, Hungary went ahead, and led at the half, 1–0. But Poland rallied in the second half to defeat the defending champions, 2–1.

The Polish team was good enough to again finish third in the 1974 World Cup, indicating the high standard of Eastern European football. Poland played East Germany in the finals at Montreal and fell two goals behind at the half, losing by a score of 3–1.

In Moscow (1980), for the third straight time, the defending champion lost in the final. This time Czechoslovakia defeated East Germany, 1–0. The USSR beat Yugoslavia for the bronze.

RULES

Perhaps the popularity of football lies in its simplicity. The clear objective of the eleven man team is to move upfield and put the nine-inch diameter leather ball into the opponent's goal. The goal is 24 feet wide and 8 feet high and is defended by a goalkeeper, the only player on the team who can use his hands. The other ten players can only use their legs, trunk, and head to play the ball, except when it is thrown in from the sideline after going out of bounds.

The game is played on a field approximately 120 yards by 70 yards, slightly larger than an American football field. A rectangular penalty area, 18 by 44 yards, surrounds each of the two goals. If a foul is committed within this area by the defending team, a penalty is awarded. This is a direct shot on goal from the penalty spot, just 12 yards in front of the goal. It is a one-on-one situation and a very difficult shot for the goalkeeper to save.

Fouls committed on any other part of the playing field result in a free kick. Fouls usually take the form of "hand-ball" or a tackle, in which a player does not play the ball, but trips or pushes the opposing player.

If a ball flies out of bounds along the sidelines, it is thrown in by a player from the team which did not put the ball out of play. Should a defending player cause the ball to go out of play across the goal line, the attacking team is awarded a corner-kick. With a corner-kick, the ball can be chipped into the goal mouth from the corner, another scoring opportunity for the attacking team. If a goal is scored, the game is restarted from the center of the field.

Football is a game of continuous action lasting for two halves of 45 minutes each. Only two substitutions are allowed, which are usually employed only in case of injury. Throughout the 90 minutes, players may run more than 8 miles, often having to accelerate to full speed to reach a ball before an opponent. Endurance often becomes a critical factor, especially during the closing stages of a game.

Each team attempts to move the ball toward the opponent's goal, either by maintaining possession through a series of short passes, or by breaking open the defense with a long pass down-field. In the latter case, a player will be ruled "offside" if he is between the goal and the last defensive player when the ball is passed to him. This will result in a free-kick for the defending team.

The objective is to create an opening in front of the goal for one of the team's strikers. These are the glory boys of football whose speed and instinct are used in the attacking forward positions where they seek openings in the defense for shots on goal.

Football is generally a low-scoring game. No team has ever scored more than four goals in an Olympic final. Often the margin of victory is a single goal. Although the spectator thirsts for a score, the appreciative viewer recognizes the skills and strategy of the total game as each team works toward creating opportunities.

A shot on goal is the outcome of a sequence of moves requiring ball skills, good offensive decisions, and accurate passing. Equally, defensive play requires careful positioning, concentration, and bold challenges for the ball. It is the appreciation of the total game which provides enjoyment for the fans, who possess a level of passion toward football, which may be unequaled in all of sport.

1984 PROSPECTS

It is possible that Eastern European teams will again take the field for the '84 final. Each will be comprised of a squad of twenty-two "nonprofessional" players who practice together every day, are supported by the state, and play world-class football, often gaining experience against the best professional teams.

If anyone can upset this monopoly it could be the Brazilians, too young to have signed professional contracts, but maybe with the magic of a Pele or a Revelino in their feet. Some of the Arabian Gulf countries may also have a few surprises. They are beginning to profit from an Arabian love of football and some of the best training programs that oil revenues can buy.

The international passion for football (soccer) has bypassed the United States, although in the last decade hundreds of thousands of youngsters have taken to the game with enthusiasm. U.S. teams still have a long way to go, however.

17

GYMNASTICS

— *17* —

1984 VENUE

Both men and women's gymnastics events will be held at Pauley Pavilion on the campus of the University of California, Los Angeles. The Pavilion was completed in 1965, seats 12,500 spectators and is the home of the UCLA Bruins basketball team.

EVENTS AND SCHEDULE (Finals)

Men

Team Competition	July 29, 31
Individual All-Around	August 2
Floor Exercise	August 4
Pommel Horse	August 4
Rings	August 4
Vault	August 4
Parallel Bars	August 4
Horizontal Bar	August 4

Women

Team Competition	July 30, August 1
Individual All-Around	August 3
Vault	August 5
Uneven Bars	August 5
Balance Beam	August 5
Floor Exercise	August 5
Rhythmic All-Around	August 11

WOMEN'S, GIRL'S . . . OR IS IT CHILDREN'S GYMNASTICS?

Larisa Latynina was twenty-two years old when she won her first Olympic Gold Medal in 1956, winning the all-around title and helping to establish the Soviet Union's domination of the women's team competition. She went on to win a gold medal in the world championship in 1958, while five months pregnant.

In Rome (1960), she defended her all-around title en route to gaining a record eighteen Olympic medals, nine of them gold. When her daughter Tanya was five years old, Larisa, almost thirty years old, won her last Olympic gold medal on the floor exercises in her final Olympic appearance at Tokyo (1964).

Latynina belonged to a different era of gymnastics, when adult women sought to impress the judges with technical proficiency, character, and grace. Today's teenagers impress the judges with incredible pizzazz, risk, virtuosity, and acrobatics and charm their audience with youthful exuberance.

The great popularity of women's gymnastics is a recent phenomenon and a direct result of worldwide television exposure. The popularity boom began with Vera Caslavska, the queen of the Mexico Games (1968). Her magnetic personality enthralled the audience with every move on both floor and apparatus.

In Mexico, Caslavska added four gold medals to the three she had won in Tokyo four years earlier. Then she added to the drama and romance by getting married during the period of the Games. She returned to Czechoslovakia as Mrs. Joseph Odlozil. Her proud husband added to Vera's seven gold medals his silver, which he'd gained in the 1,500-meter run at the 1964 Olympics.

Olga Korbut came to the 1972 Munich Olympic Games as a complete unknown, but left with a small bag of gold medals and superstar status. Her Olympic adventure was pure storybook. Olga captured the hearts of a worldwide television audience with her elfin charm and energy and became the catalyst for a dramatic growth of gymnastics after Munich. Suddenly, U.S. parents were taking their daughters to gymnastic classes, dreaming of creating the next Olga, establishing the foundation for the development of the sport in the United States.

As the 1972 gymnastics competition neared its finish, Olga seemed to have the all-around title locked up. Then triumph turned into tragedy when she lost her composure during the uneven bars event. Simply swinging through to mount the apparatus, her legs dragged along the floor, stopping her motion. This disastrous performance on the uneven bars caused her to drop from first to seventh in the all-around competition, allowing Ludmilla Turischeva to attain the most coveted title.

Then, as if by magic, Olga came back with superlative performances on the final day on the individual apparatus, securing two gold medals, one on the balance beam and, then, thrilling the enraptured crowd by winning a gold in the floor exercise.

After her Munich triumphs, Olga Korbut appeared the following March at Madison Square Garden in New York City before 20,000 people. It was by far the largest and most enthusiastic audience ever to see a gymnastics performance in U.S. history. The audience showed affection and held out their hearts to this charming heroine.

The next superstar was Nadia Comaneci at the 1976 Games in Montreal. This fourteen-year-old Romanian schoolgirl was well known to insiders of the

Olga Korbut USSR the darling of Munich 1972, won gold medals for beam and floor exercise.

Olga attracted a world audience.

Ludmilla Turischeva won all-around.

gymnastics world, but the ever growing television audience had not seen any of her previous exploits, which included the European Championship of the previous year.

During the team event, Nadia went through her daring uneven bar routine, performing difficult combinations with the ease and energy of a child at play. Her dismount was crisp and she jogged back to the team bench. Suddenly, a new era of gymnastics was born as the judges recognized an ultimate gymnastics performance, and the scoreboard flashed her perfect score, a 10. It was the first 10 ever awarded in Olympic gymnastics competition. With this historic score, gymnastics was no longer a women's event; it belonged to the girls.

At fourteen, Nadia signaled what was to come. The more flexible physique of youth during the early teens is not only competitive with the mature woman's physique, but is actually a physical advantage. Tiny Nadia had touched a state of perfection that merged art and beauty with the athletic ideals of strength and agility.

The first 10 in gymnastics history was to be repeated six times as Nadia made perfection a common sight and created a pleasant dilemma in the judging of the sport: where does it go from here?

In the frenzy of adulation that pursued Nadia, the almost equally superlative performances of Nelli Kim were almost overlooked in Montreal. She won two individual golds and another for her part in the Soviet team championship. Nelli's unique problem was that her two perfect scores would always be thought of as secondary to Nadia's great achievement.

Following the Games of Montreal, as Nadia grew toward womanhood, her performances declined, rumors about her health circulated, and even her interest in gymnastics was questioned. At the 1979 World Championship in Fort Worth, Texas, she had matured, adding fifteen pounds and growing four inches. She fueled rumors of possible retirement by not finishing the competition, dropping out on the first day with a reported wrist injury.

Yet, she was ready to compete in the 1980 Games, making a comeback at age eighteen. Nadia performed brilliantly, starting out with another perfect 10. But now she had to contend with a younger generation of great competitors.

Natalia Shaposhnikova countered Nadia's 10 on the beam with a 10 in the vault, although Nadia still held the lead after the first day. Then, at the outset of the second day, Nadia's magic disappeared as her almost legendary consistency failed. As she mounted the uneven bars, the event which upset Olga's bid for the '72 title, she slipped off. She received a score of only 9.5, opening the door for the determined Soviet athlete, Yelena Davydova. This 4 foot 8 inch, seventy-five pounder, went on to defeat Nadia for the coveted all-around title.

Nadia won two gold medals the final day, the first on the balance beam and then, during the last individual event of the program, tied Nelli Kim in floor exercise. Thus ended a dramatic era in Olympic gymnastics.

Nadia Comaneci ROM won three golds in Montreal 1976 and scored the first perfect 10.

The tie in this last event symbolically underscored the accomplishments of the two foremost innovators in the women's gymnastics revolution. As they stood side-by-side on the victory stand, it seemed sad that Nadia, at the age of eighteen, and Nelli, aged twenty-two, would retire to relative obscurity from both the Olympics and their huge world audience.

The premature age at which gymnasts reach their peak is a major problem for the sport. Can the enormous strain of international competition be good for tiny, teenaged girls? Becoming world class in the sport requires an all-consuming mechanical training discipline, molding exercise units through endless repetitions.

Nadia is said to have been discovered at the age of seven, then placed in a gymnastics school. She competed in her first international competition at the age of eleven. A limitation on age will be put into effect in time for the 1984 Olympics, specifying that an athlete must be at least fifteen years of age at the time of the competition.

Girls of tiny proportions are favored with more flexibility and a physique which adapts easily to the flips, somersaults and acrobatic feats required of international gymnastics. Gymnasts often starve themselves to attain maximum strength-to-weight ratio and to increase flexibility.

Because of the daring of the young gymnasts, many fear that the stunts are becoming far too adventuresome, causing frequent injuries detrimental to the athlete. The girls are performing tricks on the 10-centimeter balance beam that were once considered daring even in floor exercise.

RULES

The scoring on the team, all-around, and individual competitions is closely interrelated. Every exercise performed has a cumulative effect upon the results of the following competitions. Medalists must have all-around gymnastics skills and make almost no mistakes throughout four days of intensive effort and concentration.

TEAM COMPETITION

Sixteen national teams of six gymnastics performers (ninety-six gymnasts) participate first in the compulsory exercises, consisting of four events for women and six for the men. They then repeat each event, choosing their own optional routines. The team title is determined by adding the two round totals of the top five gymnasts of each team.

INDIVIDUAL ALL-AROUND

The top thirty-six scorers from team competition, but not more than three from any one country, compete in the all-around championship. Each individual contestant begins with one-half his total score from the team competition. Competitors perform each optional exercise again, six more for the men, four for the women.

Natalia Yurchenko USSR, new princess of gymnastics winning 1983 world all-around title.

The total score determines the individual championship, among the most prestigious of Olympic gold medals.

INDIVIDUAL APPARATUS

The top six scorers in each of the exercises from the team competition, but no more than two per country, now compete for medals at each individual apparatus. They begin with the average score achieved on that same exercise during the compulsory and optional rounds of the team competition. This is added to the score achieved on the final performance at each particular exercise.

JUDGING

As in any event in which winners are chosen according to subjective rankings, gymnastics judging often becomes mired in controversy. Gymnastics is the most judgmental of all sports and it is doubtful that coaches, spectators, and the media could ever agree about the quality of performance.

The four judges, plus one superior judge who rules in any unusual circumstance, represent a wide variety of nations. They rate each performance on a 10-point scale. The highest and lowest of the four scores are thrown out and the other two averaged to give the score. Several times in Moscow arguments took place between national coaches and judges, and several significant scores were adjusted by the head judge.

The judges have also created a problem for themselves with the awarding of 10's. Since awarding the first perfect 10 in Montreal to Nadia Comaneci, gymnastics judges have left themselves with no means of recognizing any even more superior performances. Those close to the sport will be watching the judges carefully, expectant of more furious debates over their choices of medal winners.

WOMEN'S EVENTS

Vault

Women use the same vaulting horse as the men, but they approach it side-on whereas the men vault over the horse lengthwise. The gymnast runs almost full speed down the runway and propels herself off the springboard, headfirst. The purpose is to push off from the vaulting horse and, in a brief moment of flight, perform acrobatic stunts and make a clean landing.

Uneven Parallel Bars

This event uses the same apparatus as the men's parallel bars, except the top bar is set at 2.30 meters (7.5 feet) above the floor and the lower bar is set at 1.5 meters (almost 5 feet). The gymnast seeks to execute an uninterrupted and smooth flow of

Vera Caslavska CZE twice all-around champion, won seven golds in Mexico City & Munich.

Dalia Kutkaite USSR European rhythmic gymnastics champion in 1982.

swinging and somersaulting motions, working between the bars. Judges look for smooth movement and precise execution as well as intricate mounts and dismounts.

Balance Beam

The balance beam is 5 meters (over 16 feet) long and 10 centimeters wide, a mere 4 inches. It is raised approximately four feet off the floor. Along it, gymnasts perform amazingly complex acrobatic stunts that are difficult enough to do on the floor, yet on the narrow beam require tremendous balance, body control, and concentration. The routine must last between 70 and 90 seconds. Again, the mount and dismount of the beam are among the most dramatic stunts.

Floor Exercise

This is the most artistic of all Olympic events. It combines dance with tumbling and acrobatics, all performed to music. No other event encourages such expression of personality and freedom. There are displays of balance and flexibility as well as grace and rhythm. The floor exercise mat is a 12-meter square (40 feet). The routine is judged as a single creative unit combining beautiful athletic motion and the most daring and exciting stunts. A tumbling run performed diagonally across the mat will see the gymnasts executing triple back somersaults and double somersaults with a full twist.

Rhythmic Gymnastics

Searching for ways to remedy the problem of the sport's increasing tendency toward youthfulness, the Federation Internationale Gymnastique (FIG) has introduced rhythmic gymnastics to the 1984 Olympic program. This discipline tends to favor emotional and interpretative qualities more than acrobatics. It approaches the area of dance and tends to favor the more mature gymnast. The newest Olympic gymnastics event is a cross between floor exercise and ballet.

Rhythmic gymnastics combines smooth, graceful body movements with equally graceful movements and manipulations of a piece of equipment such as a hoop, ball, ribbon, or clubs. Unlike the floor exercise, there are no sudden, acrobatic moves. The entire routine must flow continuously. But, like women's floor exercises, it is performed to music on the 12-meter square floor exercise mat. It is judged on the same 10-point scale and evaluated according to choreographic quality and originality, harmony, precision, and execution.

1984 PROSPECTS (WOMEN)

The new princess of women's gymnastics is Natalia Yurchenko who won the 1983 world championship all-around. She is an attractive young Soviet who, at 5 feet 1

Julianne McNamara USA

Mary Lou Retton USA

Aniela Ralenkova BUL

inch and an even 100 pounds, is larger and seems more mature than many of her diminutive counterparts. In Budapest, Yurchenko maintained her brilliant consistency while her rivals fell out of contention after committing single mistakes while performing ever more miraculous tricks. Yurchenko scored early with a perfect 10 in the vault, and, with great presence, concluded with another perfect routine in the floor exercise.

While Natalia reigns, the competitive edge of superiority is very fine. A number of her teammates intend to make her Olympic aspirations hard to realize. The Soviets again won the team event and Olga Mostepanova took the beam title. The Romanians, as usual, had a share of the world championship medals, being led by Ecaterina Szabo who shared two silver medals in the apparatus finals, before winning the floor exercise with a perfect 10. Maxi Gnauck of East Germany, silver medalist in the all-around and gold medalist on the uneven bars at the Moscow Olympics, showed she recovered from ankle surgery with a win in Budapest on the uneven bars. Her challenge of Yurchenko failed when she suffered a fall from the beam.

Mary Lou Retton of the United States missed the 1983 world championships because of injury. At 4 feet, 7 inches and 90 pounds, she is a muscular, acrobatic powerhouse. She uses her strength to its fullest in her stunt-filled tumbling routines. She and outstanding vaulter Dianne Durham (also missing in Budapest) are thought to be the best U.S. hopes for a medal in Los Angeles. Both are coached by Bela Karolyi, Nadia Comaneci's former mentor who recently left Romania after being their national coach for many years. He now operates a gymnastics school in Houston, Texas. Karolyi is a notorious task master and some have suggested that the injuries suffered by his latest stars are the result of his excessive zeal.

Retton and Durham, when injury-free, join Julianne McNamara and Kathy Johnson as the best female gymnasts ever produced in the U.S. and the first individuals to have a chance at a medal.

The 1982 European rhythmic gymnastics champion was Dalia Kutkaite, a nineteen-year-old Soviet. Her technique is a more classical, dancing style, than the high energy disco or daring acrobatic style favored by other rhythmic gymnasts. She considers her performances to be a method of conveying images to her audience, or as she says, a means "of imparting both a picture of the world in which I live and the way I see the world."

Kutkaite's artistic style and interpretation is contrasted with American rhythmic gymnast Sue Soffe's more acrobatic style. Twenty-three-year-old Soffe has earned six national championships, and is America's best hope for a medal in the 1984 rhythmic gymnastics competition.

Women's gymnastics is perhaps the most difficult event to predict, yet one thing is certain: the 1984 contests will be the most competitive ever. In each Olympics there has always been a relative unknown who emerges to surprise us with the latest feats of gymnastic dexterity, displayed with artistry and verve. These qualities endear the young gymnast and the sport to their audience and make gymnastics one of the most popular events on the Olympic program.

MEN'S GYMNASTICS

Although gymnastics clubs had been formed in Europe twenty years earlier, the first truly international competition was at the first Olympic Games.

Seventy-five gymnasts from five countries came to Athens in the spring of 1896 and contested a variety of events on apparatus similar to the equipment used today. There were no all-around or floor exercise events. From that point forward, the gymnastics program suffered badly in successive Olympics due to lack of standardization. In 1904 at St. Louis, there was a 100-yard race and a shot put included in the combined event. In Stockholm, there was even a 100-meter obstacle race. But by 1924, in Paris, the Olympic gymnastics program emerged pretty much in its present form. In the succeeding games in Amsterdam (1928) women's gymnastics was added for the first time.

German gymnasts dominated the early Olympic Games, especially the '36 Games in Berlin. They were led by Alfred Schwarzmann, who was proclaimed all-around champion and also won two individual gold medals.

A turning point in the sport occurred in the Helsinki Games in 1952. In their first Olympic appearance, Soviet gymnasts proved to be the best in the world. They won all of the individual events and the team titles for both men and women.

At the 1956 Games, they repeated this triumph. For the men, however, it would be their last team championship for quite a while. Japan was a close second to the USSR in the '56 team event and Takashi Ono barely failed by the narrowest of margins (0.05 points) to catch Viktor Chukarin for the all-around title.

In Rome (1960), the Japanese men began their twenty-year dominance of the sport, taking the team title from the USSR for the first time. Takashi Ono, almost unbelievably, missed a gold again by the same tiny margin of 0.05, losing the all-around to Boris Shakhlin of the USSR. Yukio Endo took the all-around title for the host-nation at Tokyo (1964).

In Mexico (1968), Sawao Kato produced a 9.9 in the floor exercise and snatched the overall title from Mikhail Voronin by the recurring 0.05 point margin that had twice eluded Ono.

Kato's performance four years later, and that of the Japanese team in Munich, was awesome. Competing despite shoulder and elbow injuries suffered before the start of the Games, diminutive Kato kept his consistency through eighteen painful routines and hung on to take the all-around title, leading the Japanese sweep of the event. The six Japanese team members were all among the top eleven, and took away sixteen of the twenty-two possible medals in gymnastics.

Soviet Nikolai Andrianov, just twenty and making his first of several Olympic appearances, captured the floor exercise gold medal. Highlighting the finals on the

Dmitri Belozerchev USSR at sixteen won the 1983 world all-around title.

Kurt Thomas USA.

Alexandr Ditiatin USSR.

apparatus, Mitsuo Tsukahara introduced his spectacular double twisting somersault, earned a 9.9 and won the vault. Following Munich, in a burst of imitation, everyone started using the "Tsukahara Vault." It was also adopted immediately by the women, indicating a new level of daring acrobatics in women's gymnastics.

In Montreal (1976), there was a tremendous battle for the men's team championship. The Soviets had a good margin at the end of the compulsory exercises, but the Japanese team began to close the gap. Then, their fortunes suddenly changed; Shun Fujimoto broke his leg during the floor exercises. If his team was to have a chance of winning, he would have to continue.

His leg in a cast, he was helped onto the rings and somehow, in one of the most incredible feats of bravery ever seen in the Olympics, Fujimoto managed to score 9.70, the best of his life. He dismounted with a triple somersaulting twist, landing heavily on both feet, but standing straight to complete the movement. Then, overcome with excruciating pain, he collapsed to the floor.

The Japanese team continued to struggle for gold with their remaining five men, the minimum possible. No one could make a mistake. Mitsuo Tsukahara, who had won the gold on the horizontal bar, was the last man up and earned a brilliant 9.90 on the bars, clinching the team title for the Japanese.

In the individual events, no one could touch the new Soviet superstar, Nikolai Andrianov. While Nadia was queen of the women's events, Nikolai reigned in men's gymnastics, winning four gold, two silver, and one bronze medal. He won the individual all-around by a full point over the durable Kato who was performing in his third Olympic final.

In 1980, with Japan joining the United States in a boycott of the Games, the USSR had an easy time winning its first team title in twenty-four years. Andrianov, the defending champion, yielded the all-around title to his younger teammate, Alexandr Ditiatan. The powerful Ditiatan became the first person to win eight medals in a single Olympics, adding golds in the rings and team event to his all-around title and also scoring the first perfect 10 in men's Olympic competition.

MEN'S EVENTS

Floor Exercise

The men's floor exercise is done without music and lasts from 50 to 70 seconds. The routine involves dynamic tumbling skills as well as static positions that show balance and flexibility. The men emphasize their great strength, contrasting with the grace of the women.

Pommel Horse

The men use the same horse that is used for vaulting, but it is set lower. The exercise is composed of clean swings about the horse, covering the neck, saddle, and croup. Each routine must include at least three scissors, in which the legs are split and straddle the horse in pendulum swinging motions.

Rings

The rings have an inside diameter of seven inches and are suspended from a frame 18 feet high. This event requires the most strength of all the gymnastic exercises. A routine consists of handstands, bodyswings, and the holding of static positions, such as an "iron cross." It is important that while the body is swinging, the rings remain motionless. Some exciting twists and somersaults are seen on the dismount.

Vault

The vaulting horse is approached head-on at full speed. Taking off on the springboard, the vaulters gather their reserves of power, using the horse as a launching pad. They perform acrobatic twists and somersaults in midair before a final "sticking" landing.

Parallel Bars

Another of the strength events in which gymnasts push to handstand positions, as well as perform swinging movements, working from bar to bar, somersaulting above the bars, and performing a final dismount.

Horizontal Bar

Gymnasts perform giant swinging motions in a variety of positions around the bar, which is over 8 feet high. The routine requires almost static handstands at the top of the bar as well as somersaults and vaults over the bar before it is grasped again. Finally, the dismount begins with giant swings which produce a high flying arc and allow for multiple twisting and somersaulting toward the final crisp, sticking landing. The dismount is perhaps the most thrilling and dangerous moment in the sport.

1984 PROSPECTS (MEN)

Alexandr Ditiatin, twenty-six, is still in powerful form and will attempt to repeat some of his Moscow successes in 1984. However, he will have some stiff competition from the Chinese gymnasts as well as from some of his own teammates.

Dmitri Belozerchev is the latest blazing star who illuminated the 1983 world championships in Budapest and became, at age sixteen, the youngest male ever to win the all-around title. Belozerchev further displayed his strength and consistency by winning three apparatus finals, scoring tens on the pommel horse, rings, and horizontal bar.

Belozerchev was challenged the first day of the all-around by Chinese stars Li Ning and Tong Fei, who were first and second in the 1982 World Cup. In Budapest they both had falls in the all-around and lost contention.

In the team championship, China did upset the Soviets by a narrow margin. Japan was third and the U.S. fourth. Tong Fei won the floor exercise, producing a perfect routine, which he said will be more exciting in 1984 if he attempts the first triple somersault.

Yuri Korolev, a world champion in 1981, was not at his best in Budapest. His skill was more evident when he won the all-around at the world student games in Edmonton, Alberta, earlier in 1983. The Soviets swept the event, easily mastering the best U.S. Olympic hopefuls, Mitch Gaylord, Jim Hartung, and Peter Vidmar. Korolev said then that his stiffest competition in Los Angeles will be, "first my teammates then the Chinese." Certainly the results from Budapest substantiated his prediction.

18

HANDBALL (TEAM)

— *18* —

1984 VENUE

Cal Poly, Pomona, and California State University, Fullerton, will host the preliminary and semifinal rounds of the handball tournament, while the men's final will be held at the Forum.

EVENTS AND SCHEDULE

Men

Team championship	August 11

Women

Team championship (round robin tournament)	August 1, 3, 5, 7, 9

HISTORY OF HANDBALL

When most Americans hear the word "handball," they think of the two to four person, four-wall variety which is commonly played in the United States. But the handball played in the Olympics is an entirely different sport and is often called team handball to distinguish between the two. Team handball, which was introduced in Europe, is similar to water polo and basketball.

Handball did not develop in one particular country. It is more the result of a conglomeration of many games from several European nations. These various games include the Czechoslovakian game of hazena, the German torball, and the Danish handbold, as well as association football and basketball. A gradual mixing of these sports occurred in the early 1900's as neighboring European countries combined the sports in order to compete with one another.

In 1928, the International Amateur Athletic Federation (IAAF) brought together representatives of eleven of these nations in an effort to draw up international rules for handball. The initial formulation called for eleven players on each team, but because this large number of players prevented indoor play, Scandinavian countries developed a seven-a-side variation. Seven-a-side handball became an indoor sport and adopted many characteristics and tactics used in basketball.

OLYMPIC HISTORY

The eleven-a-side version of handball was a demonstration sport in the 1928 and 1932 Olympics, and finally became an official Olympic sport in Berlin. For various reasons, particularly the lack of standardization, handball was removed from the Olympic program after the Berlin Games and was not reinstated until Munich, even though it was pursued enthusiastically throughout Europe during the interim years. The Munich version was seven-a-side, which became most popular in Europe and had been a demonstration sport in 1952.

The seven-a-side version has proven so popular in Eastern and Western Europe that it is now a permanent Olympic sport. Unfortunately, in 1972, it had still not gained much recognition or participation in the United States. The United States did field a team, but, not surprisingly, the U.S. finished sixth out of six teams. Yugoslavia won the '72 gold over the Czechoslovakians, with Eastern European teams capturing the first five places.

In Montreal, where women's handball was introduced, the USSR won both the men's and women's competitions and other Eastern European nations swept the medals in each competition. The highest finishing non-Eastern bloc nation was Denmark, which took fourth in the men's competition.

In Moscow, the Soviet women easily maintained their supremacy, beating Yugoslavia, 18–9, in the final, but the Soviet men narrowly lost their title to East Germany in a very fast and fierce final, 23–22.

RULES

Olympic handball is played by two teams of seven players on a 20-meter wide by 40-meter long indoor court, slightly larger than a basketball court. The goals at each end are about half the size of soccer goals, 2 meters by 3 meters, and are fired upon with a small leather ball, 19 centimeters (8 inches) in diameter.

The seven players, six court players and one goal tender, play two 30-minute halves. Each half begins with a throw-off at center court, in which the team which has won ball possession via a coin flip starts to move the ball toward the opponents' goal. The ball may be touched with any part of the body above the knee, but usually only the hands are used. The ball is moved up and down the court by passing or dribbling.

Dribbling in handball is similar to basketball, whereby a player is subject to a traveling penalty if the ball is carried without touching the floor for more than three steps. Passing, however, is a much more efficient method of moving the ball and scoring goals. Because most handball teams rely on passing during offensive play, the game moves very quickly.

Defense is much like that used in basketball. Because it is, at least in theory, a noncontact sport, a player is not permitted to push, grab, or tackle his opponent. However, he may use his arms, legs, and torso to block an opponent.

1984 PROSPECTS

It is unlikely Eastern European dominance will be threatened in Los Angeles. The support and enthusiasm which team handball enjoys in Europe, as contrasted to the nearly total ignorance of the sport in the United States, makes it difficult to compete on the same level. However, handball is such a fast and exciting sport, it is surely only a matter of time until it becomes a popular sport in the United States.

19

HOCKEY (FIELD)

1984 VENUE

East Los Angeles College stadium, located 10 miles east of downtown Los Angeles, has seats for 22,000 spectators. The facility has played host to many of the region's track and American football events. At a cost of $4 million, donated principally by the Weingard foundation, the facility has been refurbished with a new synthetic track and artificial turf infield.

EVENTS AND SCHEDULE

Men

Team Championship	August 11

Women

Team Championship (round robin)	July 31–August 10

HISTORY OF FIELD HOCKEY

Almost every culture has its traditional ball and stick game, with many dating back before written history. The game that we know today as field hockey was fashioned in Britain late in the last century. It is really a merger of an existing European version of hockey and the ancient Celtic games of hurling, shinty, and banty. Formulation of the present rules began with a code drawn up by the Wimbledon Hockey Club in west London during the 1880's.

The game was carried by British troops throughout the empire, thus developing widespread international participation. For the British, the attraction was natural. To them, field hockey was polo without horses or soccer with sticks.

OLYMPIC HISTORY

Affirming its essentially British origins, hockey was introduced at the 1908 Olympic Games in London. England easily defeated Ireland in the final match, 8–1. The British team won again when hockey was included for a second time in the 1920 Olympic Games in Antwerp.

Hockey finally achieved permanent Olympic status in Amsterdam in 1928. Nine teams were entered. India, then under British rule, won five matches going into the final without yielding a single goal. More than 42,000 spectators watched the final against the host team of Holland.

The Indians, led by center-forward Dhyan Chand, overpowered and defeated the Dutch, 3-0. Captain Chand, who is considered by many to be the greatest hockey player of all time, also led his team to victories in 1932 and 1936. Thus began a remarkable series of six Olympic championships, a reign of almost thirty years, which established India as the worldwide master of field hockey.

In 1960, Pakistan, the silver medalist from Melbourne (1956), avenged its previous Olympic loss, taking the championship and India's streak away in the final, 1-0. In Tokyo, the result was again reversed, with India regaining the championship from Pakistan, also by a score of 1-0. Pakistan regained its title in 1968, winning the gold medal from fast improving Australia, with India slipping to third and a bronze.

Hockey success returned to Europe in Munich (1972) when the German team applied the principle that had brought Australia to world prominence. The German team was extremely fit, fast, and strong and wore down Pakistan as the final progressed. Late in the game, Michael Krause of Germany scored the only goal in the game from a penalty corner. There were protests at the end of the game and during the lineup for the medal presentations, the Pakistan team showed open contempt and hostility toward the German team. This ugly behavior brought suspension to the individuals involved.

The 1976 results came as a complete surprise as India finished a disappointing seventh, while Australia and New Zealand got to the final by winning tie-breaking playoffs in their divisions. These games were noted for extremely rough play. Again, the Olympic final saw just one goal, a penalty shot in the second half, to bring victory to New Zealand.

Due to the boycott, the defending champions did not defend their title in Moscow in 1980 and it was India who became the world leader in field hockey, defeating Spain, 4-3 in the finals.

Women's field hockey was introduced to the Olympics at Moscow in 1980 and the women from Zimbabwe, continuing a British colonial hockey tradition, won the round robin tournament of six teams.

RULES

Hockey demands great teamwork, skill with ball and stick, and tremendous running endurance. It is played on a field 100 yards long and 60 yards wide. At each end are goals 12 feet wide and 7 feet high. The field is marked into four 25-yard long sections. Originally, the ball was a cricket ball, similar to but slightly larger than a baseball. Plastic balls of the same size are now utilized. They are hit with a laminated stick 36 to 40 inches long and curving to a 6-inch long head, flat on one side and

India fires on goal during a game with Germany at Montreal 1976.

Spain defeats India in 1982 world championship in Melbourne.

rounded on the back. The ball may only be hit with the flat side of the stick.

There are eleven players on a team, each attempting to advance the ball toward the opponents' goal and score from the "striking zone," a 16-yard semicircle. This zone is inscribed from the center of the goal. The players compete for two periods of 35 minutes each, with only a 5-minute halftime break. There are no substitutions, not even for injury. If an injury does occur, the player must grit his teeth and continue in spite of it, or allow his team to play one short.

The game is started and resumed after each goal with a "bully-off" from the center of the field. If an attacking player hits the ball over his opponent's goal line without a score, the game is restarted from the 25-yard line with another bully.

If a defender deflects the ball across his own goal line, a corner is taken. A free hit is taken from the corner nearest the point where the ball went out. The defenders line up along the goal line and the attackers position themselves outside the 16-yard striking circle until the corner is taken.

If a defender commits a foul within the striking circle, a penalty-corner is taken. A penalty-corner is like a corner except the attacker hits the ball out from a point at least 10 yards from either goal post toward his teammates, who must be outside the striking circle. If the foul is deliberate or interrupts a shot on goal, a penalty stroke is awarded. This is a direct shot on goal from a spot just seven yards in front of the goal. All players except the striker and goalkeeper must remain outside the 25-yard line.

Other fouls on the field result in a free hit against the offending team from the point where the infraction took place. Like soccer, the "advantage rule" is played, in which the umpire will not enforce a penalty if the nonoffending team still maintains possession of the ball.

The "offside rule" is also similar to soccer, although three defensive players, rather than two, must be in front of an attacking player when the ball is passed. No obstruction is allowed, so a player may not place his body between the opponent and the ball. The heavily-padded goalkeeper is allowed to stop and kick the ball with his foot, while other players are only allowed to stop the ball with their hands and let it to drop immediately to the ground.

Some of the factors which determine success in team hockey are:

1. Skill with Ball And Stick. A player's ability to drive the ball accurately toward teammates and, with a dexterous wrist, change the direction of a short pass.

2. Team Sense. The capability for all eleven players to work together as a unit, predicting each other's moves, while keeping their eyes on the play, the movement of the other players, and the position of the ball.

3. Physical Endurance. Seventy minutes of a championship hockey game may require 7 miles of running, including acceleration, sharp cuts, and explosive motions, all of which are very tiring and require a high level of physical endurance. The endurance training of the team is most important as the team lacking it can simply be outrun by their opponents.

4.   Defensive Skills. Tight man-to-man marking, acompanied by tough, aggressive tackling are vital to protection of the goal.

1984 PROSPECTS

When U.S. players, both male and female, make their field hockey appearance in 1984, it will be the first time in twenty-eight years they will be seen in Olympic competition. The United States made its first appearance in 1932, and captured a bronze medal. Because of the great distance involved in going to Los Angeles, only three teams entered the 1932 hockey event, allowing the U.S. team to lose to Japan and India and still get a medal. In fact, their 24–1 loss to India still remains as the highest score in Olympic history.

As the host nation, the U.S. teams automatically qualify for the Los Angeles tournament. The men have made some progress, but are unlikely to threaten any of the traditional hockey powers. The Montreal finalists (Australia and New Zealand) will be back in action following the Moscow boycott, while India and Pakistan should be as good as ever. Pakistan won the 1982 World Cup from a surprising West German team. Later, an under-twenty-one German team won the Junior World Cup in unfamiliar conditions in tropical Kuala Lumpur.

United States' women have gained much respect in international hockey, yet must still be considered outsiders in the '84 medal race. They finished a disappointing sixth in the 1982 World Cup, but are now training harder than ever at the team's training center in Philadelphia, Pennsylvania. Led by top scorer Beth Anders and defensive stalwart Anita Miller, the United States could have an emotional edge and upset some of the favorites.

The number one women's team in the world is the Netherlands, winner of the World Cup. Holland's players are renowned for brilliant stick handling and Fieke Boekhorst, the team's star, may be the best shooter in the world.

Australia and Canada are considered to be the best of the rest. Australia has a long history of international success and took third in the World Cup, while Canada caused the biggest surprise by finishing second.

20

JUDO

— 20 —

1984 VENUE

All judo matches will be held at California State University, Los Angeles, gymnasium. The gymnasium has seating capacity for 4,200 spectators.

EVENTS AND SCHEDULE (Finals)

Weight Classes	Maximum Bodyweight	
Extra-Lightweight	Up to 60 kg—132.3 lbs.	August 4
Half-Lightweight	65 kg—143.3 lbs.	August 5
Lightweight	71 kg—156.5 lbs.	August 6
Half-Middleweight	78 kg—172.0 lbs.	August 7
Middleweight	86 kg—189.6 lbs.	August 8
Half-Heavyweight	95 kg—209.4 lbs.	August 9
Heavyweight	Over 95 kg—209.4 lbs.	August 10
Open Category	OPEN	August 11

HISTORY OF JUDO

Judo is a relatively young sport, although its direct ancestor, jujitsu, is one of the oldest sports in existence. Jujitsu is an early form of wrestling practiced as far back as 230 B.C. At that time, it was used for self-defense by the common people of Japan, who were forbidden to carry swords and by Japanese priests, who sought a nonviolent form of self-defense.

Judo was established by Jigoro Kano in the late nineteenth century. Kano had studied jujitsu for many years, but was dissatisfied with its violent nature and large number of resultant injuries. He developed his new sport by combining the best of various jujitsu techniques, along with his own inventions and modifications.

Kano's modifications were based on the principle that an opponent can be effectively defeated by using his movements against him to get him off-balance and, once he is off-balance, he can be thrown. Judo combines ancient beliefs that "soft prevails over hard" and that one may "conquer by yielding." Kano called this new fighting technique judo, a word literally meaning "soft-way." In 1882, he opened the first judo institute in Tokyo and began to teach the sport to the public.

Judo immediately became popular and spread quickly throughout Japan, eventually encompassing the world. From the time judo was introduced, until the early twentieth century, it was practiced mainly as a form of self-defense and recreation. Not until after World War II did it become popular as a competitive sport. Europeans introduced strength and constant pressure to the pure technique-oriented Japanese style. The first international judo competition was held in Tokyo in 1956, where, predictably, it was dominated by the Japanese.

Kano believed technique was the only important factor in determining competitive ability. Early judo competitions were, therefore, classified according to the judoka's or judo athlete's skill level, which was indicated by the color of his belt. Olympic judokas are now classified and separated into competitive divisions, according to weight. This new classification system for judo competitions became necessary due to one man, Anton Geesink of the Netherlands.

Geesink was unusual because, besides having the superior judo skills necessary to compete with the best in the world, he also had the size, (he was 6 feet 6 inches tall and weighed 253 pounds), to beat those with equal technical skill. As a result of Geesink's success in the 1956 World Championships (which was not judged according to weight classes) four weight divisions were included when judo was introduced in the 1964 Olympics.

OLYMPIC HISTORY

In keeping with the historic roots of the sport, judo was first included in the 1964 Games in Tokyo. The Japanese won three of the four divisions. Geesink won the heavyweight division and prevented the Japanese from making a clean sweep.

Judo was not included in the Mexico City Games, but became a permanent Olympic sport in 1972. Willem Ruska of Holland was the outstanding performer in Munich, capturing the gold in both the heavyweight and open divisions. He then announced his retirement after a very long and successful competitive career.

Ruska's performance and that of Soviet star Shota Khokhoshvili humiliated the once-dominant Japanese judoka and their government. After the Games, the Japanese Olympic trainers were dismissed and a new, more rigorous training program was adopted in an effort to regain Japan's former supremacy. The new program was very successful as the Japanese team won three of six gold medals in Montreal and finished second to Soviet judoka in two other events.

There were eight events in Moscow, the most divisions ever in Olympic judo competition. With the Japanese boycott of the Games, there was no clear national dominance. The USSR, France, Cuba, and East Germany provided most of the medal winners. Two particularly outstanding performers were Angelo Parisi of France, who won the heavyweight division and finished second in the open division and Dietmar Loranz of East Germany, winner of the open division and bronze medal winner in the half heavyweight division.

RULES

Judo competition begins with a ceremonial bow. The bow was initiated by Kano, who felt judo should be used for mutual recreation and benefit rather than battle and destruction. Olympic judo matches last up to five minutes for preliminary bouts, and seven minutes for the finals. They are won when one judoka scores a single point. If the match goes the full duration, the judges determine which athlete has proven his superiority over the other.

The point necessary to win a match may be gained when one judoka throws his opponent so the opponent's back hits the mat. If done with perfect form, one full point is awarded, and the referee announces, "Ippon." Fractions of a point, which are combined throughout the match, may also be accumulated to gain the full point necessary to win. Fractions are awarded for partial holds or for throws with less than classic textbook execution.

Olympic judo is regulated by the International Judo Federation (IJF). Each nation is allowed to enter one competitor per weight division. The United States representatives for each event are chosen via an Olympic trial in which judoka compete head-to-head for that single position. The judoka are invited to the trials only if they have proven their ability in previous competitions.

1984 PROSPECTS

The United States' best hope for a judo medal in 1984 is probably Mike Swain, reigning national champion in the lightweight division. He has trained extensively in Japan and employs a technique which emphasizes skill rather than pure strength. Swain was a member of the 1980 Olympic team and has several years of experience in international competition.

21

MODERN PENTATHLON

— 21 —

1984 VENUE

For the first time, the modern pentathlon will have all five events scheduled at the same site. Coto de Caza is a secluded community located approximately 50 miles south of Los Angeles in the foothills of Orange County. This community, with its thousands of acres of equestrian trails and beautiful landscape, is perfect for the variety of events involved with the modern pentathlon.

EVENTS AND SCHEDULE (Finals)

Men

Equestrian	July 29
Fencing	July 30
Swimming	July 31
Shooting	August 1
Running	August 1

OLYMPIC HISTORY

The modern pentathlon is a uniquely Olympic event. It is the brainchild of the founder of the Modern Olympics, Baron Pierre de Coubertin. Coubertin wanted to develop an Olympic competition for the complete all-around athlete. The modern pentathlon's five events are based on military skills practiced at the turn of the century.

In a four day period, the modern pentathletes ride a horse, drawn by lot, over a 1,000-meter obstacle course; fence a one-touch epee bout with every other competitor; shoot at targets 25 meters away that are displayed for only three seconds; swim 300 meters freestyle; and conclude with a grueling 4-kilometer cross-country run. Each athlete's achievements are measured against a predetermined standard performance in each event, worth 1,000 points.

Pierre de Coubertin's aim was to create the ultimate heroic event that would test and identify the true athlete par excellence. The failure of the event to grow to the Olympic stature Coubertin envisioned is due to the complexity of staging a modern pentathlon and the high cost of training for the five expensive disciplines. These factors have made the sport the domain of state- or military-supported athletes, greatly limiting participation.

Working with the Stockholm organizing committee, Coubertin succeeded in installing the modern pentathlon in the 1912 Olympics. The first victor was a Swede, Gustaf Lilliehook. Only one competitor out of the top six was not Swedish, a young American cavalry Lieutenant named George Patton.

Although Patton finished fifth in the modern pentathlon, he actually defeated Lilliehook, the champion, in three of the five events. Patton displayed the spirit and tenacity which would later make him famous as the World War II general who led the Allied advance across Europe. Patton was applauded for his skill and relentlessness in the fencing competition.

His performance in the final event, the cross-country run, in which he finished third, was described as follows: "After a moment's waiting came Patton, of the U.S.A., who had started like a 100 meter sprinter and it was only by an incredible degree of energy that he managed to stagger past the tape."

Patton's only, yet devastating, mistake was using an army revolver instead of a more precise target pistol during the shooting competition. He finished twenty-first in shooting and lost any chance of a gold medal.

The Swedish, who helped write the rules for the events, won every modern pentathlon in the first five Olympic outings. The 1936 Games in Berlin saw the first non-Swedish gold medalist, a German named Gotthard Handrick.

In subsequent Olympics, the Swedish regained and held their monopoly of the individual championships through 1956. That year, in Melbourne, Lars Hall became the first modern pentathlon competitor to regain his Olympic title and win a second individual gold medal.

Since 1952, the modern pentathlon has included a team championship in addition to the individual title. The team event has since been dominated by the USSR and Hungary, with the exception of Montreal (1976), where the surprising British team moved from fifth place before the final cross-country run to capture the gold.

Perhaps the greatest of all of the Hungarian modern pentathletes was Andras Balczo, who was a five-time world champion. He competed in four Olympics before getting a gold medal. In Rome (1960) he placed fourth in a tight finish. In Tokyo (1964), he placed well down the field, but in Mexico (1968), was runner-up, missing the title by a mere 9 points. Finally, in Munich, coming from behind with a brilliant cross-country run, Balczo passed the leading Soviets to win his long-awaited gold medal.

The 1972 Games produced one of the biggest controversies in the sport when tests revealed that sixteen modern pentathletes had taken tranquilizers before the shooting events, supposedly to steady the arm, wrist, and overall nervous

Dean Glenesk USA fires a .22 caliber pistol in the fourth modern pentathlon test.

Equestrian: The first of five tests.

Fencing: Each pentathlete duels all others.

system. Faced with disaster, the International Federation, under a Swedish president, quickly ruled that not all nations had been adequately informed of the prohibition of such drugs; thus, no action was taken.

EVENTS

There are two gold medal events to be won in the modern pentathlon: the individual and the team. Each team is comprised of four competitors from each nation. Three actually score in the team event. The low score of the fourth team member is dropped.

Riding

Each pentathlete is allowed to view the 1,000-meter jumping course the day before competition. The course has twenty widely varied obstacles with which the competitor must contend. Another obstacle to be overcome is the horse, which is assigned by lot. Horses are provided by the Olympic Organizing Committee in cooperation with the International Equestrian Federation.

An athlete can only hope he draws a good horse. The rider is allowed twenty minutes to get to know the horse's mannerisms before competition. A rider who finishes the course within the prescribed time is awarded 1000 points. Two points are added or deducted for every second by which his finishing time is faster or slower than the prescribed performance. Points are subsequently deducted for any faults or refusals of the horse and rider during the execution of the course.

There have been numerous proposals in recent years to replace the riding portion of the pentathlon with canoeing or cycling. Procuring the large number of horses needed for this event with equal abilities is difficult and introduces an element of unfairness in the lottery and makes the event difficult to stage.

Fencing

The fencing portion of the pentathlon is an epee pool competition. All pentathletes must fence each other in bouts decided on one hit. Competitors are given a total of 1,000 points for winning seventy percent of their bouts. Points are gained or lost for each victory or defeat, above or below this percentage. A deciding match is usually held to determine the overall winner in this particular event. This, however, does not change the points toward the modern pentathlon score.

Shooting

Athletes use 5.6 millimeter (.22) caliber weapons to fire at silhouette targets that are placed 25 meters away. They fire four series of five shots at the target. For a score of 194 points of a possible 200, 1,000 points are awarded. Points are gained or lost for each target point over or under 194.

Swimming

The swimming race is 300 meters freestyle, in which competitors race the clock. Swimmers are given 1,000 points for a completion time of 3 minutes, 54 seconds. Any period of .5 seconds faster or slower will increase or decrease the 1,000 points by 4.

Cross-Country Running

The modern pentathlete's final and most grueling event is the 4-kilometer cross-country race. The athlete is allowed to view the course the morning of the race and is given a contour map of the course. Competitors start at one-minute intervals.

　　　The course may have a total climb of up to 100 meters in elevation. Completion of the course in 14 minutes and 15 seconds gives the runner a score of 1,000. Each second below or above that time will result in 3 points being added to or deducted from the competitor's initial 1,000 points.

22

ROWING

— 22 —

1984 VENUE

Rowing events will be held at Lake Casitas, 80 miles north of Los Angeles, near Ojai. There will be seating for approximately 10,000 spectators.

EVENTS AND SCHEDULE (Finals)

Men

Single Sculls	August 5
Double Sculls	August 5
Coxless Quadruple Sculls	August 5
Coxless Pairs	August 5
Coxed Pairs	August 5
Coxless Fours	August 5
Coxed Fours	August 5
Eights	August 5

Women

Single Sculls	August 4
Double Sculls	August 4
Coxed Pairs	August 4
Coxed Quadruple Sculls	August 4
Coxed Fours	August 4
Eights	August 4

HISTORY OF ROWING

The sport of rowing extends far back into history. Like canoeing, it began as a mode of transportation and gradually evolved into its present recreational form as other, more efficient means of transport became available. There are records of competitive rowing events as far back as 6,000 B.C., when the Chinese included boat races in their major festivals. Rowing races were also included in ancient Greek and Roman festivals, but not in the Ancient Olympic Games.

The first organized competition most resembling modern rowing was probably the event held in 1715 to honor the accession to the British throne. To mark the day of accession, the well-known Irish comedian Thomas Dogget announced a prize would be given to the winner of a 4½ mile race from London Bridge to Chelsea. Contestants were chosen from among the professional transport boatmen of the Thames. This race is still held annually, a constant reminder of the historic roots of competitive rowing.

In the early nineteenth century, rowing became something of an upper-class sport, practiced mainly in exclusive clubs and private eastern Universities. In 1839, the first Royal Henley Regatta was held. The regatta continues today, another link in Britain's long rowing tradition.

Henley was also the scene of a major innovation which is primarily responsible for today's rowing style. There, in 1872, the sliding seat was used for the first time. The seat, which moves a total of about sixteen inches back and forth, allows the rower to use his legs, rather than his arms, as the primary power source. This improvement, along with design improvements in the oarlocks and hull, gave rise to the efficient shells and rowing styles used today.

OLYMPIC HISTORY

Etes vous pret? (Are you ready?) *Partez!* (Go!) These are the commands used to begin every Olympic rowing race, an acknowledgment to France, where five rowing events were first introduced to the modern Olympic program at the Paris Games (1900).

Both the popularity of the sport and number of competitors grew quickly in succeeding Games. Predictably, the Games in London (1908), the birthplace of modern competitive rowing, provided a huge boost to Olympic rowing's popularity and participation. The events took place along the famous course of the Royal Henley Regatta and Great Britain won every gold medal.

Britain again dominated the sport in 1912 at Stockholm, but these games marked the end of Britain's preeminence. Britain has never lost its rowing strength, but by 1920, North America and other European nations began to show they could also produce superior rowers.

In Antwerp (1920), the U.S. oarsmen were led by John B. Kelly, father of the late Princess Grace of Monaco and 1956 bronze medalist Jack Kelly, Jr. John B. Kelly won golds in the single sculls and double sculls, which helped to form his series of 126 consecutive victories during 1919 and 1920.

Earlier in 1920, Kelly, a Philadelphia bricklayer, showed up to compete in the Royal Henley Regatta. Organizers, however, excluded him from the competition because of a Henley rule that classified manual laborers as nonamateurs. Presumably, bricklayers had muscles that might give them an unfair advantage over the English gentry, who were determined to maintain the upper-class tradition of success in the Royal regatta.

Double sculls, Canadian team on Lake Casitas, the 1984 Olympic venue.

Coxless pairs

By winning the 1920 single sculls, Kelly beat Britain's Jack Beresford, then competing in his first of five consecutive Olympics, which would eventually bring him three gold medals and two silver, making him the most successful Olympic rower of his time.

Kelly returned to the Paris Olympics (1924) with the same doubles partner, cousin Paul Costello, to win another gold. Four years later, in Amsterdam, Costello went on to win his third consecutive double sculls gold, this time with a new partner.

Between 1920 and 1956, the United States dominated the eight-oar event, the most prestigious on the rowing program. During this time, the United States, represented by a variety of collegiate teams, won eight consecutive eight-oar golds.

Australian Henry Pearce completely outclassed his competition in the single sculls event in Amsterdam (1928), where he won his first heat by ten lengths, the third heat by twenty lengths, and the semifinal by three lengths. This was quite a distance in races which are often won and lost by inches. Pearce achieved another single scull victory in Los Angeles, becoming the first man to ever repeat.

In Helsinki (1952), with a record thirty-three nations competing in the seven events, a new force made its presence felt: the USSR. Although Soviet athletes won only one event, the single sculls, they showed their potential for future rowing greatness. The United States managed to retain its dominance until 1956, where they went out in a blaze of glory, winning three golds, two silvers, and one bronze. The up-and-coming Soviets won golds in the single and double sculls.

In Tokyo (1964), Vyacheslav Ivanov won his third consecutive single sculls gold, becoming history's most successful Olympic sculler, an unequivocal symbol of the USSR's emergence as an Olympic power. In recent years, East Germany has shared prominence in the sport.

Women's events were first included in Montreal (1976), adding six events to the existing program. As in the men's competition, East Germany was most successful in the women's events, with the Soviets close behind.

East German men were led by coxless pairs champions, the brothers Bernd and Jorg Landvoight, and by coxed pairs champions, Jahring and Ulrich. Both pairs returned in Moscow (1980) to collect their second consecutive golds. In fact, East German men won seven out of eight events in Moscow, foiled from achieving a clean sweep by Pertti Karppinen of Finland. Karppinen won the single sculls, defending his Olympic championship, won in Montreal.

U.S. rowing fortunes have declined since Tokyo, when the Vesper Boat Club, supported by the Kellys, beat the German favorites in the eights final and won one of two U.S. gold medals. Since then, the United States has been without an Olympic rowing champion.

RULES

Rowing is often used as an all-encompassing term to refer to both rowing and sculling. In reality, they are two different techniques. Rowing uses one large oar, which is held with both hands, while sculling uses two smaller oars, one in each hand. Sculling is probably the more difficult of the two strokes, requiring more intense concentration and more balance. Olympic events are classified according to the type of stroke, the number of crew members in the shell, and the presence or absence of a coxswain.

The coxswain, or simply "cox," who must weigh at least 50 kilograms, steers the shell, provides a rhythm and cadence by calling the strokes, and supplies leadership and encouragement to the crew, but does no rowing or sculling. It's a big job for the smallest member of the crew.

The cox is the only crew member who actually faces the direction the boat is moving, so he must steer the shell by directing the crew to row "heavy on port" or "heavy on starboard," to pull harder on one side, thereby bringing the shell into proper alignment. The most famous of all coxswains is Edgar the Peaceful, King of England. In 973 A.D., Edgar led an eight-man crew, calling out their strokes as they rowed him down the Dee River to his coronation at St. John's Church.

Not all crews require the leadership of a coxswain. In coxswainless or "coxless" crews, one member is designated to control the rudder and another member sets the stroke pace. The bowman of a coxless crew must row as well as cox, using a foot controlled rudder to steer the shell. An expert bowman uses the rudder as little as possible, since it provides steering at the expense of increased resistance on the flat surface of the rudder. A far more efficient method of steering is to call for increased pull on one side as a coxswain would do.

Every nation is permitted to enter one boat and crew in each race. The crew must make it through a series of elimination heats until only six crews remain for the final. However, a crew which loses only one race in the series, has a second chance in repechage heats to earn entry in the semifinals. Depending upon the number of initial entries, heats and repechage heats can add up to quite a number of races. The only consolation for the tired athletes is that no crew is required to race more than once on a single day.

23

SHOOTING

— 23 —

1984 VENUE

Prado Regional Area, located near Chino in San Bernardino County, will host the 1984 Olympic shooting competition.

EVENTS AND SCHEDULE

Men

Free Pistol (50 meters)	July 29
Small Bore Rifle: Prone position	July 30
Small Bore Rifle: Three positions	August 1, 2
Rapid Fire Pistol	August 1, 2
Running Game Target	July 30, 31
Air Rifle	July 31

Women

Standard Rifle	August 3
Air Rifle	July 29
Pistol Match	

Mixed

Skeet Shooting	August 2–4
Trap Shooting	July 29–31

HISTORY OF SHOOTING

Shooting is the modern day counterpart to the ancient military skill of archery. While archery dates back to the Stone Age, shooting traces its roots to the fifteenth century, when guns were invented. Competitive shooting started almost immediately because of man's natural inclination to test and compare skills. The first recorded competition took place in Germany in 1477.

Today, most Olympic shooters are affiliated with the military, which provides them with equipment, facilities, training; support which can be difficult or impossible for civilians to find.

OLYMPIC HISTORY

Shooters point with pride to the fact that shooting was one of the eight sports in the first modern Olympic Games in Athens (1896). Eight nations were represented in the five events, where the Greeks were most successful.

Since many different sizes and types of guns are used throughout the world, it has taken time for shooting competition to become standardized. The target distance, type of target, time requirement, and size and type of gun are just a few of the many variables. With so many possibilities, events kept being added to the Olympic schedule and by 1920, in Antwerp, there were nineteen different events, nearly three times as many as there will be in Los Angeles. As the Union Internationale de Tir (UIT), the international governing body for shooting, attempted to standardize the sport, the number of events gradually decreased to the present eight for men, while three new events exclusively for women will be introduced in 1984.

United States entrants performed very well in these early Olympic contests. Some notable U.S. shooters were Alfred Lane and Morris Fisher who each won five golds in 1912 and 1920. Scandinavian shooters were the most successful from the early 1900's to the 1950's. Their power came from a strong military tradition which contributed to the development and support of competitive shooters. These systems produced such shooting legends as Torsten Ullman of Sweden, who competed in three Olympic Games, and the Swedish father-son team of Oscar and Alfred Swahn, who combined for six Olympic golds, four silvers, and five bronzes.

Scandinavian shooting ability was superseded by other military powers from the Eastern European nations, particularly Hungary and the USSR. Karoly Takacs of Hungary was an outstanding right-handed pistol shooter in the 1930's, until he lost his right hand in a grenade explosion. In an inspiring display of determination, he learned to shoot with his left hand and came back to win Olympic golds in the rapid-fire pistol event in 1948 and 1952.

The Scandinavians and Eastern Europeans still dominate Olympic shooting, but U.S. shooters are beginning to challenge. In 1956, President Dwight Eisenhower initiated an Army Marksmanship Unit to help develop skills for enlisted personnel for military and competitive purposes. There had been reports of poor shooting skills among U.S. soldiers during World War II. Eisenhower's concern is paying off as U.S. Olympians earn more and more medals in Olympic competition.

In Munich, United States shooters won two golds and two silvers, led by four-time Olympian Lones Wigger. The other gold was won by John Writer in the small-bore free rifle, three positions. Although most shooters, for purposes of accuracy and concentration, use up every bit of their allotted time, Writer needed only thirty-five minutes of his two hours to complete the forty-shot standing phase of this event. He set a world record for accuracy, and probably for speed as well, earning 1,166 points.

Shooting survives as an Olympic sport despite early problems concerning amateurism and more recent problems of arms control and public image. The credibility of amateur status was questioned throughout the thirties and forties. Small cash prizes were often given at shooting tournaments, but because the amount rarely covered the shooter's expenses and equipment, they felt these cash awards should not count against their amateur standing. Cash prizes have since been banned from shooting tournaments to avoid any conflict.

Arms control issues and public image have been more difficult to resolve. The UIT enforces several rules concerning conduct of the shooters. The rules are designed to protect shooting's public image. In Munich, after winning the small-bore prone rifle event, North Korean soldier Ho Jun Li was forced to retract his statement that, "I thought I was aiming at my enemies. Prior to the Games our Prime Minister told us to shoot as if we were fighting our enemies."

Statements and attitudes such as this cannot help but erode public enthusiasm toward shooting. Few communities build shooting facilities and parents tend not to encourage their children to practice the sport.

However, 1976 Olympic gold medalist and consultant to the U.S. training program for shooters, Lanny Bassham, is concerning himself with changing public perception of the sport. Bassham believes the primary purpose of sport is to build self-image. To win without heeding one's self-image, or that of his opponents, cannot truly be called a victory. Olympic hopefuls are being taught this philosophy by Bassham himself. Hope for a change in attitude concerning the sport of shooting isn't nonexistent; rather, it is a little farther down the road.

Despite these image problems, the competitive fortunes of the top U.S. shooters continue to prosper. Veteran Lones Wigger garnered eight medals at the 1983 Pan Am Games in Caracas, while Eric Buljung won three more U.S. golds in the pistol shooting events. U.S. medal prospects for 1984 appear to be excellent.

RULES

Each nation is permitted to enter two competitors in each of the Olympic shooting events. In 1984, for the first time, separate events will be held for men and women. Until now, men and women have competed in the same division. In the Los Angeles Games there will be six men's events, three women's events, and two mixed events.

There are eight different kinds of events. Three involve moving targets, the remaining five stationary targets. The events are further classified according to the type of gun used or type of target.

In trap shooting, the contestant uses a 12-gauge shotgun to hit a moving target. The target, called a clay pigeon, is actually a disc, 11 centimeters in diameter, that is propelled from a mechanical trap. There are several traps positioned at various distances and angles from the shooter, so skill in judgment of projectile speeds, angles, and distances is very important. Competition is spread over three days. Seventy-five pigeons are shot on the first and second days and fifty pigeons on the third day. Each competitor is allowed only two shots from a shotgun for each of the total 200 pigeons.

The clay pigeon is also used as the target in skeet shooting. The main differences between skeet and trap events are only one shot per pigeon is allowed in skeet. Also, the shooter must move through a series of seven shooting stations, forcing him to shoot at a greater variety of angles.

These two events are competitive equivalents to duck and bird hunting, with a medal replacing the bird as the reward for skillful shooting. The competitions originated from game shooting, popular in Britain in the eighteenth century. The game ranged from wild birds and ducks in field hunting to live pigeons in competitive shooting.

As live pigeons became scarce, clay discs were substituted, but the early terminology is still in use. The discs are called pigeons and the spring-loaded devices from which they are propelled are called pigeon-traps. In Los Angeles, men and women will compete together in the trap and skeet shooting events.

The third moving target competition, the running game target event, uses as its target a life-size paper representation of a wild boar. The boar, marked with a series of scoring rings representing scores from one to ten points, runs along a 10-meter track, 50 meters away from the shooter. The boar runs at two speeds, normal and rapid. The shooter is permitted thirty shots at each speed. This event is derived from boar hunting, a sport enjoyed by European aristocracy in the fourteenth and fifteenth centuries.

Pistols are used in two of the five stationary target events and rifles in three. The rapid-fire pistol competition uses a paper representation of a person as the target. Competitors fire sixty shots over two days, each day consisting of three phases. In the first phase, five targets are simultaneously presented and the shooter is allowed only eight seconds to hit each. In the second phase, the five targets are presented again, this time for only six seconds. In the third and final phase, presentation is reduced to four seconds.

The free pistol competition uses a ten-ring target with point regions ranging from one to ten with a two-inch bull's-eye. The target is 50 meters from the shooter, and metallic sights are used in aiming. This event is also timed. Shooters have a total of three hours (180 minutes) to fire sixty shots, averaging one shot every three minutes.

The small-bore prone rifle event, often called "English Match," is similar to the free pistol competition in that the ten-point bull's-eye is again 50 meters from the shooter. In this case, the bull's-eye is only 5/8 of an inch in diameter. The time limit is reduced to two hours for the sixty shots and the rifle is fired from the prone position.

The last event is the small-bore free rifle event. As the name suggests, the event is similar to the small-bore prone rifle event in all respects but position, which is "free" rather than prone. Position isn't free in the ordinary sense of the word, though. In this event, the shooter takes forty shots at the same small bull's-eye from each of three positions: prone, kneeling, and standing. This event is generally considered to be the most difficult of all shooting events.

The newest event, added to the 1984 program, is the air rifle, which will have men's and women's divisions.

24

SWIMMING, DIVING, AND WATER POLO

— 24 —

1984 VENUE

The construction of a new world-class swimming and diving facility at the University of Southern California was one of the few major construction needs of the Games. McDonald's Corporation financed the pool, the temporary bleachers, and necessary amenities.

The new pool was criticized during its opening at an international meet in July, 1983. Soviet swimming coach Anatoly Pimenov complained of the lack of dressing rooms on the site and that the temporary bleachers looked like scaffolding, hardly up to the standard of the Moscow facilities. True, in these low budget Games, the money for the USC pool was spent on the technical quality of the pool, not on expensive stands that would never again be full once the Olympics were over.

Even the pool itself came under criticism. Some Eastern European swimmers said it was slow. This concern was quickly dispelled, however, when Victor Salnikov broke his own 800-meter freestyle world record by 0.5 seconds.

EVENTS AND SCHEDULE (Finals)

Men

SWIMMING

100-meter Freestyle	July 31
200-meter Freestyle	July 29
400-meter Freestyle	August 2
1,500-meter Freestyle	August 4
100-meter Backstroke	August 3
200-meter Backstroke	July 31
100-meter Breaststroke	July 29
200-meter Breaststroke	August 2
100-meter Butterfly	July 30
200-meter Butterfly	August 3
200-meter Medley	August 4
400-meter Medley	July 30
4 X 100-meter Medley Relay	August 4
4 X 100-meter Freestyle Relay	August 2
4 X 200-meter Freestyle Relay	July 30

DIVING
Springboard	August 8
Platform	August 12

WATER POLO
Team Competition	August 10

Women

SWIMMING
100-meter Freestyle	July 29
200-meter Freestyle	July 30
400-meter Freestyle	July 31
800-meter Freestyle	August 3
100-meter Backstroke	July 31
200-meter Backstroke	August 4
100-meter Breaststroke	August 2
200-meter Breaststroke	July 30
100-meter Butterfly	August 2
200-meter Butterfly	August 4
200-meter Medley	August 3
400-meter Medley	July 29
4 X 100-meter Medley Relay	August 3
4 X 100-meter Freestyle Relay	July 31

DIVING
Springboard	August 6
Platform	August 10

SYNCHRONIZED SWIMMING
Duets	August 9

HISTORY OF SWIMMING

The history of mankind is filled with tales and legends of swimming feats, including those of great leaders such as Caesar, Charlemagne, Louis IX, and Mao Tse-Tung. But competitive swimming as we know it only dates back to the early nineteenth century when swimming pools were first introduced. At the time, swimmers favored the breaststroke and sidestroke, considered the fastest and most efficient strokes.

In the late nineteenth century, James Trudgen, having observed the two-handed overhead swimming style of South American Indians, introduced the technique in England. It was the forerunner of the modern butterfly. Several years later, another Englishman, Alec Wickman, introduced a stroke in Australia which he had observed being used by Solomon Island natives. Richard Cavill, observing this "Australian Crawl," improved upon it and taught it in England, while his brother, Sydney, introduced it in the United States.

Through gradual improvement, came the evolution of three of the four Olympic strokes: the breaststroke, backstroke, and freestyle (or crawl). The fourth, the butterfly, resulted from a loophole in the breaststroke style regulations. Instead of thrusting his arms forward in the water, Erich Radmacher of Germany improved upon the breaststroke by thrusting his arms forward through the air, where he encountered less resistance. In 1952, this overhead stroke was officially separated from the breaststroke, and the modern day butterfly was introduced as the fourth Olympic stroke.

OLYMPIC HISTORY: MEN

There were only four swimming events in the first modern Olympic Games at Athens and competitors were free to use any stroke. Style restrictions were first imposed in Paris (1900), with a backstroke race and an underwater swimming competition. In the latter, a Frenchman named Devendeville managed to swim 60 meters for the winning distance.

The swimming competitions became increasingly more organized as style, distances, and facilities were regulated and improved. By Stockholm (1912), there were ten men's events, including three diving competitions.

Duke Kahanamoku of Hawaii, winner of the 100-meter freestyle in Stockholm and again, eight years later in Antwerp, was an early indicator of U.S. swimming strength. Kahanamoku, a native Hawaiian, burst upon the U.S. swimming scene in 1912, shortly before the Olympic Games. In Hawaii, he was isolated from other U.S. swimmers, allowing him to develop a new and very efficient type of kicking style, the flutter kick. This new technique revolutionized swimming and was subsequently adopted by most freestyle swimmers. Kahanamoku later went on to become an innovator and champion in the sport of surfing.

Kahanamoku was succeeded in Paris (1924) by Johnny Weissmuller, the first man to swim 100 meters in less than one minute. Weissmuller collected a total of five gold medals in two Olympiads before going to Hollywood to become the first talking "Tarzan" of the movies.

In 1950, the Associated Press voted Johnny Weissmuller the greatest swimmer of the first half of the twentieth century, capping a career which included five golds, sixty-seven world records, fifty-two national championships, and not a single loss.

Unlike most of today's Olympic swimming champions who begin serious training before the age of ten, Weissmuller did not begin competitive swimming until age sixteen. But age and training disadvantages were only minor compared to the other disadvantages young Johnny had to overcome. Johnny grew up in Chicago, where his parents, who had recently emigrated from Austria, rarely had money for everyday necessities, much less the luxury of swimming lessons. Weissmuller's father was often drunk, out of work, and occasionally beat Johnny and his younger brother.

As a result of his family's poverty, Johnny had to quit school and work at odd jobs, first as an errand boy and later as a hotel bellhop and elevator operator, in order to help support the family. He never finished high school and was desperate

Johnny Weissmuller USA won 100-meter freestyle in Paris 1924 and Amsterdam 1928.

for a way out of poverty. His chance came in 1921, when a friend took him along to a swim team practice, where he met Bill Bachrach, who went on to coach Weissmuller through a legendary nine years of championship swimming.

Weissmuller was a natural athlete and a fierce competitor, who took to competitive swimming quite naturally. His first national championship and first world record came in 1921, the same year he began competitive swimming. In his first Olympic Games in Paris (1924), Weissmuller won the 100-meter freestyle, 400-meter freestyle, and helped his team to another victory in the 800-meter relay. He repeated the 100-meter and 800-meter relay victories in the Amsterdam Olympics (1928), thereby bringing his gold medal total to five.

In 1930, Weissmuller married the first of an eventual five wives. Becoming a family man meant Weissmuller would have to start earning a living, so he became a professional, promoting BVD swimsuits for $500 a week. That same year, Weissmuller was invited by Metro-Goldwyn-Mayer to do a screen test for the part of Tarzan in Tarzan of the Apes. His wife Bobbe, who feared what show business might do to him, asked MGM to fail him on his screen test. MGM refused her request and awarded Weissmuller the contract. Over the next twenty years, Weissmuller made nineteen Tarzan movies, more than ten Jungle Jim movies, had four more wives, and four children.

Although his life had its ups and downs, with marriage, alcohol, and financial problems offsetting his many successes, Weissmuller always maintained a positive outlook on life. He served as an inspiration to young men and women seeking a path out of poverty. Weissmuller, after a long period of poor health, died early in 1984 in Acapulco, Mexico, at the age of eighty.

U.S. leadership in men's swimming was short-lived, cut short by the Japanese, who won five of six events in Los Angeles (1932), and three of six events in Berlin (1936). Japanese domination eventually gave way to Australia, as the number of events on the Olympic program continued to climb.

In Tokyo (1964), Don Schollander of the United States won gold medals in four of ten events. A freestyle specialist from Oregon, Schollander won the 100 meters, 400 meters, and anchored two relay teams, setting world records in the last three. In Mexico City (1968), Schollander added a fifth gold medal in the 4 X 200-meter relay. It was a victory he shared with teammate Mark Spitz, the man who would replace him as swimming's most productive gold medalist.

After falling far short of his prediction of five or six gold medals, winning only two relay golds in Mexico City (1968), Mark Spitz returned in Munich to win four individual gold medals in the 100- and 200-meter freestyle and butterfly events and three more in relay events. It was the most gold ever won at a single Olympic Games in any sport. Each of Spitz's victories was accompanied by a world record.

Spitz was a remarkably versatile swimmer, having also achieved world records outside Olympic competition in the 400-meter freestyle, and coming within a fraction at 1,500 meters. A poster depicting Spitz wearing his seven gold medals,

Mark Spitz USA winner of seven gold medals in Munich 1972, most ever at a single Games.

Michael Gross GER, dominant swimmer at 1983 European championships & top '84 prospect.

and a lucrative offer from Shick Corporation made him an instant millionaire, when he turned professional following the Munich Games.

In Montreal (1976), John Naber led a U.S. aquatic gold rush, winning both backstroke events and sharing two relay victories. Brian Goodell won two freestyle events, setting world records at 400 meters and 1,500 meters. The U.S. men's team won twelve of thirteen golds and ten of eleven individual silvers.

Predictably, Soviet men dominated the 1980 Olympics, winning seven of thirteen gold medals. The star of men's swimming in Moscow is the same man who is expected to lead the Soviet team in Los Angeles, Victor Salnikov. He won both the 400- and 1,500-meter freestyle events. In the latter, he became the first man to break the 15-minute barrier as he swam fifteen consecutive 100- meter legs, averaging less than one minute on each, a feat that had not been achieved even once until Weissmuller first did it in the 1924 Games. This comparison is a vivid indicator of the advances in swimming over the past sixty years.

Improvements in swimming times over the six decades are the result of many factors, including improved style techniques, better coaching and training methods, and greater dedication by the athletes. When describing training techniques which made him a two-time Olympic champion, Duke Kahanamoku said, "We didn't train too rigorously in those early days. I swam as far as I felt like swimming and then I would quit."

Compare that with the training techniques used by the internationally-known Mission Viejo Nadadores of California. The Nadadores, many of whom begin serious swimming at age five, work out six or seven days per week, swimming up to ten or more miles daily. Athletes sometimes wear extra suits or panty hose to increase water resistance and hand weights or paddles to increase arm and shoulder strength. These athletes also run, lift weights, and essentially devote their lives to becoming the best swimmers possible.

The training requirements to compete at a world-class level are demanding when an athlete hopes for an Olympic medal. Salnikov swims over sixty miles per week. "It's not always fun," he has said, "The training is so hard that I can't always relax. But to stay on top, I must show no weakness." Perhaps the strain of his five years as the world's supreme male swimmer is beginning to show. His successor might well emerge at the '84 Games.

WOMEN'S SWIMMING

From three events in Stockholm (1912), women's swimming continued to grow, dominated by women from Australia, Great Britain, and the United States. Led by Helene Madison, U.S. swimmers won six of the seven swimming and diving events in Los Angeles (1932). In describing Madison's 100-meter freestyle victory, the *Los Angeles Times* said, "Queen Helene, cutting through the sparkling waters like some finny denizen of the deep, left her competitors behind during the first fifty

Kornelia Ender GDR swam to three individual golds and one relay title in Montreal 1976.

Shane Gould of Australia won four golds, one silver and a bronze medal in Munich 1972.

meters and coasted home well in front."

In Berlin (1936), U.S. women swimmers won only three bronze medals. One woman, who had won the 100-meter backstroke in Los Angeles, and who might have made a difference in Berlin, was Eleanor Holm. She did not compete, however, because she had been suspended from the U.S. Team on the boat trip for the unladylike act of sipping champagne.

After World War II, a strong Australian team emerged, led by Dawn Fraser. Fraser controlled the sprint events through three Olympic Games: 1956, 1960, and 1964. She finally retired at age twenty-seven, several years older than most other competitive swimmers. She left behind world records which would take younger girls several years to surpass.

Fraser's successor was Californian Debbie Meyer, the star of the Mexico City Games (1968). At age sixteen, Meyer won individual golds in the 200-, 400-, and 800-meter freestyle events and was named America's outstanding amateur athlete in 1968. Meyer exemplified a new trend in women's swimming, youth replacing and surpassing older, more experienced swimmers.

The increasing tendency toward youth amoung champion swimmers is evident in both men's and women's events. This is due in part to financial reasons, since few athletes can afford to train full-time unless thay are on scholarships or are supported by parents.

The long hours of practice, sometimes up to five hours a day, can become exhausting and tedious. Imagine swimming ten or more miles per day, hour after hour, in the same repetitive pattern in the same chlorinated pool.

In Munich (1972), with twenty-year-old Meyer already in retirement, a fifteen-year-old continued the youthful trend. Australian Shane Gould provided the perfect female counterpart to Mark Spitz, winning four golds, one silver, and one bronze. Another fifteen-year-old, Melissa Belote of the United States, won two individual golds and one relay gold.

Munich saw the last of the American-Australian dominance in women's swimming as the East German women won eleven of thirteen golds in Montreal. The star was eighteen-year-old Kornelia Ender, who earned three individual golds and one relay gold.

Shirley Babashoff proved to be the greatest U.S. female swimmer to date, with a series of U.S. records. She lagged behind Ender for a silver in the 200-meter freestyle and won silvers behind Petra Thurmer in the 400- and 800-meter freestyle. Babashoff did, however, win a relay gold to add to four silvers.

A similar experience occurred four years earlier in Munich, when Shane Gould edged out Shirley in the 200-meter freestyle. Babashoff came back to lead the United States to a freestyle relay gold, completing her record collection of eight Olympic medals, six silver and two gold.

The East German women, continuing to display the effects of an intensive government training program, won eleven of thirteen races in Moscow, led this time by fifteen-year-old Rica Reinisch. Reinisch won three golds, setting three world records along the way. Her teammate, Barbara Krause, also won three golds in the 100- and 200-meter freestyle and the freestyle relay, setting Olympic records in all.

1984 PROSPECTS

For over twenty years, the United States was the major power in both men's and women's world swimming. The emergence of the East German women became fully evident with their monopoly of the Montreal Games. The U.S. men, however, continued to be a bastion of strength.

The first sign of a challenge to U.S. dominance came with the poor U.S. performance at the 1982 world championships at Guayaquil, Ecuador. The United States won only six gold medals in men's competition and two golds in women's, the fewest ever in world championship competition. The rest of the world finally had caught up, especially the USSR, West Germany, and East Germany. The question remains: Can the U.S. men make the resurgence needed to regain their world stature?

Victor Salnikov is currently the world's outstanding male swimmer, holder of all the freestyle world records from 400 meters to 1,500 meters. His form was as strong as ever in 1983 when he improved his world record for 800 meters to 7:52.83 during the international meet inaugurating the Los Angeles Olympic pool. Afterward, he sat in the bleachers and watched his Soviet teammates continue the massacre, crushing the remainder of the U.S. opposition.

Vladimir Shemetov, a 1980 Olympic finalist at the 200-meter backstroke, managed victories in both the 200-meter freestyle and 100-meter backstroke, before losing his specialty to teammate Sergey Zabalotnov, who, with 2:00.95, came very close to his own European record.

Many of the U.S. hopefuls avoided the Soviets at Los Angeles to save themselves for the national championships at Clovis, California, a few weeks later. The Clovis competition provided the best news U.S. swimming has had in recent years. Five world records were established by the men, most notable the performance of Rick Carey, who erased John Naber's two 1976 Olympic backstroke world records, the oldest left in the book. Carey, a University of Texas senior, clocked 55.38 for the 100-meter backstroke and 1:58.93 for the 200 meters.

Matt Gribble established a world mark in the 100-meter butterfly in 53.44 seconds in the preliminaries before winning the final in 53.64. Gribble narrowly defeated Pablo Morales who, with a time of 53.71, also bettered the old record. Steve Lundquist first set a U.S. record in the 200-meter breaststroke, then lowered his record at 100 meters to 1:02.34.

Among the U.S. women competing at Clovis, seventeen-year-old Tiffany Cohen from Mission Viejo, California, appeared to be in the best form, winning the

Steve Lundquist USA.

Rowdy Gaines USA.

Victor Salnikov USSR.

Tracy Caulkins USA.

Birgit Meineke GDR.

Dara Torres USA.

400-, 800-, and 1,500-meter freestyle events by wide margins. Her performances, however, fell short of threatening Eastern-bloc world leadership and world records in these events.

If anyone is to challenge East Germany's supremacy in the women's events, it could well be the emerging Japanese. Hiroko Nagasaki, fourteen years of age, was impressive in a Los Angeles pre-Olympic meet, clocking a 2:29.51 200-meter breaststroke, close to the world record. Yaori Yanase, also from Japan, won the 100- and 200-meter freestyle races, both in fast times.

In the first Los Angeles Olympics (1932), Japan proved to be the world power, winning golds in five of the six men's races. Japanese swimmers, who have not been prominent since, hope to repeat some of their historical success in Los Angeles.

POOLS

The first Olympic swimming events were held in the Bay of Zea, near Athens, and the "swimming pools" could only improve upon this initial site. In Paris (1900) and St. Louis (1904), open air pools were marked off in larger bodies of water, the Seine and an artificial lake, respectively. None of these provided clear boundaries for competitors or adequate views for spectators, so it was a great advance when London provided the first real Olympic swimming pool, unfiltered and unheated though it was.

Today's Olympic pools carefully avoid such surprises as they are built to specific standards. The racing pool must be 50 meters long by at least 21 meters wide and 1.8 meters deep, with eight lanes, each 2.5 meters wide. In every event but the backstroke, during which competitors take off with explosive, backward dives from the side of the pool, the swimmers spring from platforms one meter above the water's surface.

STYLES AND STROKES

In the first Olympic Games, an unregulated variety of styles were used for all events, thus the name freestyle was born and applied to the crawl, which was the most commonly used stroke. Freestyle, backstroke, and breaststroke have been accepted styles in the Olympic Games since 1908, while the butterfly was added in the Games of 1956.

The strokes represent the four basic techniques of swimming. Their relative efficiency can be appreciated by the relationship between the four world record times for each mode of propulsion. Sprint swimmers from the United States presently hold records for each of the four strokes at 100 meters:

WORLD RECORD TIMES

FREESTYLE	BUTTERFLY	BACKSTROKE	BREASTSTROKE
Rowdy Gaines	Matt Gribble	Rick Carey	Steve Lundquist
49.36 sec.	53.44 sec.	55.19 sec	1:02.28

Matt Gribble USA, world record holder, 100-meter butterfly.

Rica Reinisch GDR set world records in winning both backstroke events, Moscow 1980.

Swimming starts and turns have evolved since the early days of swimming and are regulated in Olympic competition by the International Swimming Federation (FINA). The pool wall must be touched simultaneously with both hands in the breaststroke and butterfly and with the feet in the backstroke and freestyle.

Electronic devices are used to record both the swimmer's accuracy in touching the wall during a turn and the final time of the event. Electronic timing, capable of thousandth-of-a-second accuracy, was introduced in Tokyo (1964).

The need for such equipment and accuracy was dramatically displayed in the 100-meter freestyle in the Rome Olympics. Lance Larson of the United States was timed at 52.1 seconds, with John Devitt of Australia right behind at 52.2 seconds. However, the judges ruled Devitt had actually touched first and declared him the winner, despite his slower finishing time.

DIVING

Competitive diving began as "graceful diving" from platforms in the late nineteenth century and later branched into springboard diving. Diving was first introduced into the Olympic Games in St. Louis in 1904.

The diving pool must be a minimum of five meters deep. Platform divers take off from a 10-meter high platform, approximately 33 feet in the air. Springboard divers leave from a 3-meter high board.

In diving, each competitor must complete a series of compulsory dives, then a series of dives of his own choosing. Five judges rate the divers on a ten-point scale similar to that used in gymnastics. The high and low scores are thrown out and the three remaining ones are totaled and multiplied by a number between 1.2 and 3.0 which reflects the "degree of difficulty" of the dive. Thus, a diver must choose his optional dives according to a trade-off between increasing difficulty and increased scoring potential. Finally, the scores of all the dives are added together.

The first women's Olympic diving contest, "plain diving," was held in 1912. Swedes won both men's and women's diving in Stockholm, but when modern day springboard and platform diving were introduced in Antwerp (1920), the United States began a long lasting string of success. In Antwerp, the women's winner was thirteen-year-old Aileen Riggin. In Berlin (1936), an even younger woman won a diving gold medal. Marjorie Gestring, also of the United States, at age thirteen years and four months, became the youngest Olympic champion ever.

Unlike swimming, where stars rarely last longer than one Olympiad, divers are capable of repeating medal winning achievements. Pat McCormick earned golds in both springboard and platform diving in two successive Olympics in 1952 and 1956, and fellow team member Sammy Lee earned gold medals in the 1948 and 1952 highboard diving competitions. Lee also earned a bronze in the springboard event in 1948. He subsequently became a successful diving coach and directed

Wendy Wyland USA world champion 1982 in platform diving.

Bob Webster to a duplication of his own back-to-back highboard golds in 1960 and 1964.

Klaus Dibiasi of Italy achieved the legendary feat of winning the platform competition in Mexico City (1968), repeating the performance in Munich and doing it again in Montreal. His father, Carlo Dibiasi, coached Klaus throughout his career. Carlo, also an Olympic diver, was affectionately known as "Papa" throughout the international diving community.

Klaus' first Olympic medal was a silver, earned in the 1964 platform contest at the age of seventeen. His performance inspired the people of Bolzano, his hometown, to finance and build an indoor pool for him so he could train year-round. The gold medals that followed were a far greater reward for their act of kindness than the people could have imagined.

In Montreal, Dibiasi's win was contested to the last dive by U.S. diving star Greg Louganis, who settled for the silver. Louganis has replaced Dibiasi as king of divers, the one who sets the standard for which all divers strive. Louganis, only twenty-three years old and coached by Ron O'Brien, already has won twenty-three national championships. He has not been defeated in major springboard competition since 1978 and with previous Olympic experience to his credit, must be rated as a strong gold medal prospect for 1984.

Usually, diving is associated with the beautiful, graceful acrobatics which Louganis and his fellow divers seem to perform so effortlessly. Diving was recently subjected to criticism when a Soviet diver died after hitting his head on the board in an international competition in Edmonton, Canada.

Sergei Chalibahsvili was performing a reverse 3½ somersault in tuck position, an extremely difficult dive which many thought was beyond Chalibashvili's capability. The incident caused several athletes in the competition to question whether diving risks are worth the gains. Throughout the extensive media coverage, prominent divers repeatedly reminded all who would listen that the incident was isolated, the first serious injury in competitive diving. The tragedy will certainly help athletes keep sport in its proper perspective. Health and enjoyment should far outweigh the importance of any victory if it can only be achieved through excessive risk and danger.

SYNCHRONIZED SWIMMING

Synchronized swimming for women will be introduced to the Olympic program in Los Angeles. This is a ballet-like event, comparable in many ways to gymnastics floor exercises, full of expression and grace.

The duet is the only event adopted thus far. Each team member first performs a solo of various standard movements. A four-minute optional duet follows in which innovative teamwork and synchronization are key factors in scoring.

1984 PROSPECTS

America's foremost duet team, Tracie Ruiz and Candy Costie, are renowned for their creative routines which are punctuated with dolphin-like tricks and hip-high leaps from the water. Their claims on 1984 gold medals will be strongly contested by the current world champions, Canadians Sharon Hambrook and Kelly Kryczka, who are most effective at figures.

Another Canadian duet team, identical twins Penny and Vicky Vilagos, might well become the one team to represent Canada, having defeated Hambrook and Kryczka in their 1983 national championships. Ruiz and Costie also defeated the world champions at the inaugural synchronized swimming event at the new Olympic pool in Los Angeles.

As in gymnastics, judges use a ten-point scale to score performers, evaluating them on body position, figure control, content, difficulty, and synchronization with music and each other. Seven judges, with elevated positions at poolside, decide the scores. The high and low scores are thrown out and the average is added to the score from the figures, which counts equally in the final tally.

WATER POLO

Water polo is a relatively young sport. Its predecessor was developed in the midnineteenth century by British pool and resort owners in an effort to attract customers with games and friendly competition. The contests were, as the name implies, polo in the water. Poloists straddled "horses," actually round wooden barrels, and hit a ball around the pool with kayak paddles. The first recorded game took place in 1870 at Bournemouth, a British resort. Soon after, rules were formulated for competitive play and the extraneous paddles and horses were abandoned.

Water polo quickly became known as a rough game because pools were so shallow even nonswimmers could play. Thus, strength and roughness, rather than skill and swimming ability, were the important factors. In fact, the game was so rough and resulted in so many injuries it was barred from U.S. collegiate competition. Referees, though able to enforce above-water rules and fair play, were unable to control the underwater infractions.

Although water polo was introduced early in the series of modern Olympic Games (Paris, 1900), it did not gain worldwide popularity until the 1920's. Predictably, it was Britain, the nation responsible for its invention, that dominated early Olympic water polo games. As water polo began to gain international attention, the power shifted first to Western European nations, then to Eastern European nations.

The first European water polo championships did not take place until 1926. At that time, Hungary reigned supreme in water polo, partly due to the attention and

Tracie Ruiz USA and Candy Costie are favorites in 1984 synchronized swimming duets.

popularity it received as its national sport, and partly due to the many effective innovations introduced. These innovations included the wet pass, which allows for very fast ball transport and the use of one guard as a forward during offensive play.

Hungary won its first water polo gold in 1932 and continued to dominate the game the next thirty years. Hungary won the gold in 1932, 1936, 1952, 1956, 1964, and 1976 and took the silver in every other Olympic Games, except in 1980 when it won the bronze.

One of the most exciting of these Olympic water polo contests came in Melbourne. Just before the Games opened, the Hungarian uprising had been put down by the Soviets. The water polo player's nationalistic feelings were apparent in the pool. Hungary retaliated by beating the Soviets before going on to win the finals. In the last three Olympic Games, the Hungarians have been led by Tamas Farago, a 6-foot 6-inch forward who scored a phenomenal twenty-two goals at Montreal.

The United States does not have a successful history in Olympic water polo. Other than at St. Louis (1904), when there were no foreign opponents, the U.S. team has earned three bronze medals over the years, first in Paris (1924), a second time in Los Angeles (1932), and a third time in Munich (1972). One member of the medal-winning 1924 Olympic water polo team was Johnny Weissmuller, well-known for his swimming and acting talents, but less for his polo talent.

RULES

Water polo is much like soccer and basketball in rules and strategy. There are seven players on each team: one goalie, three forwards or offensive players, and three guards or defensive players. The winner of each game is the team scoring the most goals.

The water polo pool is 30 meters long, 20 meters wide and at least 2 meters deep; thus players are unable to touch the pool bottom and must swim or tread water continuously throughout the four seven-minute periods. Such constant activity requires stamina, as well as quickness and strength, for offensive and defensive play. Water polo teams create plays just as basketball teams do, the main difference being water polo players must contend with the water, as well as with the ball and the opposing team members.

As in ice hockey, when a water poloist is penalized, he must sit out of the game for 45 seconds. The absence of a penalized player leaves a team one man short, giving the opposition a powerful scoring advantage. To prevent stalling play while a team has this disadvantage, there is a 35-second stall clock, during which time a team must attempt a goal or turn the ball over to the other team.

Players catch and pass the hard rubber ball with one hand, sometimes using a technique known as an "eggbeater." The eggbeater is a rapid series of leg movements which enable the poloists to rise hip-high in the water. This resulting height, which can usually be held for only a few seconds, gives the player a momentary advantage during a goal shot or defensive play.

Twelve national teams are chosen to compete in the Olympic water polo tournament, based upon performances in international competition. These teams compete in a series of elimination games in which six successful teams move into a championship round and the other six compete for places seven through twelve in the consolation round.

1984 PROSPECTS

The 1984 U.S. team, training harder than ever, is hoping to improve on its dismal water polo record. The United States traditionally has exceptionally fast swimmers and, with the addition of outstanding forward Kevin Robertson and hole man Terry Schroeder, may be able to turn things around.

The traditional European powers, however, remain strong, with the USSR leading the way, having won the 1983 European championships over Hungary and Spain.

25

VOLLEYBALL

— 25 —

1984 VENUE

All volleyball matches will be held in the Long Beach Arena, which has a seating capacity of 11,329. The arena will undergo a $1 million facelift for the Games, which includes a new lighting system and ceiling.

EVENTS AND SCHEDULE (Finals)

Men

Team Competition	August 11

Women

Team Competition	August 7

HISTORY OF VOLLEYBALL

Volleyball was invented in 1895 as an alternative to basketball, by William G. Morgan, a YMCA director who felt basketball was too strenuous for most people. Thus began volleyball's long evolution toward its present day form. Morgan would scarcely recognize the diving, leaping, ball-smashing players of today as participants in the same leisurely, passive game he first developed.

Volleyball's popularity stems from its ease of play. It requires only a ball, a net or rope, and two or more players. It can be played indoors or outdoors, on the beach, in vacant lots, even on aircraft carriers. During World Wars I and II, more than 16,000 volleyballs were spread by U.S. troops to military and refugee camps throughout the world. As refugees traveled to new places, the game of volleyball went with them, thus making volleyball a truly international sport.

Because equipment is minimal and the rules easy to learn, it has become a worldwide sport. In Japan in 1945, the sport was dubbed "volleyball for a million people," and in 1925 the Soviet Communist Party's Central Committee encouraged volleyball "for farmers and the working class . . . it should be brought to the level of the people at large, not only the youth, but the aged also."

The involvement of so many nations in the development of the sport has given volleyball some distinctive styles and characteristics. The Japanese introduced a tireless, never-give-up defense, diving and scrambling for balls most players would have thought impossible to reach. The Japanese wore down their opponents with endurance and their incredible ability to keep any ball in play.

The Soviets introduced powerful offensive play to the game with very strong, tall players who could hit the ball with enough force to knock an opponent to the ground. In order to be competitive in today's international games, a team must be able to combine all of these tactics.

OLYMPIC HISTORY

Volleyball was introduced as an Olympic sport in Tokyo (1964) with men's and women's competitions. By this time, volleyball was being played throughout the world, but it was the Soviet men and Japanese women who prepared most seriously and organized the training necessary to capture the gold. Such dedication was exquisitely exhibited by the Japanese women, who were driven seven days a week by Hirofumi Diamatsu, a fanatical coach who drilled team members endlessly in defensive skills.

While horrifying some people with their intensity, films of their training sessions inspired many others and showed the world how demanding volleyball training must be in order to succeed. Other nations developed similar intensive volleyball programs in an effort to keep up with the Japanese. The most successful team was the USSR, which introduced a real power offense into the game. The Soviets won the gold in both men's and women's competitions in Mexico City (1968), beating out the still powerful Japanese women and the up-and-coming Japanese men.

In Munich (1972), with twelve teams in the men's competition, the Japanese men dethroned the USSR and East Germany surprised everyone by winning the silver. The Soviets retained the gold in the women's competition, beating the Japanese for the second straight Olympics. The Soviet women were led by the experienced Inna Ryskal and Ludmila Buldakova, both competing in their third Olympic final against the Japanese.

The big surprise in Montreal was the Polish men's team, which broke through years of Japanese and Soviet domination to win the gold from the Soviets in a long, tension-filled game. Luckily, the Polish coach had anticipated the need for endurance, putting his athletes through eight-hour training sessions in preparation for the Games.

Recounting two previous Olympic losses to the Soviet women, Japanese star Takoko Shirai said, "We decided that we must win the gold medal here (Montreal) at all costs." We can only guess what the costs must have been, but they paid off as the Japanese women decisively beat the Soviets in three straight games.

Debbie Green (10) sets for Rita Crockett (3) during 1983 game against Cuba at Long Beach.

USA celebrates victory reversing their loss to Cuba at the 1983 PanAm Games.

In Moscow, with Japan boycotting the Games, the Soviets easily captured the gold in both men's and women's competition. The USSR should find it more difficult in 1984, however, as the Japanese, Chinese, and the up-and-coming United States will be ready to challenge for Olympic titles in both men's and women's divisions.

Ten men's and eight women's teams will be competing in Los Angeles. In both tournaments, teams are separated into two pools. Each team plays every other team in their pool in round robin fashion. Then the overall winners of each pool play the runner-up from the other pool in a semifinal match. Winners of these semifinal matches play for the gold and silver medals. Semifinal losers play for third and fourth.

RULES

Volleyball is played on a court 18 meters by 9 meters (roughly 60 by 30 feet). It is divided in half by a net which extends one foot beyond each sideline. The men's net is 8 feet high, the women's is 7 feet 4½ inches. Both are 3 feet deep. The net separates the teams, which are not allowed to touch or step under the net.

A team consists of six players, who must abide by specific rules governing touching the ball. Each team may hit the ball up to three times, unless the first hit is on a deflected block. In this case, four total hits may occur before returning a ball. No player may touch the ball twice in succession unless the second touch is a recovery from an unsuccessful block which has just been attempted.

Besides the serve, which is made with a flat, open palm, there are three basic techniques for hitting the ball, although technically it is legal to hit it with any part of the body above the waist. The successful completion of these three hits, the recovery, set, and spike, is the goal of every good volleyball team.

The first hit, essentially a recovery from the "attack" or spike of the opposing team, places the ball in a position where the "setter" can get it. Both hands are connected, while bumping or "lifting" the ball as it bounces off the inner forearms. With top hitters spiking the ball at speeds over 100 MPH, the forearms of defensive players can take quite a bit of punishment.

The setter positions the ball for the hitter. This requires a delicate touch and exact positioning. The setter delivers the set from the middle front position. The set must be exactly the right height and distance from the net to allow the hitter maximum power and control. Almost all good setters learn the preferences of each of their hitters and set the ball accordingly. They are like football quarterbacks who determine the plays and make the passes.

Finally, the hit, or spike, completes the trio and is done with an open palm. Although a clenched fist is allowed, the open-palm spike allows more control and power, since the wrist acts like a whip and extends the power of the arm and elbow. While only the three forward players are legally designated as hitters, all players may do so. Some stipulations apply, however.

Cuban attempt to block a USA hit. Their ongoing rivalry will continue in Los Angeles.

Extending from one sideline to the other, 10 feet from the center line on both sides of the court, is a restraining line which back row players may not touch or cross when they "spike." Also, their feet must remain on the floor, thereby preventing the ball from being hit powerfully downward. Clearly, it is to the offensive team's advantage to use the front row players to spike in the hopes of overpowering opponents.

After the serve, volleying continues until one team fails to return the ball or keep it off the floor. If the receiving team makes the error, the serving team retains the ball and acquires one point. If the serving team commits the foul, or simply is unable to continue the volley, the opposite team is given the ball with no points earned on either side. Whenever the serve is awarded to the previously receiving team, the six players "rotate" in a clockwise direction, moving a new player into the serving position.

A match consists of five, fifteen-point games, each of which must be won by at least two points. If the score is 14–14, the final score must go to 16–14 or more.

Offensive play involves complex strategies for drawing the other team out of position, thereby opening holes in the defense. The setter usually calls signals to set up the elaborate plays. Because six players must operate with such coordination and synchronization, good communication and emotional support are vital.

1984 PROSPECTS

The U.S. men's team has not qualified for an Olympic tournament since 1968, but now qualifies automatically because the United States is the host country. The team has a permanent training center in San Diego, California, and also has some of the financial and public support it needs to challenge the more established volleyball powerhouses. For the first time, the team has had an opportunity to train together consistently, which has resulted in great progress during the last two years.

In the past, the United States has been defeated by the USSR because of the Soviets' powerful serving, great size, and strength. The Soviets remain in top form, undefeated since the last Olympics. The U.S. men are gaining consistency and are learning to use their quickness and finesse with great success.

The U.S. men's team will be led by Dusty Dvorak and Karch Kiraly. Paul Sunderland, another key figure on the team, is a veteran of international volleyball competition and will add experience to the young, 1984 Olympic team. Dvorak, though still young and improving, is regarded as one of the world's foremost setters. He and Kiraly are both natural leaders as well as outstanding players. The U.S. men could well be the surprise of the tournament. They have come from nowhere and could perhaps be the sensation of '84, much like the U.S. ice hockey team of 1980.

Los Angeles will also provide the U.S. women's team another chance at the medal it felt so sure of winning, had it gone to Moscow. The main competition will come from the ever-powerful Soviets, the quick moving, defensive Japanese, and the 1982 world champion, China. China plays a style similar to that of the U.S. women, combining power and quickness. These three will be formidable teams to overcome, but the U.S. women, coached and motivated by Arie Selinger at their training center at Coto de Caza, in Orange County, California, have the training and commitment such a task requires.

The U.S. women also have some strong and outstanding individual players in Flo Hyman, Rita Crockett, and Debbie Green. Flo Hyman, at 6 feet 5 inches, is one of the most respected women players in the world. At the 1981 World Cup, she was named the best overall hitter. Rita Crockett's power comes from her thirty-nine inch vertical leap, highest in women's volleyball. Although only 5-feet 4-inches tall, Debbie Green is one of the world's best players in a sport dominated by taller women. Her excellent setting abilities allow hitters such as Hyman and Crockett to make the most of every attack.

These women, who would have been part of the 1980 Olympic team, and eight others on the Olympic roster, should prove a tough challenge for the powerful Japanese, Chinese, and Soviet women's teams.

26

WEIGHTLIFTING

— 26 —

1984 VENUE

The Olympic weightlifting competition will be held at the Gerston Pavilion on the campus of Loyola-Marymount University, located close to Los Angeles International Airport. The facililty was completed in 1982 and has a seating capacity of 4,500 spectators.

EVENTS AND SCHEDULE (Finals)

Weight Classes	Maximum Bodyweight	
Flyweight	Up to 52 kg—114.6 lbs.	July 29
Bantamweight	56 kg—123.5 lbs.	July 30
Featherweight	60 kg—132.3 lbs.	July 31
Lightweight	67.5 kg—148.8 lbs.	August 1
Middleweight	75 kg—165.4 lbs.	August 2
Light-Heavyweight	82.5 kg—181.9 lbs.	August 4
Middle-Heavyweight	90 kg—198.4 lbs.	August 5
First Heavyweight	100 kg—220.5 lbs.	August 6
Second Heavyweight	110 kg—242.5 lbs.	August 7
Super Heavyweight	Over 110 kg—242.5 lbs.	August 8

HISTORY OF WEIGHTLIFTING

Weightlifting probably originated with prehistoric man, who lifted rocks rather than barbells to demonstrate his strength. Feats of strength had very practical applications; thus, strong men were highly esteemed in ancient societies. The Greeks exercised with dumbbells of lead and stone, but weightlifting was not contested in the Ancient Olympics. Many localities in the British Isles have large, heavy rocks which, for centuries, strong men of the region have attempted to move off the ground.

As a competitive sport with standardized rules, weightlifting first began in Germany and spread quickly to adjacent European countries and throughout the continent. The types of contests were prescribed by the equipment. Weights were somewhat crude and could not be adjusted; therefore, the first forms of competition required certain weights to be lifted several times. Italian Louis Attila is said to have introduced the hollow barbell which could be filled with leadshot, allowing the weight to be adjusted.

OLYMPIC HISTORY

Weightlifting was among the charter sports when the Olympic Games were revived in Athens in 1896. There were two events: a one-handed lift and a two-handed lift, both contested without regard to the lifter's bodyweight. In the latter event, Viggo Jensen of Denmark managed to heave 111.5 kilograms (245.5 lb.) overhead.

Weightlifting, much as we know it today, appeared on the Olympic program in 1920 with three styles of lifting: press, snatch, and clean and jerk. This system lasted until 1972, when the press was eliminated.

In Amsterdam (1928), five weight categories comprised the competition. In the lightweight division, both Kurt Helbig of Germany and Hans Haas of Austria lifted the same total weight, thus sharing the title. This happened again in 1936, also in the lightweight event, when Mohammed Mesbah of Egypt and Robert Fein of Austria were both awarded gold medals. Subsequently, a rule which resolves a tie in favor of the lighter man has been applied.

Early Olympic contests were dominated by the European nations. The United States was slow to develop competitive prowess in the sport. It was not until 1936, when Anthony Terlazzo won the featherweight lifting title, that the United States achieved its first gold medal in a weightlifting event. Terlazzo lifted a world and Olympic record total of 312.5 kilograms (688.5 lb.).

A brief period of U.S. supremacy in the sport began at the postwar Games in London. The United States won four of six weightlifting categories, deprived of a clean sweep by two Egyptian lifters.

The streak continued in Helsinki in 1952, despite the three gold medals won by the Soviet Union in its first Olympic appearance. John Davis retained the heavyweight title for the United States, repeating his London performance. Tommy Kono won his first Olympic championship in the lightweight class, a feat he would duplicate four years later in Melbourne.

In both Helsinki and Melbourne, all weightlifting gold medals were won either by U.S. or Soviet lifters. In both cases, United States competitors gathered the majority with four golds to the Soviets' three. In Melbourne, with the medal count tied, three to three and one event remaining, it was left to mammoth heavyweight Paul Anderson to break the deadlock. In a tense duel, Anderson hoisted the same weight as Argentinian Humberto Selvetti. But Anderson, at 302 pounds, was awarded the gold because his bodyweight was less than Selvetti's.

The Rome Olympics proved to be a harbinger of things to come. The Soviets had applied scientific methods to weightlifting technique and training. This time they won five of seven weight categories. In the middleweight division, Tommy

Vasily Alexeev USSR won consecutive heavyweight golds in Munich 1972 & Montreal 1976.

Sultan Rakmanov USSR assumed heavyweight title in Moscow 1980.

Sultan Rakmanov USSR.

Kono saw his world record fall to Soviet Aleksandr Kurynov, who also deprived Kono of a chance to become the only man to win three Olympic weightlifting golds. Kono finished second. In the heavyweight division, Yuri Vlasov won by a huge margin of 25 kilograms (55 lb.), easily outlifting James Bradford and Norbert Schemansky of the United States. On his way to victory, Vlasov raised 202.5 kilograms (446 lb.) overhead, the most weight ever raised by man.

The USSR–United States rivalry in weightliftng became history as the Soviets again captured the majority of weightlifting honors in Tokyo. Five of the seven divisions were won with world records, emphasizing the almost ceaseless revision of the weightlifting record books that continues today. Leonid Zhabotinsky deprived his teammate, Vlasov, of a second heavyweight championship by a mere five pounds. Zhabotinsky jerked a world record 217.5 kilograms (479.5 lb.) to edge the seemingly unbeatable Vlasov in the last of the three lifts.

In Mexico City, Zhabotinsky lifted the same total to become the second heavyweight in Olympic history to retain his title. Not only did he star on the weightlifting platform, but many Olympic fans will never forget how the 6-foot 4-inch, 330-pound giant, the world's strongest man, led his team into the arena for the opening ceremony, carrying the Soviet banner at arm's length as if it were a toy.

Soviet lifters fell short of prior expectations by winning only three gold medals, but easily exceeded the fifty-three other competitive nations.

The story of weightlifting at Munich (1972) was the emergence of other Eastern European nations, notably Bulgaria, which shared the gold rush with the Soviet Union. Each nation won three. The program had been expanded to nine weight divisions. Poland, Hungary, and Norway each won golds while the United States failed to win a single medal of any variety.

All Olympic records were rewritten and four world record totals were established. The performance of Mikharbi Kirzhinov of the USSR was perhaps the most convincing. A lightweight of less than 148 pounds, he broke through the 1,000-pound barrier with a performance of 464 kilograms (1014 lb.), adding a 22-pound increment to the previous world record.

Everything went according to plan for Vasily Alexeev, who had established himself indisputably as the world's strongest man. He performed up to his usual high standards, taking the super-heavyweight title by an enormous margin of 30 kilograms (66 lb.).

In 1976, the lifting contests in Montreal were tests of strength between Russia and Bulgaria, the Soviets retaining the edge, 5-3, while Poland earned the remaining gold.

The long awaited super-heavyweight clash between the two strongest men in the world failed to materialize when Christo Plachkov, the new world record holder from Bulgaria, was withdrawn at the last minute for unknown reasons.

Even reigning champion Vasily Alexeev's participation was questionable when he failed to show up for a routine steroid test. After a stern warning, he showed up, took the test, and passed. Weighing in at 345 pounds, he was in the greatest form of his life. On his second attempt at the clean and jerk, Alexeev, with seeming ease, hoisted 255 kilograms (562 lb.) overhead to establish a world record, earned his second gold medal, and revised his own Olympic record in the process.

A few weeks after the close of the weightlifting events at Montreal, the International Weightlifting Federation announced ten lifters had been suspended for one year as a result of positive post-competition tests for steroids. Three of the ten had been Olympic Champions: Kaczmarek of Poland and two of the Bulgarian champions.

After the medals were returned to the IOC and reissued, the final count for weightlifting supremacy became seven for the Soviets and two for the Bulgarians. These were the first disqualifications for steroid use in Olympic history. The short, one-year suspension seemed an admission by the IOC that they were aware of the widespread use of steroids.

The Moscow Olympic competitions were, as expected, an Eastern European affair, with the exception of the bantamweight championship, which was won by Daniel Nunez of Cuba, who set a world record.

In Montreal, Alexeev became the ninth weightlifter in Olympic history to win two gold medals. He returned to Moscow with a chance to become the only man to ever triple, seeking three successive Olympic victories. But, the career of one of the Soviet Union's greatest sports figures came to a sudden end when he failed to make his opening snatch of 180 kilograms (396 lb.) and was eliminated, probably never to compete again. In his wake, teammate Sultan Rakhmanov went on to win and equal Alexeev's Olympic record total.

Perhaps the greatest weightlifting performance was that of Yurik Vardanyan. He set world records for both snatch and clean and jerk, as well as the combined total. Although weighing less than 82.5 kilograms (181 lb.), his 400 kilograms (880 lb.) total exceeded the winning performances of the next two higher weight categories.

RULES

1. Each weightlifter has three chances in the snatch and in the clean and jerk. If he misses on all three opportunites to. lift, he is eliminated.
2. The greatest weight lifted in each of the two lifts is combined to give a total lift and determine the final placings.
3. In the case of two lifters with the same total, the winner is the lifter with the lesser bodyweight.
4. Three referees decide if a lift has been performed successfully. A good lift is indicated by a white light and a failed attempt by a red light. The majority decision rules. A jury of three other referees from the International Weightlifting Federation (IWF) observes the performance of the officiating judges to insure accurate standards and impartiality.

Blagoi Blagoev BUL 1983 world champion in the 90kg division.

Viacheslav Klokov USSR 1983 world champion in the 110kg division.

THE LIFTS

The two lifts currently used in Olympic competition are the snatch and the clean and jerk. Following the Munich Olympics, the format of international weightlifting was reduced from three lifts to two. The military press was abandoned because it was too questionable to judge. The rules were being stretched to the limit, resulting in partiality in judging. Also, the military press caused great stress on the lower back, causing frequent injury to novice lifters.

Today, judging is simplified. The most common causes of disqualification are pressing the bar out at the top of the snatch and having the bar touch the knees or thighs during the clean and jerk.

Snatch

The bar is pulled in a single movement from the ground to the full overhead extension, both arms locked, supporting the bar vertically above the head. The lifter attempts to pull the bar as high as possible, and then either splits or squats under the bar. Most squat and, with power from the thighs, push to a standing position. The weight must be maintained in a final static position, arms and legs extended, until the referee signals with a clap that the weight can be returned to the platform.

Clean and Jerk

The clean and jerk is the name given to the technique that has been devised to raise the greatest amount of weight overhead. It consists of two distinct motions. In the clean, the weight is gripped palm downward and pulled in a single movement as high as one's power will allow.

The lifter attempts either to split or squat underneath the bar while it is at the highest point of this initial pull. The bar is then brought to shoulder level and the lifter recovers to a standing position. To begin the jerk, the lifter bends his legs and extends them with all his power to drive the bar upward. Again, at the bar's apex, the lifter attempts to split underneath the bar, dropping to a point where his arms can be extended. The lifter then recovers, holding the weight in a fully extended position overhead until the referee signals him to return it to the floor.

THE LIFTER'S APPROACH TO THE BAR

The bar and its weights are merciless. To understand the approach to competition, one has only to watch the lifters approach the bar. The bar sits inert, while the lifter approaches with extreme ceremony, almost reverence. He steps into a tray of resin to improve the grip of his lifting boots and coats his hands and thighs with chalk. All the time he paces back and forth, gathering his wits for the climactic confrontation with gravity. As the weight increases, the intensity of this one-sided drama increases.

Animal-like grunts are not for the audience. The "psyching" of the lifter is a self-hypnotic affair in which he tries to approach a totally confident and physical plane of being. The lifter tries to overpower his own doubt, pulling the bar with a great "aargh," believing only in the successful outcome of the lift with a vision of the bar overhead. The reward of the sport is extreme satisfaction. One look at a successful lifter's sweet smile makes it all very clear.

1984 PROSPECTS

Bulgaria and the Soviet Union dominated the world rankings in 1983, and are favored in the race for gold in '84. During the 1983 World Championships in Moscow, Eastern Europeans swept all weightlifting categories.

These teams will be limited only by the Olympic rule which specifies that each team may enter only ten lifters, spread among the ten weight categories. The rules further stipulate that a country may enter up to two lifters in a category. This means Bulgaria and the Soviet Union will be restricted as to the number of competitors and many of their great lifters will have to stay home.

One of the most sensational Bulgarian lifters is Nam Suleimanov who, in 1983 at Allentown, Pennsylvania, set world records of 125 kilograms (275.5 lb.) in the snatch and 160 kilograms (352.5 lb.) in the clean and jerk. Suleimanov is only fifteen-years-old, stands 5 feet 5 inches and weighs 123 pounds, yet his amazing weightlifting capabilities equal those of the world's strongest men.

Experts had predicted that Suleimanov might become the first weightlifter to raise three times his bodyweight overhead. Another Bulgarian teenager, however, earned the distinction first. Nineteen-year-old Stefan Tuporov, competing in the 132-pound division, clean and jerked 396 pounds at the world championships.

The United States will be hard pressed to win any medals. The best prospect was Jeff Michaels, twenty-one years of age, from Chicago, current national champion in the 110 kilograms (242 lb.) category. Michels jeopardized his chances, however, when drug tests following his 1983 Pan Am victories revealed the presence of testosterone. His suspension of two years will keep him out of the 1984 Olympic Games. U.S. hopes may therefore rest with Curt White who, in the 82.5 kilogram (182 lb.) class, has clean and jerked over 440 pounds and is improving rapidly. None of the seven U.S. lifters competing at the '83 world championships were able to complete both the required lifts. All were eliminated in one of the most dismal U.S. performances in international sport.

The United States was the world power in weightlifting until the 1960's. Now, no U.S. weightlifter ranks in the top ten in any division. In the Soviet Union, there are hundreds of thousands of active participants. Elsewhere in Eastern Europe, weightlifting is a sport strongly supported by government. In the United States, there are only 2,000 serious participants.

Progress in the development of world weightlifting records has been astonishing. Every year the record book is rewritten. In 1982, sixty-two world records were set by twenty-nine competitors in the different bodyweight categories. Only five record performances remained unsurpassed. At the '83 World Championships twenty-three world records were established.

Perhaps the number one lifter in the world is Blagoi Blagoev from Bulgaria, who became world champion in the 90 kilograms (198 lb.) category. He has snatched 195 kilograms (431 lb.) and clean and jerked 230 kilograms (504 lb.). In Los Angeles, another impressive lifter to watch will be four-time world champion Yurik Vardanian, whose 400 kilogram (880 lb.) total in the 181-pound division at the Moscow Olympics was considered the greatest feat ever in weightlifting.

In the super-heavyweight class, Alexeev's records have been erased by Anatoli Pisarenko of the Soviet Union, who has the honor of being the man to raise the greatest poundage overhead with a clean and jerk of 574 pounds. This, and his 457.5 kilograms (1,009 lb.) total, currently stand as world records. In winning the 1983 world championship, Pisarenko added a 455-pound snatch to his world record collection.

Weighing 270 pounds, Pisarenko is an extremely solid athlete in relation to the huge super-heavyweight predecessors, acclaimed as the world's strongest men. Lifting techniques have become so precise that an Olympic champion lifter, as Pisarenko aspires to be, must have the agility of a gymnast and the reflexes of a world-class sprinter to overcome the sheer bulk of the heavyweight giants.

27

WRESTLING

— 27 —

1984 VENUE

The Anaheim Convention Center, with a seating capacity of 8,892, is the site of the 1984 wrestling events. The convention center is located adjacent to Disneyland, 27 miles from downtown Los Angeles.

EVENTS AND SCHEDULE (Finals)

Freestyle Classes	*Maximum Bodyweight*	
Light Flyweight	Up to 48 kg—105.8 lbs.	August 9
Flyweight	52 kg—114.6 lbs.	August 10
Bantamweight	57 kg—125.7 lbs.	August 11
Featherweight	62 kg—136.7 lbs.	August 9
Lightweight	68 kg—149.9 lbs.	August 11
Welterweight	74 kg—163.1 lbs.	August 10
Middleweight	82 kg—180.8 lbs.	August 11
Light Heavyweight	90 kg—198.4 lbs.	August 9
Heavyweight	100 kg—220.5 lbs.	August 11
Super Heavyweight	Over 100 kg—220.5 lbs.	August 10
Greco-Roman Classes	*Maximum Bodyweight*	
Light Flyweight	Up to 48 kg—105.8 lbs.	August 1
Flyweight	52 kg—114.6 lbs.	August 2
Bantamweight	57 kg—125.7 lbs.	August 3
Featherweight	62 kg—136.7 lbs.	August 1
Lightweight	68 kg—149.9 lbs.	August 3
Welterweight	74 kg—163.1 lbs.	August 2
Middleweight	82 kg—180.8 lbs.	August 3
Light Heavyweight	90 kg—198.4 lbs.	August 1
Heavyweight	100 kg—220.5 lbs.	August 3
Super Heavyweight	Over 100 kg—220.5 lbs.	August 2

HISTORY OF WRESTLING

Wrestling is one of the most ancient competitive sports, dating back to thousands of years B.C. Pictorial representations of wrestlers in classic wrestling poses have been found in archaeological excavations of the ancient civilizations of Japan, China, Babylonia, and Greece. Egyptian hieroglyphics from 2250 B.C. depict wrestlers in positions recognizable today.

The sport was introduced in the Ancient Olympic Games in 708 B.C., where it was one of the most popular events, as well as the deciding contest in the all important pentathlon. One of the greatest wrestlers of the ancient era was Milo of Croton, who won six consecutive Olympic championships. Milo was more than a great wrestler. He took pleasure in performing all types of strong-man feats, such as carrying a bull, breaking cords tied around his neck by tensing his neck muscles, and consuming record amounts of food and drink.

Wrestling evolved through the ages, with each nation practicing and developing its own particular style. Iceland had the glima and Switzerland the schwingen. The cumberland style developed in Ireland, the sumo in Japan, and the yagli in Turkey. From these various styles, evolved two international styles, the freestyle and the Greco-Roman, which were adopted for Olympic competition.

Of the two styles of wrestling, Greco-Roman is the classic, European style which involves upper-body grappling, while freestyle involves the entire body in a less regulated battle. Greco-Roman favors upper-body strength and technique as the wrestler attempts to pin his opponent without using his legs and without grasping his opponent's legs.

Europeans tend to excel in Greco-Roman wrestling, since their best wrestlers favor this more classical style. The opposite occurs in the United States, where the best wrestlers are attracted to freestyle. U.S. collegiate wrestling is very similar to international freestyle.

Greco-Roman matches are upright and involve a lot of classic throws in which a wrestler grasps his opponent above the waist and actually throws him over his head. It is a spectacular sight to see a wrestler's huge body flying in high, sweeping motions through the air. Between throws, the game can become quite slow as the wrestlers "pummel" (spar and dig) to attempt to gain the position necessary to make another throw.

Freestyle wrestlers use their legs to attack as well as to counter-attack, using moves such as a foot-sweep in which one wrestler attempts to take the other off his feet, or a simple leg grab with which leverage can be applied to take an opponent down to the mat.

OLYMPIC HISTORY

Only one wrestling event, the Greco-Roman heavyweight, was contested in the first modern Olympic Games. It was not until the 1904 Games that freestyle events were added. For the next twenty years the styles, divisions, and rules varied according to which nation was hosting the Games. The events tended to favor athletes of the host nation, thus it is difficult to say which nations produced the best wrestlers.

Dave Schultz USA (blue) wins 1983 Kiev world freestyle wrestling championship at 74kg.

Arsen Fadzaev USSR pins opponent to win 68kg. class at 1983 world championships.

Finally, by 1924 in Paris, the sport achieved some measure of standardization as well-officiated contests in both freestyle and Greco-Roman were held. Scandinavians, particularly the Finns and the Swedes, dominated Greco-Roman competition, while U.S. wrestlers proved themselves the best at freestyle.

Wrestling expanded greatly after World War II and in London (1948), 266 athletes representing twenty-seven nations competed in the various divisions. Turkey and Sweden won most of the medals but the United States, led by light-heavyweight champion Henry Wittenberg, also did well. Wittenberg was generally considered to be the top wrestler in the '48 Games as well as the top U.S. wrestler of all-time. Due to the cessation of the Games during World War II, Wittenberg received only one Olympic gold, but his long success record encompasses four years and over 300 successive undefeated wrestling matches.

In Helsinki (1952), an unfortunate delay in the arrival of entry forms prevented Turkey from repeating its victories of 1948 and opened the door to the Soviet wrestlers who were competing in their first Olympics. The Turks and Soviets remained dominant for many years after that, especially in Greco-Roman events.

In 1960, 336 wrestlers competed in a sixteen hundred-year-old building amid the ruins of ancient Rome, an appropriate site for such an ancient sport. Here, the star was West German heavyweight Wilfried Dietrich. Dietrich, who won the Greco-Roman silver in Melbourne, performed a rare double in winning the freestyle and taking a second successive silver in Greco-Roman. By this time, wrestling had become so competitive that most wrestlers were forced to concentrate on one style or the other. Dietrich went on to compete in five straight Olympics, winning medals in four.

After Rome, where the United States won three gold medals, U.S. wrestling experienced a gradual decline while Eastern bloc wrestlers showed improvement. Alexandr Medved of the USSR became the first wrestler to earn three successive gold medals (1964 through 1972).

A light-heavyweight in Tokyo, Medved moved up to heavyweight where he often faced and defeated men more than 100 pounds heavier. Weighing just 230 pounds in Munich, he had to use all his experience to overcome the great strength of Chris Taylor of the United States who weighed 420 pounds.

There are currently twenty different wrestling divisions in the Games, ten categories in each of the two styles. With respect to total medals, wrestling is the third most important sport in the Games, with a total of twenty gold medals available.

Eastern bloc nations seem to excel in sports with many categories, such as wrestling. This may be a reason why wrestling receives such attention and support in the USSR. It is certainly a gold rich sport which provides good pay-offs on the medal table.

In Munich (1972), all ten Greco-Roman divisions were won by Eastern Europeans, four of them Soviets. Five freestyle golds were also won by the USSR.

World champion Dave Schultz USA stalks Magomedova USSR.

Soviet Ivan Yarygin pinned all seven of his foes on his way to the 220-pound class title. The United States put on its best performance ever, garnering three gold medals, including the impressive victory of Dan Gable, now the 1984 Olympic coach.

Between 1968 and 1980 the Soviets have produced a number of repeat winners such as Ivan Yarygin in the 1972 and 1976 heavyweight freestyle, Valeri Rezantsev in the 1972 and 1976 light-heavyweight Greco-Roman, Sosian Andiev in the 1976 and 1980 super-heavyweight freestyle, and Alexandr Kolchinski in the 1976 and 1980 super-heavyweight Greco-Roman.

RULES

The goal in wrestling is to pin an opponent within a circle 9-meters in diameter, marked on a 12-meter square mat. If no action occurs within a smaller, 7-meter circle, the wrestlers are returned to the center to restart. The pin is comparable to a knockout in boxing, both constituting an automatic victory. If no pin occurs, the victory goes to the wrestler who has gained the most points during the two three-minute rounds.

In freestyle, points may be earned for taking a man to the mat (one point); gaining the upper position while on the mat (one point); touching an opponent's elbow, shoulder, or head to the mat (two points); taking an opponent directly from his feet to his back (three points); or any of the many other successful offensive moves.

In Greco-Roman wrestling, spectacular throws are awarded the greatest number of points. These moves, which usually earn three points, are quite risky even for the executor, who must place himself in a vulnerable position just to achieve them. A fourth point may be earned in the throw for grand amplitude. It is essentially an appreciation point in recognition of the extra effort the throw requires.

A referee oversees all action on the mat. The majority decision of the referee, judge, and mat chairman rules on any decision. Although no penalty points are subtracted for illegal throws or holds, a wrestler may be disqualified for any move, such as choking, hitting, kicking, or finger twisting. The referee also keeps the match moving by calling the wrestlers to their feet if the action on the mat reaches an impasse.

1984 PROSPECTS

The USSR is the number one power in wrestling. In October 1983, at the world freestyle championships at Kiev, the Soviets won seven events, took two seconds, and one third. They have world champions in most weight categories, several of whom are also Olympic champions.

The United States should be strong in Olympic freestyle competition. Dave Schultz from Oklahoma rallied to win the only U.S. gold at the world championships. Lee Kemp is a former three-time world champion in the same 163-pound division. Kemp will face Schultz in the U.S trials to determine which representative is the best U.S. gold medal prospect.

Joe Gonzales, from California State University, Bakersfield, won the nationals twice and is one of the best in the world. He is an excellent technician with his feet, probably the result of his extensive training in Japan. Chris Campbell, who missed the Kiev trip due to injury, and Leroy Smith and Greg Gibson, who gained silver medals in Kiev, should also be prominent freestyle contenders for the United States.

In the Greco-Roman events, Mark Fuller is probably the best hope for the United States. He won the Junior World Championship two years ago and is wrestling for the senior team. Fuller has beaten some of the best wrestlers in the world, including several top Hungarians and East Germans. But this style of wrestling is still seriously underdeveloped in the United States and the Eastern Europeans, led by the Soviet Union, will again dominate, challenged only by West Germany and Japan.

28

YACHTING

— 28 —

1984 VENUE

The Long Beach Marina will be headquarters for the Olympic yachting events, the only sport for which no tickets are sold. The Pacific Ocean off Long Beach has long been the site of much sailing activity, including the 1932 Olympic yachting competition. Gentle onshore breezes, from the west–southwest, are fairly reliable in the summer months, as is the consistent Alaskan current that moves down the coast of the Western United States.

EVENTS AND SCHEDULE

All Classes

First Race	July 31
Second Race	August 1
Third Race	August 2
Fourth Race	August 3
Fifth Race	August 6
Sixth Race	August 7
Seventh Race	August 8

HISTORY OF YACHTING

The racing of ships under sail is as old as the boats themselves. The competitive spirit of the ancient Greeks inspired the racing of sailing ships in the Mediterranean during the classical period.

The word "Yacht" is an English derivation of the Dutch "Haght," the word for the small, fast cargo boats used in Holland as early as the fifteenth century. According to *The Diary of Samuel Pepys*, King Charles II of England raced his brother, the Duke of York, in 1662 along the Thames in a small yacht imported from Holland. Soon the English nobility adopted the royal sport, which has remained popular ever since.

The involvement of the United States in international yachting began in 1851 when the New York Yacht Club built a 101-foot schooner, "America," and sailed her to England where she defeated the best British sailing ships. This was the genesis of the America's Cup, the most prestigious yachting race held today.

OLYMPIC HISTORY

Sailing has been an Olympic sport since 1896, when the first modern Games were held in Athens. Not much is known about the results or the types of boats used. It seems many of the planned events were canceled due to bad weather and lack of entries. Olympic yacht racing was not held in 1904, presumably because of difficulties involved in transporting the boats to St. Louis.

Early yachting contests suffered from lack of craft standardization until 1906, when the International Yacht Racing Union was formed and formulas of length, girth, and sail areas were agreed upon. These were first applied in the 1908 Olympic Games, in which yachting was held off the Isle of Wight, England. This was also the year motor boats made their appearance in the Olympics for the first and only time.

Interest and participation grew steadily throughout post-World War I Olympic Games, and by the 1928 Olympic regatta, twenty-three countries were represented. The Northern European maritime nations, Norway, Sweden, Holland, and Britain, continued to dominate the competition.

Not surprisingly, things were much different in 1932, when yachtsmen from eleven countries competed in the Pacific Ocean near Los Angeles. The United States won its first yachting medals, capturing the Star Class and the eight-meter category.

Olympic yachting returned to Northern European waters at Kiel, Germany in 1936, where twenty-six nations took part. There were many newcomers to the sport, all taking advantage of sailboats provided by the host country's Olympic Organizing Committee.

Paul Elvstrom of Denmark revolutionized competitive small boat sailing by introducing land training and athleticism into a sport in which very little physical conditioning had been thought necessary. His physical conditioning permitted him to hang over the side of the boat or "hike" for long periods of time. The hike allows the sailor to take full advantage of the wind without capsizing the boat.

Elvstrom, who practiced in stormy weather in order to test and exercise his skills, won eleven world championships between 1957 and 1974. His Olympic record includes four gold medals, one in each of the Games between 1948 and 1960.

The 1952 Olympic yachting events saw more participants than ever before in five sailing events. A contest was held to design a new singlehanded sailboat to replace the previous Firefly Class. Ricard Sarby, a competitor in the 1948 Olympics, produced the design for the Finn, named for the nation in which it was first used in Olympic competition. The Finn has been a part of the Olympics ever since. Sarby excelled in this event, winning the bronze medal in the Helsinki yachting competition.

At Helsinki, the USSR entered Olympic yachting competition for the first time. The large number of nations competing affirmed the efforts of the IOC to establish yachting as a popular sport, not one to be enjoyed only by the wealthy.

The Soviets won their first gold medal in the 1960 Olympic competition at Naples, taking the Star Class in an American built boat. The Dragon Class gold medal was won by Crown Prince Constantine of Greece. It was the first Olympic yachting medal to be won by his country. His mother, Queen Frederika, was at quayside to congratulate him and in the traditional manner, pushed him into the water. Also in the bay of Naples, Paul Elvstrom of Denmark won his third straight gold medal in the Finn Class.

In 1972, yachting returned to Kiel, the city where the '36 Olympic regatta had been held. A lavish new facility had been built for the yachtsmen from forty-two countries. Medals were well distributed, ending earlier European dominance. The traditional European yachting nations won only two medals. Australia collected two and the United States and USSR went home with one apiece.

The United States' win went to Harry "Buddy" Melges, at the helm in the Soling Class. He previously won a bronze medal, sailing a Flying Dutchman in Tokyo and posted a wide variety of world titles and international regattas in the intervening years. Melges recently won two more world championships in the Star Class.

In 1976 at Kingston, Ontario, five nations again shared six gold medals, West Germany topping the count with two. The Soling Class competition was the closest ever in Olympic yachting. John Knowles of the U.S. started the final leg of the course in sixth place and failed by the narrowest margin to catch the Danish crew, finishing second. Tie-breaking procedures gave the bronze medal to East Germany with the same point score.

In Moscow, despite the absence of traditionally strong yachting countries due to the boycott, the USSR and Eastern European countries failed to dominate the Olympic regatta. The medals were awarded to yachtsmen from twelve countries, the widest medal distribution yet in the sport.

OLYMPIC CLASSES

Soling

The largest of the seven Olympic classes with a length of 8.2 meters (26 feet 9 inches) and a sail area of 21.7 square meters. It has a keel and carries a three-man crew. The Soling is the most tactical of Olympic boats.

Star

Adopted first at the Los Angeles Olympics in 1932, it is the oldest class of boat now in Olympic competition. It measures 6.90 meters (22 feet 8 inches) in length, has a fixed keel, and carries 285 square feet of sail. It is sailed by a crew of two. The Star is the class in which the United States has enjoyed the most success in world championship competition.

Flying Dutchman

The Flying Dutchman is a centerboard dinghy, measuring 6.60 meters long and requiring a crew of two. This class is usually dominated by Europeans and is probably the weakest U.S. event. Considered the fastest two-man dinghy in the world, its performance requires the utmost of skill and teamwork from the crew.

470

Another centerboard dinghy, this light and small two-man boat made its first Olympic appearance at Kingston on Lake Ontario in 1976. The 470 has become popular as a result of its uncomplicated design and capability to double as a recreational and competitive sailboat.

Finn

This is the smallest Olympic class (14 feet 9 inches long) and the only boat other than the windglider sailed by a single person. As a result, this event requires the most physical endurance of the Olympic classes, providing a most athletic form of yacht racing. The Olympic organizers of the host country traditionally provide the Finns for all competitors.

Tornado

This two-man, twin hulled, Catamaran-type boat made its Olympic debut in 1976. The Tornado is the fastest of the Olympic classes, with top speeds of 30 knots under ideal conditions.

Windglider

Boardsailing will be making its first Olympic appearance in 1984. It is a physically demanding event and among the most affordable forms of sailing. A fleet of identical windglider sailboards is provided by the organizing committee, each made of fiberglass with a board length of 3.90 meters, or just under 13 feet.

SAILING SKILLS

Good sailing requires agility, strength, and plenty of good judgment. To attain complete command of one's sailboat, the sailor must know the technical capabilities of the craft and be able to judge the effects of the wind and wave pattern.

The talented sailor has quick reactions and is very observant. He has good eyesight to perceive the subtle variations of wind and water which tell him things lesser skilled yachtsmen do not see. He possesses an ability for sensing how the

Sailors experience the challenge of wind and water.

Yachting: Star class.

boat is performing relative to the elements, enabling him to adjust sail shape to gain maximum speed.

At the start of each race, boats congregate behind the starting marker, maneuvering for position as the start time approaches. The proximity to the starting line, the angle at which each boat is moving in relationship to the wind, and the degree to which its air is effected by the other boats are all vital to the outcome.

In each race, competitors sail the upwind leg three times. They sail downwind either on reaches (across the wind) or runs (more directly with the wind). Each aspect of sailing requires different skills.

Because of the unpredictable nature of the wind, luck sometimes plays a part in the placings of the events. Such variations of wind tend to be balanced since the sailors race each other seven times, accumulating points in each race. The best six scores of the seven races are totaled to establish the final placings and determine the medalists.

The Olympic scoring system rewards first place with zero (0) points, second 3 points, third 5.7 points, fourth 8 points, fifth 10 points, sixth 11.7 points, and seventh and above scores the placing plus 6 points.

Women are eligible to enter and compete on equal terms with men. However, few women have done so successfully. No woman has yet to win an Olympic medal. While some classes, particularly Finn and Boardsailing, require a great deal of physical strength, others, especially the 470, are not as demanding and actually favor smaller sailors.

THE COURSE

Triangular courses are laid out for all yachting categories. All race around the triangle at least once in a counterclockwise direction, which brings them back near the starting line. Next, they make the upwind first leg again, round the marker, and return on a direct run toward the start. The race is finished by taking the first leg into the wind for a third time. All classes of Olympic yacht racing follow the same sequence: "triangle," "up," "back," and "up."

Each course is determined by the judges a few minutes before a race begins so any shifting wind pattern is accounted for, assuring that the windward legs will be directly into the prevailing wind. The course can be altered if the wind changes direction.

A yacht and its crew will be disqualified if, during the course of the race, they violate right-of-way rules, whether or not a collision takes place. If a marker is hit, it must be rerounded.

STATUS OF YACHTING

There are several issues unique to the sport of yachting. Sailboat racing is almost exclusively a participant sport, since spectators must be kept far from the competition so as not to hinder the boats. As a result, those most able to view a race are the competitors themselves. Therefore, the sport gets little attention from the media.

The IOC has made great efforts to hold contests in events with affordable equipment, but technology necessary for competitive Olympic sailing is still expensive as are the costs of shipping boats around the world to Olympic venues. A Finn costs around $3,500, a fully equipped Soling $14,000, and a Flying Dutchman a bit more. But equipment has a high resale value; thus, sailboat racing does not cost much more than equestrian or kayaking, or many other recreational activities.

Because of the rapid worldwide growth of boardsailing, the International Yacht Racing Union added the event to the sailing program in Los Angeles. Boardsailing equipment is less expensive than other sailboats, so more individual participation and enjoyment of wind and water is encouraged.

1984 PROSPECTS

The limit of one boat per class in each nation's fleet means potential Olympic medalists must first win selection trials before they can set sail in the Olympic Games. In many traditionally powerful yachting nations, Britain, Holland, Germany, and the United States, trials are as competitive as Olympic races themselves.

The U.S. trials are to be staged in the spring of 1984, off Long Beach, in the same waters where the Olympic events will be held. To reward consistency and eliminate the element of luck, each class trial will entail ten races, scored as one series, with two races discarded in computing the score.

United States medal prospects looked good following the 1982 world championships, in which the United States won four of the seven classes. In the 1983 pre-Olympic Regatta, held to enable sailors to practice on Olympic courses, U.S. sailors were left in the wake of their foreign rivals, winning only two classes. Regardless, the United States should have a good year in 1984 and maintain their "unofficial" team leadership of Olympic yachting.

Soling Prospects

The United States has been very successful with the Soling. Several U.S. sailors could have a shot at a medal, but only one boat can carry the U.S. banner. Dave Curtis, the 1979 Pan Am winner, showed good form in 1983 with a win in the pre-Olympic Regatta, where the United States went 1–2–4–5. But Curtis was runner-up to Robin Haines of San Diego in the world championships earlier in 1983. Buddy Melges, the 1972 Olympic champion, and Australian Mark Bethwaite will lead the other challengers.

Star Prospects

The 1982 World Champion, Antonio Gorostegui of Spain, successfully defended his title in '83 when the Star Class championships were held off Marina del Rey,

California. Gorostegui overcame a premature start which caused his elimination in the second race. Thereafter, his consistent helmsmanship enabled him to hold off the challenge of Joachim Griese of West Germany, who finished second. Bill Buchan was the top U.S. yachtsman, finishing third.

Flying Dutchman Prospects

Britain's Jonathon Richards was so far ahead in the pre-Olympic Regatta, he just pulled his boat up on the beach and watched the seventh race since his lead was unassailable. "Our trials will be tougher than this competition," he said.

The Flying Dutchman is the United States' weakest class, and is traditionally dominated by Europeans. The United States, however, is making a concerted effort to catch up. With the introduction of a domestic "high-tech" boat-building effort, as well as a team training concept, U.S. fortunes have improved. Kelson Elam finished seventh in the 1983 World Championship, ahead of 1982 champion Batzill of Germany. Although there's still a long way to go, it was the best U.S. showing in ten years.

470 Prospects

Dave Ullman of Southern California is a three-time world champion and will be sailing in familiar waters in the Games. Steve Benjamin has been the dominant 470 skipper over the last three years. If their boat is challenged, it will be by one of several successful crews from New Zealand. The Kiwi 470's skippers, current world champion Dave Barnes, Murray Jones, and Chris Dixon, will provide formidable competition.

Finn Prospects

Lasse Hjortnaes of Denmark swept the major events of 1982 and is considered the man to beat, despite the fact that he lost to Paul Ven Cleve of the United States in the world championships off Milwaukee. Hjortnaes, at 6 feet 4½ inches and 210 pounds, characterizes the physical demands of Finn sailing. A large, strong man, he is able to counterbalance the craft and remain fully hiked out, often for many hours. Hjortnaes trains very hard, sailing year-round. "Sometimes the water is blocked with ice," he says, "and you can't get out, but that's only a few days a year."

U.S. prospects have slipped since U.S. sailors dominated the world-class Finn event in 1978–80.

Tornado Prospects

The team of Randy Smyth and Jay Glaser of Newport Beach, California, is undefeated in major regattas for over three years and has dominated the last three world championships. There is no reason to believe their string of successes will stop. Their speed is still improving as a result of greater concentration, an essential skill at Tornado speeds. Reg White, Britain's 1976 Olympic champion, will be the most experienced of the challengers.

Boardsailing Prospects

This is a type of sailboard of which the windsurfer equipment is most common in the United States. In Europe, boardsailing is contested on lakes in round-the-buoy races and utilizes windglider equipment.

Boardsailing is currently dominated by Europeans. Stephen Van den Berg is the 1982 world champion, considered to be well ahead of his rivals. At the 1983 OCR pre-Olympic Regatta, Van den Berg again led the boardsailing ahead of Klaus Maran of Italy. No U.S. boardsailor finished in the top ten.

SELECTED OLYMPIC RECORDS

This section lists the 1896—1980 gold medalists in events that are to be contested in the 1984 Olympic Games in Los Angeles.

COUNTRY ABBREVIATIONS

ARG	Argentina	JAM	Jamaica
AUS	Australia	JPN	Japan
AUT	Austria	KEN	Kenya
BAH	Bahamas	KOR	South Korea
BEL	Belgium	LUX	Luxembourg
BRA	Brazil	MEX	Mexico
BUL	Bulgaria	NOR	Norway
CAN	Canada	NZL	New Zealand
CUB	Cuba	PAK	Pakistan
CZE	Czechoslovakia	PER	Peru
DEN	Denmark	POL	Poland
EGY	Egypt	PRK	North Korea
EST	Estonia	ROM	Romania
ETH	Ethiopia	SAF	South Africa
FIN	Finland	SPN	Spain
FRA	France	SUI	Switzerland
GBR	Great Britain	SWE	Sweden
GDR	German Democratic Republic *	TRI	Trinidad & Tobago
GER	German Federal Republic	TUN	Tunisia
GRE	Greece	TUR	Turkey
HOL	Holland (Netherlands)	UGA	Uganda
HUN	Hungary	URU	Uruguay
IND	India	USA	United States of America
IRL	Ireland	URS	Soviet Union
IRN	Iran	VEN	Venezuela
ITA	Italy	YUG	Yugoslavia
		ZIM	Zimbabwe

* 1968 on

METRIC CONVERSION

1 centimeter = 0.394 inch
1 meter = 3.281 feet
100 meters = 109.36 yards
1,500 meters = 0.93 mile
1 kilogram = 2.2046 pounds

OLYMPIC HISTORICAL CHART

Olympiad	Year	Site	Sports	Contests	Nations	Athletes
I	1896	Athens	10	42	13	295
II	1900	Paris	14	60	20	1,066
III	1904	St. Louis	13	67	10	496
IV	1908	London	21	104	22	2,059
V	1912	Stockholm	15	106	28	2,541
VI	1916	World War I	*			
VII	1920	Antwerp	20	154	29	2,606
VIII	1924	Paris	20	137	44	3,092
IX	1928	Amsterdam	17	120	46	3,015
X	1932	Los Angeles	17	124	37	1,408
XI	1936	Berlin	22	142	49	4,069
XII	1940	World War II	*			
XIII	1944	World War II	*			
XIV	1948	London	19	138	59	4,689
XV	1952	Helsinki	19	149	69	4,925
XVI	1956	Melbourne	17	145	67	3,184
		Stockholm	1**	3	29	159
XVII	1960	Rome	18	150	84	5,337
XVIII	1964	Tokyo	20	162	94	5,558
XIX	1968	Mexico City	18	182	112	6,123
XX	1972	Munich	21	195	122	7,830
XXI	1976	Montreal	21	198	95	6,189
XXII	1980	Moscow	21	203	80	5,503
XXIII	1984	Los Angeles	21	220		

* Canceled
** Equestrian events only, held in Stockholm

ARCHERY

Men

1972	John Williams	USA	2,528
1976	Darrell Pace	USA	2,571
1980	Tomi Poikolainen	FIN	2,455
1984			

Women

1972	Doreen Wilber	USA	2,424
1976	Luann Ryon	USA	2,499
1980	Keto Losaberidze	URS	2,491
1984			

ATHLETICS (Men)

100 Meters

1896	Thomas Burke	USA	12.0
1900	Francis Jarvis	USA	11.0
1904	Archie Hahn	USA	11.0
1908	Reginald Walker	SAF	10.8
1912	Ralph Craig	USA	10.8
1920	Charles Paddock	USA	10.8
1924	Harold Abrahams	GBR	10.6
1928	Percy Williams	CAN	10.8
1932	Eddie Tolan	USA	10.3
1936	Jesse Owens	USA	10.3
1948	Harrison Dillard	USA	10.3
1952	Lindy Remigino	USA	10.4
1956	Bobby Morrow	USA	10.5
1960	Armin Hary	GER	10.2
1964	Robert Hayes	USA	10.0
1968	James Hines	USA	9.95
1972	Valeri Borzov	URS	10.14
1976	Hasely Crawford	TRI	10.06
1980	Allan Wells	GBR	10.25
1984			

200 Meters

1900	Walter Tewksbury	USA	22.2
1904	Archie Hahn	USA	21.6
1908	Robert Kerr	CAN	22.6
1912	Ralph Craig	USA	21.7
1920	Allan Woodring	USA	22.0
1924	Jackson Scholz	USA	21.6
1928	Percy Williams	CAN	21.8
1932	Eddie Tolan	USA	21.2
1936	Jesse Owens	USA	20.7
1948	Mel Patton	USA	21.1
1952	Andrew Stanfield	USA	20.7
1956	Bobby Morrow	USA	20.6
1960	Livio Berruti	ITA	20.5
1964	Henry Carr	USA	20.3
1968	Tommie Smith	USA	19.83
1972	Valeri Borzov	URS	20.0
1976	Don Quarrie	JAM	20.23
1980	Pietro Mennea	ITA	20.19
1984			

400 Meters

1896	Thomas Burke	USA	54.2
1900	Maxwell Long	USA	49.4
1904	Harry Hillman	USA	49.2
1908	Wyndham Halswelle	GBR	50.0
1912	Charles Reidpath	USA	48.2
1920	Bevil Rudd	SAF	49.6
1924	Eric Liddell	GBR	47.6
1928	Ray Barbuti	USA	47.8
1932	William Carr	USA	46.2
1936	Archie Williams	USA	46.5
1948	Arthur Wint	JAM	46.2
1952	George Rhoden	JAM	45.9
1956	Charles Jenkins	USA	46.7
1960	Otis Davis	USA	44.9
1964	Michael Larrabee	USA	45.1
1968	Lee Evans	USA	43.86
1972	Vincent Matthews	USA	44.66
1976	Alberto Juantorena	CUB	44.26
1980	Viktor Markin	URS	44.60
1984			

800 Meters

1896	Edwin Flack	AUS	2:11.0
1900	Alfred Tysoe	GBR	2:01.2
1904	James Lightbody	USA	1:56.0
1908	Melvin Sheppard	USA	1:52.8
1912	James Meredith	USA	1:51.9
1920	Albert Hill	GBR	1:53.4
1924	Douglas Lowe	GBR	1:52.4
1928	Douglas Lowe	GBR	1:51.8
1932	Thomas Hampson	GBR	1:49.7
1936	John Woodruff	USA	1:52.9
1948	Mal Whitfield	USA	1:49.2
1952	Mal Whitfield	USA	1:49.2
1956	Thomas Courtney	USA	1:47.7
1960	Peter Snell	NZL	1:46.3
1964	Peter Snell	NZL	1:45.1
1968	Ralph Doubell	AUS	1:44.3
1972	David Wottle	USA	1:45.9
1976	Alberto Juantorena	CUB	1:43.5
1980	Steve Ovett	GBR	1:45.4
1984			

1,500 Meters

1896	Edwin Flack	AUS	4:33.2
1900	Charles Bennett	GBR	4:06.2
1904	James Lightbody	USA	4:05.4
1908	Melvin Sheppard	USA	4:03.4
1912	Arnold Jackson	GBR	3:56.8
1920	Albert Hill	GBR	4:01.8
1924	Paavo Nurmi	FIN	3:53.6
1928	Harri Larva	FIN	3:53.2
1932	Luigi Beccali	ITA	3:51.2
1936	Jack Lovelock	NZL	3:47.8
1948	Henry Eriksson	SWE	3:49.8
1952	Joseph Barthel	LUX	3:45.1
1956	Ronald Delaney	IRL	3:41.2
1960	Herbert Elliott	AUS	3:35.6
1964	Peter Snell	NZL	3:38.1
1968	Kipchoge Keino	KEN	3:34.9
1972	Pekka Vasala	FIN	3:36.3
1976	John Walker	NZL	3:39.17
1980	Sebastian Coe	GBR	3:38.4
1984			

3,000–Meter Steeplechase

1900	George Orton	USA	7:34.4	†
1904	James Lightbody	USA	7:39.6	†
1908	Arthur Russell	GBR	10:47.8	§
1920	Percy Hodge	GBR	10:00.4	
1924	Ville Ritola	FIN	9:33.6	
1928	Toivo Loukola	FIN	9:21.8	
1932	Volmari Iso-Hollo	FIN	10:33.4	*
1936	Volmari Iso-Hollo	FIN	9:03.8	
1948	Thore Sjostrand	SWE	9:04.6	
1952	Horace Ashenfelter	USA	8:45.4	
1956	Chris Brasher	GBR	8:41.2	
1960	Zdzislaw Kryszkowiak	POL	8:34.2	
1964	Gaston Roelants	BEL	8:30.8	
1968	Amos Biwott	KEN	8:51.0	
1972	Kipchoge Keino	KEN	8:23.6	
1976	Anders Garderud	SWE	8:08.02	
1980	Bronislaw Malinowski	POL	8:09.7	
1984				

* Extra lap run in error.
† Distance only 2,500 m.
§ Distance 3,200 m.

5,000 Meters

1912	Hannes Kolehmainen	FIN	14:36.6
1920	Joseph Guillemot	FRA	14:55.6
1924	Paavo Nurmi	FIN	14:31.2
1928	Ville Ritola	FIN	14:38.0
1932	Lauri Lehtinen	FIN	14:30.0
1936	Gunnar Hockert	FIN	14:22.2
1948	Gaston Reiff	BEL	14:17.6
1952	Emil Zatopek	CZE	14:06.6
1956	Vladimir Kuts	URS	13:39.6
1960	Murray Halberg	NZL	13:43.4
1964	Robert Schul	USA	13:48.8
1968	Mohamed Gammoudi	TUN	14:05.0
1972	Lasse Viren	FIN	13:26.4
1976	Lasse Viren	FIN	13:24.76
1980	Miruts Yifter	ETH	13:21.0
1984			

10,000 Meters

1920	Paavo Nurmi	FIN	31:45.8
1924	Ville Ritola	FIN	30:23.2
1928	Paavo Nurmi	FIN	30:18.8
1932	Janusz Kusocinski	POL	30:11.4
1936	Ilmari Salminen	FIN	30:15.4
1948	Emil Zatopek	CZE	29:59.6
1952	Emil Zatopek	CZE	29:17.0
1956	Vladimir Kuts	URS	28:45.6
1960	Pyotr Bolotnikov	URS	28:32.2
1964	William Mills	USA	28:24.4
1968	Naftali Temu	KEN	29:27.4
1972	Lasse Viren	FIN	27:38.4
1976	Lasse Viren	FIN	27:40.38
1980	Miruts Yifter	ETH	27:42.7
1984			

Marathon

1896	Spyridon Loues	GRE	2:58:50.0
1900	Michel Theato	FRA	2:59:45.0
1904	Thomas Hicks	USA	3:28:53.0
1908	John Hayes	USA	2:55:18.4
1912	Kenneth McArthur	SAF	2:36:54.8
1920	Hannes Kolehmainen	FIN	2:32:35.8
1924	Albin Stenroos	FIN	2:41:22.6
1928	Mohamed El Ouafi	FRA	2:32:57.0
1932	Juan Zabala	ARG	2:31:36.0
1936	Kitei Son	JPN	2:29:19.2
1948	Delfo Cabrera	ARG	2:34:51.6
1952	Emil Zatopek	CZE	2:23:03.2
1956	Alain Mimoun	FRA	2:25:00.0
1960	Abebe Bikila	ETH	2:15:16.2
1964	Abebe Bikila	ETH	2:12:11.2
1968	Mamo Wolde	ETH	2:20:26.4
1972	Frank Shorter	USA	2:12:19.8
1976	Waldemar Cierpinski	GDR	2:09:55.0
1980	Waldemar Cierpinski	GDR	2:11:03.0
1984			

110–Meter Hurdles

1896	Thomas Curtis	USA	17.6
1900	Alvin Kraenzlein	USA	15.4
1904	Frederick Schule	USA	16.0
1908	Forrest Smithson	USA	15.0
1912	Frederick Kelley	USA	15.1
1920	Earl Thomson	CAN	14.8
1924	Daniel Kinsey	USA	15.0
1928	Sydney Atkinson	SAF	14.8
1932	George Saling	USA	14.6
1936	Forrest Towns	USA	14.2
1948	William Porter	USA	13.9
1952	Harrison Dillard	USA	13.7
1956	Lee Calhoun	USA	13.5
1960	Lee Calhoun	USA	13.8
1964	Hayes Jones	USA	13.6
1968	Willie Davenport	USA	13.33
1972	Rodney Milburn	USA	13.24
1976	Guy Drut	FRA	13.30
1980	Thomas Munkelt	GDR	13.39
1984			

400–Meter Hurdles

1900	Walter Tewksbury	USA	57.6
1904	Harry Hillman	USA	53.0
1908	Charles Bacon	USA	55.0
1920	Frank Loomis	USA	54.0
1924	F. Morgan Taylor	USA	52.6
1928	David Burghley	GBR	53.4
1932	Robert Tisdall	IRL	51.8
1936	Glenn Hardin	USA	52.4
1948	Roy Cochran	USA	51.1
1952	Charles Moore	USA	50.8
1956	Glenn Davis	USA	50.1
1960	Glenn Davis	USA	49.3
1964	Warren Cawley	USA	49.6
1968	David Hemery	GBR	48.12
1972	John Akii-Bua	UGA	47.82
1976	Edwin Moses	USA	47.64
1980	Volker Beck	GDR	48.70
1984			

20–Kilometer Walk

1956	Leonid Spirin	URS	1:31:27.4
1960	Vladimir Golubnichy	URS	1:34:07.2
1964	Kenneth Matthews	GBR	1:29:34.0
1968	Vladimir Golubnichy	URS	1:33:58.4
1972	Peter Frenkel	GDR	1:26:42.4
1976	Daniel Bautista	MEX	1:24:40.6
1980	Maurizio Damilano	ITA	1:23:35.5
1984			

50–Kilometer Walk

1932	Thomas Green	GBR	4:50:10.0
1936	Harold Whitlock	GBR	4:30:41.4
1948	John Ljunggren	SWE	4:41:52.0
1952	Giuseppe Dordoni	ITA	4:28:07.8
1956	Norman Read	NZL	4:30:42.8
1960	Donald Thompson	GBR	4:25:30.0
1964	Abdon Pamich	ITA	4:11:12.4
1968	Chrisoph Hohne	GDR	4:20:13.6
1972	Bern Kannenberg	GER	3:56:11.6
1980	Hartwig Gauder	GDR	3:49:24.0
1984			

4 X 100–Meter Relay

1912	Great Britain	42.4
1920	United States of America	42.2
1924	United States of America	41.0
1928	United States of America	41.0
1932	United States of America	40.0
1936	United States of America	39.8
1948	United States of America	40.6
1952	United States of America	40.1
1956	United States of America	39.5
1960	Germany	39.5
1964	United States of America	39.0
1968	United States of America	38.2
1972	United States of America	38.19
1976	United States of America	38.33
1980	Soviet Union	38.26
1984		

4 X 400–Meter Relay

1908	United States of America	3:29.4
1912	United States of America	3:16.6
1920	Great Britain	3:22.2
1924	United States of America	3:16.0
1928	United States of America	3:14.2
1932	United States of America	3:08.2
1936	Great Britain	3:09.0
1948	United States of America	3:10.4
1952	Jamaica	3:03.9
1956	United States of America	3:04.8
1960	United States of America	3:02.2
1964	United States of America	3:00.7
1968	United States of America	2:56.1
1972	Kenya	2:59.8
1976	United States of America	2:58.56
1980	Soviet Union	3:01.10
1984		

High Jump

1896	Ellery Clark	USA	1.81 m	5 ft. 11¼ in.
1900	Irving Baxter	USA	1.90 m	6 ft. 2¾ in.
1904	Samuel Jones	USA	1.80 m	5 ft. 11 in.
1908	Harry Porter	USA	1.90 m	6 ft. 2¾ in.
1912	Alma Richards	USA	1.93 m	6 ft. 4 in.
1920	Richmond Landon	USA	1.94 m	6 ft. 4¼ in.
1924	Harold Osborn	USA	1.98 m	6 ft. 6 in.
1928	Robert King	USA	1.94 m	6 ft. 4¼ in.
1932	Duncan McNaughton	CAN	1.97 m	6 ft. 5½ in.
1936	Cornelius Johnson	USA	2.03 m	6 ft. 7¾ in.
1948	John Winter	AUS	1.98 m	6 ft. 6 in.
1952	Walter Davis	USA	2.04 m	6 ft. 8½ in.
1956	Charles Dumas	USA	2.12 m	6 ft. 11¼ in.
1960	Robert Shavlakadze	URS	2.16 m	7 ft. 1 in.
1964	Valery Brumel	URS	2.18 m	7 ft. 1¾ in.
1968	Dick Fosbury	USA	2.24 m	7 ft. 4¼ in.
1972	Yuri Tarmak	URS	2.23 m	7 ft. 3¾ in.
1976	Jacek Wszola	POL	2.25 m	7 ft. 4½ in.
1980	Gerd Wessig	GDR	2.36 m	7 ft. 8¾ in.
1984				

Pole Vault

1896	William W. Hoyt	USA	3.30 m	10 ft. 9¾ in.
1900	Irving Baxter	USA	3.30 m	10 ft. 9¾ in.
1904	Charles Dvorak	USA	3.50 m	11 ft. 6 in.
1908	Albert Gilbert	USA	3.71 m	12 ft. 2 in.
	& Edward Cook	USA	3.71 m	12 ft. 2 in.
1912	Harry Babcock	USA	3.95 m	12 ft. 11½ in.
1920	Frank Foss	USA	4.09 m	12 ft. 5½ in.
1924	Lee Barnes	USA	3.95 m	12 ft. 11½ in.
1928	Sabin Carr	USA	4.20 m	13 ft. 9½ in.
1932	William Miller	USA	4.32 m	14 ft. 1¾ in.
1936	Earle Meadows	USA	4.35 m	14 ft. 3¼ in.
1948	Gauinn Smith	USA	4.30 m	14 ft. 1¼ in.
1952	Bob Richards	USA	4.55 m	14 ft. 11¼ in.
1956	Bob Richards	USA	4.56 m	14 ft. 11½ in.
1960	Don Bragg	USA	4.70 m	15 ft. 5 in.
1964	Fred Hansen	USA	5.10 m	16 ft. 8¾ in.
1968	Robert Seagren	USA	5.40 m	17 ft. 8½ in.
1972	Wolfgang Nordwig	GDR	5.50 m	18 ft. 0½ in.
1976	Tadeusz Slusarski	POL	5.50 m	18 ft. 0½ in.
1980	Wladyslaw Kozakiewicz	POL	5.78 m	18 ft. 11½ in.
1984				

Long Jump

1896	Ellery Clark	USA	6.35 m	20 ft. 10 in.
1900	Alvin Kraenzlein	USA	7.18 m	23 ft. 6¾ in.
1904	Myer Prinstein	USA	7.34 m	24 ft. 1 in.
1908	Francis Irons	USA	7.48 m	24 ft. 6½ in.
1912	Albert Gutterson	USA	7.60 m	24 ft. 11¼ in.
1920	William Pettersson	SWE	7.15 m	23 ft. 5½ in.
1924	William DeHart Hubbard	USA	7.44 m	24 ft. 5 in.
1928	Edward Hamm	USA	7.73 m	25 ft. 4¾ in.
1932	Edward Gordon	USA	7.64 m	25 ft. 0¾ in.
1936	Jesse Owens	USA	8.06 m	26 ft. 5¼ in.
1948	Willie Steele	USA	7.83 m	25 ft. 8 in.
1952	Jerome Biffle	USA	7.57 m	24 ft. 10 in.
1956	Gregory Bell	USA	7.83 m	25 ft. 8¼ in.
1960	Ralph Boston	USA	8.12 m	26 ft. 7¾ in.
1964	Lynn Davies	GBR	8.07 m	26 ft. 5¾ in.
1968	Bob Beamon	USA	8.90 m	29 ft. 2½ in.
1972	Randy Williams	USA	8.24 m	27 ft. 0½ in.
1976	Arnie Robinson	USA	8.35 m	27 ft. 4¾ in.
1980	Lutz Dombrowski	GDR	8.54 m	28 ft. 0¼ in.
1984				

Triple Jump

1896	James Connolly	USA	13.71 m	44 ft. 11¾ in.
1900	Myer Prinstein	USA	14.47 m	47 ft. 4¼ in.
1904	Myer Prinstein	USA	14.33 m	47 ft. 0 in.
1908	Timothy Ahearne	GBR	14.91 m	48 ft. 11¼ in.
1912	Gustaf Lindblom	SWE	14.76 m	48 ft. 5 in.
1920	Vilho Tuulos	FIN	14.50 m	47 ft. 7 in.
1924	Anthony Winter	AUS	15.52 m	50 ft. 11¼ in.
1928	Mikio Oda	JPN	15.21 m	49 ft. 10¾ in.
1932	Chuhei Nambu	JPN	15.72 m	51 ft. 7 in.
1936	Naoto Tajimi	JPN	16.00 m	52 ft. 5¾ in.
1948	Arne Ahman	SWE	15.40 m	50 ft. 6¼ in.
1952	Ferreira da Silva	BRA	16.22 m	53 ft. 2½ in.
1956	Ferreira da Silva	BRA	16.35 m	53 ft. 7½ in.
1960	Jozef Szmidt	POL	16.81 m	55 ft. 1¾ in.
1964	Jozef Szmidt	POL	16.85 m	55 ft. 3¼ in.
1968	Viktor Saneev	URS	17.39 m	57 ft. 0¾ in.
1972	Viktor Saneev	URS	17.35 m	56 ft. 11 in.
1976	Viktor Saneev	URS	17.29 m	56 ft. 8¾ in.
1980	Jaak Uudmae	URS	17.35 m	56 ft. 11 in.
1984				

Shot Put

1896	Robert Garrett	USA	11.22 m	36 ft. 9¾ in.
1900	Richard Sheldon	USA	14.10 m	46 ft. 3 in.
1904	Ralph Rose	USA	14.81 m	48 ft. 7 in.
1908	Ralph Rose	USA	14.21 m	46 ft. 7½ in.
1912	Patrick McDonald	USA	15.34 m	10 ft. 4 in.
1920	Ville Porhola	FIN	14.81 m	48 ft. 7 in.
1924	Clarence Houser	USA	14.99 m	49 ft. 2½ in.
1928	John Kuck	USA	15.87 m	52 ft. 0¾ in.
1932	Leo Sexton	USA	16.01 m	52 ft. 6 in.
1936	Hans Woellke	GER	16.20 m	53 ft. 1¾ in.
1948	Wilbur Thompson	USA	17.12 m	56 ft. 2 in.
1952	Parry O'Brien	USA	17.41 m	57 ft. 1½ in.
1956	Parry O'Brien	USA	18.57 m	60 ft. 11 in.
1960	William Nieder	USA	19.68 m	64 ft. 6¾ in.
1964	Dallas Long	USA	20.33 m	66 ft. 8¼ in.
1968	Randy Matson	USA	20.54 m	67 ft. 4¾ in.
1972	Wladyslaw Komar	POL	21.18 m	69 ft. 6 in.
1976	Udo Beyer	GDR	21.05 m	69 ft. 0¾ in.
1980	Vladimir Kiselyov	URS	21.35 m	70 ft. 0½ in.
1984				

Discus Throw

1896	Robert Garrett	USA	29.15 m	95 ft. 7 in.
1900	Rudolf Bauer	HUN	36.04 m	118 ft. 2 in.
1904	Martin Sheridan	USA	39.28 m	128 ft. 10 in.
1908	Martin Sheridan	USA	40.89 m	134 ft. 2 in.
1912	Armas Taipale	FIN	45.21 m	148 ft. 4 in.
1920	Elmer Niklander	FIN	44.69 m	146 ft. 7 in.
1924	Clarence Houser	USA	46.16 m	151 ft. 5 in.
1928	Clarence Houser	USA	47.32 m	155 ft. 2 in.
1932	John Anderson	USA	49.49 m	162 ft. 4 in.
1936	Kenneth Carpenter	USA	50.48 m	165 ft. 7 in.
1948	Adolofo Consolini	ITA	52.78 m	173 ft. 2 in.
1952	Sim Iness	USA	55.03 m	180 ft. 6 in.
1956	Al Oerter	USA	56.36 m	184 ft. 10 in.
1960	Al Oerter	USA	59.18 m	194 ft. 1 in.
1964	Al Oerter	USA	61.00 m	200 ft. 1 in.
1968	Al Oerter	USA	64.78 m	212 ft. 6 in.
1972	Ludvik Danek	CZE	64.40 m	211 ft. 3 in.
1976	Mac Wilkins	USA	67.50 m	221 ft. 5 in.
1980	Viktor Rasshchupkin	URS	66.64 m	218 ft. 7 in.
1984				

Hammer Throw

1900	John Flanagan	USA	49.73 m	167 ft. 4 in.
1904	John Flanagan	USA	51.23 m	168 ft. 1 in.
1908	John Flanagan	USA	51.92 m	170 ft. 4 in.
1912	Matthew McGrath	USA	54.74 m	179 ft. 7 in.
1920	Patrick Ryan	USA	52.88 m	173 ft. 5 in.
1924	Frederick Tootell	USA	53.30 m	174 ft. 10 in.
1928	Patrick O'Callaghan	IRL	51.39 m	168 ft. 7 in.
1932	Patrick O'Callaghan	IRL	53.92 m	176 ft. 11 in.
1936	Karl Hein	GER	56.49 m	185 ft. 4 in.
1948	Imre Nemeth	HUN	56.07 m	183 ft. 11 in.
1952	Jozsef Csermak	HUN	60.34 m	197 ft. 11 in.
1956	Harold Connolly	USA	63.19 m	207 ft. 3 in.
1960	Vasiliy Rudenkov	URS	67.10 m	220 ft. 1 in.
1964	Romuald Klim	URS	69.74 m	228 ft. 9 in.
1968	Gyula Zsivotzky	HUN	73.36 m	240 ft. 8 in.
1972	Anatoli Bondarchuk	URS	75.50 m	248 ft. 8 in.
1976	Yuri Sedykh	URS	77.52 m	254 ft. 4 in.
1980	Yuri Sedykh	URS	81.80 m	268 ft. 4 in.
1984				

Javelin Throw

1912	Erik Lemming	SWE	60.64 m	198 ft. 11 in.
1920	Jonni Myyra	FIN	65.78 m	215 ft. 9 in.
1924	Jonni Myyra	FIN	62.96 m	206 ft. 6 in.
1928	Erik Lundkvist	SWE	66.60 m	218 ft. 6 in.
1932	Matti Jarvinen	FIN	72.71 m	238 ft. 6 in.
1936	Gerhard Stock	GER	71.84 m	235 ft. 8 in.
1948	Tapio Rautavaara	FIN	69.77 m	228 ft. 10 in.
1952	Cy Young	USA	73.78 m	242 ft. 0 in.
1956	Egil Danielsen	NOR	85.71 m	281 ft. 2 in.
1960	Viktor Tsibulenko	URS	84.64 m	277 ft. 8 in.
1964	Pauli Nevala	FIN	82.66 m	271 ft. 2 in.
1968	Janis Lusis	URS	90.10 m	295 ft. 7 in.
1972	Klaus Wolfermann	GER	90.48 m	296 ft. 10 in.
1976	Miklos Nemeth	HUN	94.58 m	310 ft. 4 in.
1980	Dainis Kula	URS	91.20 m	299 ft. 2 in.
1984				

Decathlon

1912	Jim Thorpe and	USA		
	Hugo Wieslander	SWE	7,724	*
1920	Helge Lovland	NOR	6,803	*
1924	Harold Osborn	USA	7,710	*
1928	Paavo Yrjola	FIN	8,053	*
1932	James Bausch	USA	8,462	*
1936	Glenn Morris	USA	7,900	†
1948	Robert Mathias	USA	7,139	†
1952	Robert Mathias	USA	7,887	†
1956	Milt Campbell	USA	7,937	†
1960	Rafer Johnson	USA	8,392	†
1964	Willi Holdorf	GER	7,887	§
1968	William Toomey	USA	8,193	§
1972	Nikolai Avilov	URS	8,454	§
1976	Bruce Jenner	USA	8,618	§
1980	Daley Thompson	GBR	8,495	§
1984				

* Original scoring system used up to and including 1932 Olympic Games.
† Revised scoring system used until 1960.
§ Current scoring system introduced in 1964.

ATHLETICS (Women)

100 Meters

1928	Elizabeth Robinson	USA	12.2
1932	Stanislawa Walasiewicz	POL	11.9
1936	Helen Stephens	USA	11.5
1948	Francina Blankers-Koen	HOL	11.9
1952	Marjorie Jackson	AUS	11.5
1956	Betty Cuthbert	AUS	11.5
1960	Wilma Rudolph	USA	11.0
1964	Wyomia Tyus	USA	11.4
1968	Wyomia Tyus	USA	11.0
1972	Renate Stecher	GDR	11.07
1976	Annagret Richter	GER	11.08
1980	Ludmila Kondrateva	URS	11.06
1984			

200 Meters

1948	Francina Blankers-Koen	HOL	24.4
1952	Marjorie Jackson	AUS	23.7
1956	Betty Cuthbert	AUS	23.4
1960	Wilma Rudolph	USA	24.0
1964	Edith McGuire	USA	23.0
1968	Irena Kirszenstein	POL	22.5
1972	Renate Stecher	GDR	22.4
1976	Barbel Eckhert	GDR	22.37
1980	Barbel Eckhert-Wockel	GDR	22.03
1984			

400 Meters

1964	Betty Cuthbert	AUS	52.0
1968	Colette Besson	FRA	52.0
1972	Monika Zehrt	GDR	51.08
1976	Irena Kirzenstein-Szewinska	POL	49.29
1980	Marita Koch	GDR	48.88
1984			

800 Meters

1928	Lina Radke-Batschauer	GER	2:16.8
1960	Ludmila Schentsova	URS	2:04.3
1964	Ann Packer	GBR	2:01.1
1968	Madeline Manning	USA	2:00.9
1972	Hildergard Falck	GER	1:58.6
1976	Tatyana Kazankina	URS	1:54.94
1980	Nadezhda Olizarenko	URS	1:53.5
1984			

1,500 Meters

1972	Ludmila Bragina	URS	4:01.4
1976	Tatyana Kazankina	URS	4:05.48
1980	Tatyana Kazankina	URS	3:56.6
1984			

3,000 Meters

1984

Marathon

1984

100—Meter Hurdles

1972	Annelie Ehrhardt	GDR	12.59
1976	Johanna Schaller	GDR	12.77
1980	Vera Komisova	URS	12.56
1984			

400—Meter Hurdles

1984

4 X 100—Meter Relay

1928	Canada	48.4
1932	United States of America	47.0
1936	United States of America	46.9
1948	Holland	47.5
1952	United States of America	45.9
1956	Australia	44.5
1960	United States of America	44.5
1964	Poland	43.6
1968	United States of America	42.8
1972	German Federal Republic	42.81
1976	German Democratic Republic	42.56
1980	German Democratic Republic	41.60
1984		

4 X 400—Meter Relay

1972	German Democratic Republic	3:23.0
1976	German Democratic Republic	3:19.23
1980	Soviet Union	3:20.2
1984		

High Jump

1928	Ethel Catherwood	CAN	1.59 m	5 ft. 2¾ in.
1932	Jean Shiley	USA	1.65 m	5 ft. 5¼ in.
1936	Ibolya Csak	HUN	1.60 m	5 ft. 2¾ in.
1948	Alice Coachman	USA	1.68 m	5 ft. 6¼ in.
1952	Esther Brand	SAF	1.67 m	5 ft. 5¾ in.
1956	Mildred McDaniel	USA	1.76 m	5 ft. 9¼ in.
1960	Iolanda Balas	ROM	1.85 m	6 ft. 0¾ in.
1964	Iolanda Balas	ROM	1.90 m	6 ft. 2¾ in.
1968	Miloslava Rezkova	CZE	1.82 m	5 ft. 11¾ in.
1972	Ulrike Meyfarth	GER	1.92 m	6 ft. 3¾ in.
1976	Rosemarie Ackermann	GDR	1.93 m	6 ft. 4 in.
1980	Sara Simeoni	ITA	1.97 m	6 ft. 5½ in.
1984				

Long Jump

1948	Olga Gyarmati	HUN	5.70 m	18 ft. 8¼ in.
1952	Yvette Williams	NZL	6.24 m	20 ft. 5½ in.
1956	Elzbieta Krzesinska	POL	6.35 m	20 ft. 10 in.
1960	Vera Krepkina	URS	6.37 m	20 ft. 10¾ in.
1964	Mary Rand-Toomey	GBR	6.76 m	22 ft. 2¼ in.
1968	Victoria Viscopoleanu	ROM	6.82 m	22 ft. 4½ in.
1972	Heide Rosendahl	GER	6.78 m	22 ft. 3 in.
1976	Angela Voight	GDR	6.72 m	22 ft. 0½ in.
1980	Tatiana Kolpakova	URS	7.06 m	23 ft. 2 in.
1984				

Shot Put

1952	Galina Zybina	URS	15.28 m	50 ft. 1½ in.
1956	Tamara Tishkyevich	URS	16.59 m	54 ft. 5 in.
1960	Tamara Press	URS	17.32 m	56 ft. 9¾ in.
1964	Tamara Press	URS	18.14 m	59 ft. 6 in.
1968	Margitta Gummel	GDR	19.61 m	64 ft. 4 in.
1972	Nadezha Chizhova	URS	21.03 m	69 ft. 0 in.
1976	Ivanka Christova	BUL	21.16 m	69 ft. 5 in.
1980	Ilona Slupianek	GDR	22.41 m	73 ft. 6¼ in.
1984				

Discus Throw

1932	Lillian Copeland	USA	40.58 m	133 ft.	1 in.
1936	Gisela Mauermayer	GER	47.63 m	156 ft.	3 in.
1948	Micheline Ostermeyer	FRA	41.92 m	137 ft.	6 in.
1952	Nina Romashkova	URS	51.42 m	168 ft.	8 in.
1956	Olga Fikotova	CZE	53.69 m	176 ft.	1 in.
1960	Nina Ponomaryeva	URS	55.10 m	180 ft.	8 in.
1964	Tamara Press	URS	57.27 m	187 ft.	10 in.
1968	Lia Manoliu	ROM	58.28 m	191 ft.	2 in.
1972	Faina Melnik	URS	66.62 m	218 ft.	7 in.
1976	Evelin Schlaak	GDR	68.98 m	226 ft.	4 in.
1980	Evelin Jahl	GDR	69.96 m	229 ft.	6 in.
1984					

Javelin Throw

1932	Mildred Didrikson	USA	43.68 m	143 ft.	3 in.
1936	Tilly Fleischer	GER	45.18 m	148 ft.	2 in.
1948	Hermine Bauma	AUT	45.57 m	149 ft.	2 in.
1952	Dana Zatopkova	CZE	50.47 m	165 ft.	7 in.
1956	Inese Janzeme	URS	53.86 m	176 ft.	8 in.
1960	Elvira Ozolina	URS	55.98 m	183 ft.	8 in.
1964	Mihaela Penes	ROM	60.54 m	198 ft.	7 in.
1968	Angela Nemeth	HUN	60.36 m	198 ft.	0 in.
1972	Ruth Fuchs	GDR	63.88 m	209 ft.	7 in.
1976	Ruth Fuchs	GDR	65.94 m	216 ft.	4 in.
1980	Maria Colon	CUB	68.40 m	224 ft.	5 in.
1984					

Pentathlon / Heptathlon

1964	Irina Press	URS	5,256
1968	Ingrid Becker	GER	5,098
1972	Mary Peters	GBR	4,801
1976	Siegrun Siegl	GDR	4,745
1980	Nadezhda Tkachenko	URS	5,083
1984			

BASKETBALL

Men

1936	USA	19	CAN	8
1948	USA	65	FRA	21
1952	USA	36	URS	25
1956	USA	85	URS	55
1960	USA	81	URS	57 *
1964	USA	73	URS	59
1968	USA	65	YUG	50
1972	URS	51	USA	50
1976	USA	95	YUG	74
1980	YUG	86	ITA	77
1984				

* semifinal pool

Women

1976	URS	112	USA	77
1980	URS	104	BUL	73
1984				

BOXING

Light Flyweight

1968	Francisco Rodriguez	VEN
1972	Gyeorgy Gedo	HUN
1976	Jorge Hernandez	CUB
1980	Shamil Sabyrov	URS
1984		

Flyweight

1904	George Finnegan	USA
1920	Frank De Genaro	USA
1924	Fidel LaBarba	USA
1928	Antal Kocsis	HUN
1932	Istvan Enekes	HUN
1936	Willy Kaiser	GER
1948	Pascual Perez	ARG
1952	Nathan Brooks	USA
1956	Terence Spinks	GBR
1960	Gyula Torok	HUN
1964	Fernando Atzori	ITA
1968	Ricardo Delgado	MEX
1972	Gheorghi Kostadinov	BUL
1976	Leo Randolph	USA
1980	Petar Lessov	BUL
1984		

Bantamweight

1904	Oliver Kirk	USA
1908	Henry Thomas	GBR
1920	Clarence Walker	SAF
1924	William Smith	SAF
1928	Vittorio Tamagnini	ITA
1932	Horace Gwynne	CAN
1936	Ulderico Sergo	ITA
1948	Tibor Csik	HUN
1952	Pentti Hamalainen	FIN
1956	Wolfgang Behrendt	GER
1960	Oleg Grigoryev	URS
1964	Takao Sakurai	JPN
1968	Valeri Sokolov	URS
1972	Orlando Martinez	CUB
1976	Yong Jo Gu	PRK
1980	Juan Hernandez	CUB
1984		

Featherweight

1904	Oliver Kirk	USA
1908	Richard Gunn	GBR
1920	Paul Fritsch	FRA
1924	John Fields	USA
1928	Lambertus Van Klavern	HOL
1932	Carmelo Robledo	ARG
1936	Oscar Casanovas	ARG
1948	Ernest Formenti	ITA
1952	Jan Zachara	CZE
1956	Vladimir Safronov	URS
1960	Francesco Musso	ITA
1964	Stanislav Stepashkin	URS
1968	Antonio Roldan	MEX
1972	Boris Kusnetsov	URS
1976	Angel Herrara	CUB
1980	Rudi Fink	GDR
1984		

Lightweight

1904	Harry Spanger	USA
1908	Frederick Grace	GBR
1920	Samuel Mosberg	USA
1924	Hans Nielsen	DEN
1928	Carlo Orlandi	ITA
1932	Lawrence Stevens	SAF
1936	Imre Harangi	HUN
1948	Gerald Dreyer	SAF
1952	Aureliano Bolognesi	ITA
1956	Richard McTaggart	GBR
1960	Kazimierz Pazdzior	POL
1964	Jozef Grudzien	POL
1968	Ronald Harris	USA
1972	Jan Szczepanski	POL
1976	Howard Davis	USA
1980	Angel Herrera	CUB
1984		

Light Welterweight

1952	Charles Adkins	USA
1956	Vladimir Yengibarian	URS
1960	Bohumil Nemecek	CZE
1964	Jerzy Kulej	POL
1968	Jerzy Kulej	POL
1972	Ray Seales	USA
1976	Ray Leonard	USA
1980	Patrizio Oliva	ITA
1984		

Welterweight

1904	Albert Young	USA
1920	Albert Schneider	CAN
1924	Jean Delarge	BEL
1928	Edward Morgan	NZL
1932	Edward Flynn	USA
1936	Sten Suvio	FIN
1948	Julius Torma	CZE
1952	Zyugmunt Chychla	POL
1956	Necolae Linca	ROM
1960	Giovanni Benvenuti	ITA
1964	Marian Kasprzyk	POL
1968	Manfred Wolke	GDR
1972	Emilo Correa	CUB
1976	Jochen Bachfeld	GDR
1980	Andres Aldama	CUB
1984		

Light Middleweight

1952	Laszlo Papp	HUN
1956	Laszlo Papp	HUN
1960	Wilbert McClure	USA
1964	Boris Lagutin	URS
1968	Boris Lagutin	URS
1972	Dieter Kottysch	GER
1976	Jerzy Rybicki	POL
1980	Armando Martinez	CUB
1984		

Middleweight

1904	Charles Mayer	USA
1908	John Douglas	GBR
1920	Harry Mallin	GBR
1924	Harry Mallin	GBR
1928	Piero Toscani	ITA
1932	Carmen Barth	USA
1936	Jean Despeaux	FRA
1948	Laszlo Papp	HUN
1952	Floyd Patterson	USA
1956	Gennadiy Chatkov	URS
1960	Edward Crook	USA
1964	Valeri Popenchenko	URS
1968	Christopher Finnegan	GBR
1972	Veitchesiav Lemechev	URS
1976	Michael Spinks	USA
1980	Jose Gomez	CUB
1984		

Light Heavyweight

1920	Edward Eagan	USA
1924	Harry Mitchell	GBR
1928	Victorio Avendano	ARG
1932	David Carstens	SAF
1936	Roger Michelot	FRA
1948	George Hunter	SAF
1952	Norvel Lee	USA
1956	James Boyd	USA
1960	Cassius Clay	USA
1964	Cosimo Pinto	ITA
1968	Dan Pozniak	URS
1972	Mate Parlov	YUG
1976	Leon Spinks	USA
1980	Slobodan Kacar	YUG
1984		

Heavyweight

1904	Samuel Berger	USA
1908	A. L. Oldham	GBR
1920	Ronald Rawson	GBR
1924	Otto von Porath	NOR
1928	Rodriguez Jurado	ARG
1932	Alberto Lovell	ARG
1936	Herbert Runge	GER
1948	Rafael Iglesias	ARG
1952	Edward Sanders	USA
1956	Peter Rademacher	USA
1960	Francesco de Piccoli	ITA
1964	Joe Frazier	USA
1968	George Foreman	USA
1972	Teofilo Stevenson	CUB
1976	Teofilo Stevenson	CUB
1980	Teofilo Stevenson	CUB
1984		

Super—Heavyweight (New Division)

1984	

CANOEING (Men)

Kayak Singles—500 Meters

1976	Vasile Diba	ROM	1:45.41
1980	Vladimir Parfenovich	URS	1:43.43
1984			

Kayak Singles—1,000 Meters

1936	Gregor Hradetzky	AUT	4:22.9
1948	Gert Fredriksson	SWE	4:33.2
1952	Gert Fredriksson	SWE	4:07.9
1956	Gert Fredriksson	SWE	4:12.8
1960	Erik Hansen	DEN	3:53.0
1964	Rolf Peterson	SWE	3:57.13
1968	Mihaly Hesz	HUN	4:02.63
1972	Alexsandr Shaparenko	URS	3:48.06
1976	Rudiger Helm	GDR	3:48.20
1980	Rudiger Helm	GDR	3:48.77
1984			

Kayak Pairs—500 Meters

1976	German Democratic Republic	1:35.87
1980	Soviet Union	1:32.38
1984		

Kayak Pairs—1,000 meters

1936	Austria	4:03.8
1948	Sweden	4:07.3
1952	Finland	3:51.1
1956	Germany	3:49.6
1960	Sweden	3:34.73
1964	Sweden	3:38.54
1968	Soviet Union	3:37.54
1972	Soviet Union	3:31.23
1976	Soviet Union	3:29.01
1980	Soviet Union	3:26.72
1984		

Kayak Fours—1,000 Meters

1964	Soviet Union	3:14.67
1968	Norway	3:14.38
1972	Soviet Union	3:14.02
1976	Soviet Union	3:08.69
1980	German Democratic Republic	3:13.76
1984		

Canadian Singles—500 Meters

1976	A. Rogov	URS	1:59.23
1980	Sergei Postrekhin	URS	1:53.37
1984			

Canadian Singles—1,000 Meters

1936	Francis Amyot	CAN	5:32.1
1948	Josef Holocek	CZE	5:42.0
1952	Josef Holocek	CZE	4:56.3
1956	Leon Rottman	ROM	5:05.3
1960	Janos Parti	HUN	4:33.93
1964	Jurgen Eschert	GER	4:35.14
1968	Tibor Tatai	HUN	4:36.14
1972	Ivan Patzaichin	ROM	4:08.94
1976	Ljubek Matija	YUG	4:09.51
1980	Lubomir Lubanov	BUL	4:12.38
1984			

Canadian Pairs—500 Meters

1976	Soviet Union	1:45.81
1980	Hungary	1:43.39
1984		

Canadian Pairs—1,000 meters

1936	Czechoslovakia	4:50.1
1948	Czechoslovakia	5:07.1
1952	Denmark	4:38.3
1956	Romania	4:47.4
1960	Soviet Union	4:17.94
1964	Soviet Union	4:04.64
1968	Romania	4:07.18
1972	Soviet Union	3:52.60
1976	Soviet Union	3:52.76
1980	Romania	3:47.65
1984		

CANOEING (Women)

Kayak Singles—500 Meters

1948	Karen Hoff	DEN	2:31.9
1952	Sylvi Saimo	FIN	2:18.4
1956	Elisaveta Dementyeva	URS	2:18.9
1960	Antonina Seredina	URS	2:08.08
1964	Ludmila Khvedosiuk	URS	2:12.87
1968	Ludmila Khvedosiuk-Pinaeva	URS	2:11.09
1972	Julia Ryabchinskaya	URS	2:03.17
1976	Carola Zirzow	GDR	2:01.05
1980	Birgit Fischer	GDR	1:57.96
1984			

Kayak Pairs—500 Meters

1960	Soviet Union	1:54.76
1964	Germany	1:56.95
1968	German Federal Republic	1:56.44
1972	Soviet Union	1:53.50
1976	Soviet Union	1:51.15
1980	German Democratic Republic	1:43.88
1984		

Kayak Fours—500 meters

1984		

CYCLING (Men)

1,000—meter Sprint

1896	Paul Masson	FRA	4:56.0
1900	George Taillandier	FRA	2:16.0
1908	Void, time limit exceeded		
1920	Mauritius Peeters	HOL	1:38.3
1924	Lucien Michard	FRA	12.8 *
1928	Robert Beaufrand	FRA	13.2
1932	Jacobus van Egmond	HOL	12.6
1936	Toni Merkens	GER	11.8
1948	Mario Ghella	ITA	12.0
1952	Enzo Sacchi	ITA	12.0
1956	Michel Rousseau	FRA	11.4
1960	Sante Gaiardoni	ITA	11.1
1964	Giovanni Pettenella	ITA	13.69
1968	Daniel Morelon	FRA	10.68
1972	Daniel Morelon	FRA	11.69
1976	Anton Tkac	CZE	
1980	Lutz Hesslich	GDR	
1984			

* Since 1924, only the times over the last 200 meters of the event have been recorded

1,000—Meter Time Trial

1928	Willy Falck Hansen	DEN	1:14.4
1932	Edgar Gray	AUS	1:13.0
1936	Arie van Vliet	HOL	1:12.0
1948	Jacques Dupont	FRA	1:13.5
1952	Russell Mockridge	AUS	1:11.1
1956	Leandro Faggin	ITA	1:09.8
1960	Sante Gaiardoni	ITA	1:07.27
1964	Patrick Sercu	BEL	1:09.59
1968	Pierre Trentin	FRA	1:03.91
1972	Niels Fredborg	DEN	1:06.44
1976	Klaus Jurgen Grunke	GDR	1:05.297
1980	Lothar Thoms	GDR	1:02.955
1984			

4,000—Meter Individual Pursuit

1964	Jiri Daler	CZE	5:04.75
1968	Daniel Rebillard	FRA	4:41.71
1972	Knut Knudsen	NOR	4:45.74
1976	Gregor Braun	GER	4:47.61
1980	Robert Dill-Bundi	SUI	4:35.66
1984			

4,000—Meter Team Pursuit

1920,	Italy	5:20.0
1924	Italy	5:15.0
1928	Italy	5:01.8
1932	Italy	4:53.0
1936	France	4:45.0
1948	France	4:57.8
1952	Italy	4:46.1
1956	Italy	4:37.4
1960	Italy	4:30.90
1964	Germany	4:35.67
1968	Denmark	4:22.44
1972	German Federal Republic	4:22.14
1976	German Federal Republic	4:21.06
1980	Soviet Union	4:15.70
1984		

Individual Road Race

1896	Aristidis Konstantinidis	GRE	3:22:31.0
1912	Rudolph Lewis	SAF	10:42:39.0
1920	Harry Stenquist	SWE	4:40:01.8
1924	Armand Blanchonnet	FRA	6:20:48.0
1928	Henry Hansen	DEN	4:47:18.0
1932	Attilo Pavesi	ITA	2:28:05.6
1936	Robert Charpentier	FRA	2:33:05.0
1948	Jose Beyaert	FRA	5:18:12.6
1952	Andre Noyelle	BEL	5:06:03.4
1956	Ercole Baldini	ITA	5:21:17.0
1960	Viktor Kapitonov	URS	4:20:37.0
1964	Mario Zanin	ITA	4:39:51.63
1968	Pierfranco Vianelli	ITA	4:41:25.24
1972	Hennie Kuiper	HOL	4:14:37.0
1976	Bernt Johansson	SWE	4:46:52.0
1980	Sergei Sukhoruchenkov	URS	4:48:28.9
1984			

Road Team Time Trial *

1912	Sweden	44:35:33.6
1920	France	19:16:43.2
1924	France	19:30:14.0
1928	Denmark	15:09:14.0
1932	Italy	7:27:15.2
1936	France	7:39:16.2
1948	Belgium	15:58:17.4
1952	Belgium	15:20:46.6
1956	France	16:10:36.0
1960	Italy	2:14:33.53
1964	Holland	2:26:31.19
1968	Holland	2:07:49.06
1972	Soviet Union	2:11:17.8
1976	Soviet Union	2:08:53.0
1980	Soviet Union	2:01:21.7
1984		

*Although team medals were awarded from 1912, a separate team event was not held until 1960. Since 1960, the distance has been 100 kilometers (62 miles).

Individual Points Race

1984

CYCLING (Women)

Individual Road Race

1984

EQUESTRIAN

Individual Three—Day Event

1912	Axel Nordlander	SWE
1920	Helmer Morner	SWE
1924	Adolph van Zipj	HOL
1928	Pahud de Mortanges	HOL
1932	Pahud de Mortanges	HOL
1936	Ludwig Stubbendorff	GER
1948	Bernard Chevalier	FRA
1952	Hans von Blixen-Finecke	SWE
1956	Petrus Kastenman	SWE
1960	Lawrence Morgan	AUS
1964	Mauro Checcoli	ITA
1968	Jean Guyon	FRA
1972	Richard Meade	GBR
1976	Edmund Coffin	USA
1980	Frederico Euro Roman	ITA
1984		

Team Three–Day Event

1912	Sweden
1920	Sweden
1924	Holland
1928	Holland
1932	United States of America
1936	Germany
1948	United States of America
1952	Sweden
1956	Great Britain
1960	Australia
1964	Italy
1968	Great Britain
1972	Great Britain
1976	United States of America
1980	Soviet Union
1984	

Individual Grand Prix Jumping

1912	Jean Cariou	FRA
1920	Tommaso Lequio	ITA
1924	Alphonse Gemuseus	SUI
1928	Frantisek Ventura	CZE
1932	Takeichi Nishi	JPN
1936	Kurt Hasse	GER
1948	Humberto Mariles Cortes	MEX
1952	Pierre Jonqueres d'Oriola	FRA
1956	Hans Gunter Winkler	GER
1960	Raimondo d'Inzeo	ITA
1964	Pierre Jonqueres d'Oriola	FRA
1968	William Steinkraus	USA
1972	Graziano Mancinelli	ITA
1976	Alwin Schockemoehl	GER
1980	Jan Kowalczyk	POL
1984		

Team Grand Prix Jumping

1912	Sweden
1920	Sweden
1924	Sweden
1928	Spain
1932	*
1936	Germany
1948	Mexico
1952	Great Britain
1956	Germany
1960	Germany
1964	Germany
1968	Canada
1972	German Federal Republic
1976	France
1980	Soviet Union
1984	

* No team completed course

Individual Grand Prix Dressage

1912	Carl Bonde	SWE
1920	Janne Lundblad	SWE
1924	Ernst von Linder	SWE
1928	Carl von Langen	GER
1932	Francois Lesage	FRA
1936	Heinrich Pollay	GER
1948	Hans Moser	SUI
1952	Henri St. Cyr	SWE
1956	Henri St. Cyr	SWE
1960	Sergey Filatov	URS
1964	Henri Chammartin	SUI
1968	Ivan Kizimov	URS
1972	Liselott Linsenhoff	GER
1976	Christine Stueckelberger	SUI
1980	Elizabeth Theurer	AUT
1984		

Team Grand Prix Dressage

1928	Germany
1932	France
1936	Germany
1948	France
1952	Sweden
1956	Sweden
1964	Germany
1968	German Federal Republic
1972	Soviet Union
1976	German Federal Republic
1980	Soviet Union
1984	

FENCING (Men)

Foil, Individual

1896	Emile Gravelotte	FRA
1900	Emile Coste	FRA
1904	Ramon Fonst	CUB
1912	Nedo Nadi	ITA
1920	Nedo Nadi	ITA
1924	Roger Ducret	FRA
1928	Lucien Gaudin	FRA
1932	Gustavo Marzi	ITA
1936	Giulio Gaudini	ITA
1948	Jean Buhan	FRA
1952	Christian d'Oriola	FRA
1956	Christian d'Oriola	FRA
1960	Viktor Zhdanovich	URS
1964	Egon Franke	POL
1968	Ileana Drimba	ROM
1972	Witold Woyda	POL
1976	Fabio del Zotto	ITA
1980	Vladimir Smirnov	URS
1984		

Foil, Team

1904	Cuba
1920	Italy
1924	France
1928	Italy
1932	France
1936	Italy
1948	France
1952	France
1956	Italy
1960	Soviet Union
1964	Soviet Union
1968	France
1972	Poland
1976	German Federal Republic
1980	France
1984	

Epee, Individual

1900	Ramon Fonst	CUB
1904	Ramon Fonst	CUB
1908	Gaston Alibert	FRA
1912	Paul Anspach	BEL
1920	Armand Massard	FRA
1924	Charles Delporte	BEL
1928	Lucien Gaudin	FRA
1932	Giancarlo Cornaggia-Medici	ITA
1936	Franco Riccardi	ITA
1948	Luigi Cantone	ITA
1952	Edoardo Mangiarotti	ITA
1956	Carlo Pavesi	ITA
1960	Giuseppe Delfino	ITA
1964	Grigroy Kriss	URS
1968	Gyozo Kulcsar	HUN
1972	Csaba Fenyvesi	HUN
1976	Alexander Pusch	GER
1980	Johan Harmenberg	SWE
1984		

Epee, Team

1908	France
1912	Belgium
1920	Italy
1924	France
1928	Italy
1932	France
1936	Italy
1948	France
1952	Italy
1956	Italy
1960	Italy
1964	Hungary
1968	Hungary
1972	Hungary
1976	Sweden
1980	France
1984	

Sabre, Individual

1896	Jean Georgiadis	GRE
1900	Georges de la Falaise	FRA
1904	Manuel Diaz	CUB
1908	Jeno Fuchs	HUN
1912	Jeno Fuchs	HUN
1920	Nedo Nadi	ITA
1924	Sandor Posta	HUN
1928	Odon Tersztyanszky	HUN
1932	Gyorgy Piller	HUN
1936	Endre Kabos	HUN
1948	Aladar Gerevich	HUN
1952	Pal Kovacs	HUN
1956	Rudolf Karpati	HUN
1960	Rudolf Karpati	HUN
1964	Tibor Pezsa	HUN
1968	Jerzy Pawlowski	POL
1972	Viktor Sidiak	URS
1976	Viktor Krovopuskov	URS
1980	Viktor Krovopuskov	URS
1984		

Sabre, Team

1908	Hungary
1912	Hungary
1920	Italy
1924	Italy
1928	Hungary
1932	Hungary
1936	Hungary
1948	Hungary
1952	Hungary
1956	Hungary
1960	Hungary
1964	Soviet Union
1968	Soviet Union
1972	Italy
1976	Soviet Union
1980	Soviet Union
1984	

FENCING (Women)

Foil, Individual

1924	Ellen Osiier	DEN
1928	Helene Mayer	GER
1932	Ellen Preis	AUT
1936	Ilona Elek	HUN
1948	Ilona Elek	HUN
1952	Irene Camber	ITA
1956	Gillian Sheen	GBR
1960	Heidi Schmid	GER
1964	Ildiko Uilaki-Rejto	HUN
1968	Elene Novikova	URS
1972	Antonell Ragno Lonzi	ITA
1976	Ildiko Schwarczenberger	HUN
1980	Pascale Trinquet	FRA
1984		

Foil, Team

1960	Soviet Union
1964	Hungary
1968	Soviet Union
1972	Soviet Union
1976	Soviet Union
1980	France
1984	

FOOTBALL (Soccer)

1900	GBR	4	FRA	0	*
1904	CAN	4	USA	0	*
1908	GBR	2	DEN	0	
1912	GBR	4	DEN	2	
1920	BEL	2	CZE	0	†
1924	URU	3	SUI	0	
1928	URU	2	ARG	1	
1936	ITA	2	AUT	1	
1948	SWE	3	YUG	1	
1952	HUN	2	YUG	0	
1956	URS	1	YUG	0	
1960	YUG	3	DEN	1	
1964	HUN	2	CZE	1	
1968	HUN	4	BUL	1	
1972	POL	2	HUN	1	
1976	GDR	3	POL	1	
1980	CZE	1	GDR	0	
1984					

* Demonstration events, won by club teams.

† Final abandoned in Belgium's favor when leading 2—0, the Czech team left due to expulsion of Czech player and was disqualified.

GYMNASTICS (Men)

Team

1904	United States of America
1908	Sweden
1912	Italy
1920	Italy
1924	Italy
1928	Switzerland
1932	Italy
1936	Germany
1948	Finland
1952	Soviet Union
1956	Soviet Union
1960	Japan
1964	Japan
1968	Japan
1972	Japan
1976	Japan
1980	Soviet Union
1984	

All–Around Individual

1900	Gustav Sandras	FRA
1904	Anton Heida	USA
1908	Alberto Braglia	ITA
1912	Alberto Braglia	ITA
1920	Giorgio Zampori	ITA
1924	Leon Stukelj	YUG
1928	George Miez	SUI
1932	Romeo Neri	ITA
1936	Alfred Schwarzmann	GER
1948	Veikko Huhtanen	FIN
1952	Viktor Chukarin	URS
1956	Viktor Chukarin	URS
1960	Boris Shakhlin	URS
1964	Yukio Endo	JPN
1968	Sawao Kato	JPN
1972	Sawao Kato	JPN
1976	Nikolai Andrianov	URS
1980	Alexandr Ditiatin	URS
1984		

Floor Exercise

1932	Istvan Pelle	HUN
1936	Georges Miez	SUI
1948	Ferenc Pataki	HUN
1952	Karl Thoresson	SWE
1956	Valentin Moratov	URS
1960	Nobuyuki Aihara	JPN
1964	Franco Menicelli	ITA
1968	Sawao Kato	JPN
1972	Nikolai Andrianov	URS
1976	Nikolai Andrianov	URS
1980	Roland Bruckner	GDR
1984		

Pommel Horse

1896	Louis Zutter	SUI
1904	Anton Heida	USA
1924	Josef Wilhelm	SUI
1928	Hermann Hanggi	SUI
1932	Istvan Pelle	HUN
1936	Konrad Frey	GER
1948	Paavo Aaltonen	FIN
	Veikko Huhtanen	FIN
	and Heikki Savolainen	FIN
1952	Viktor Chukarin	URS
1956	Boris Shakhlin	URS
1960	Boris Shakhlin	URS
	and Eugen Ekman	FIN
1964	Miroslav Cerar	YUG
1968	Miroslav Cerar	YUG
1972	Viktor Klimenko	URS
1976	Zoltan Magyar	HUN
1980	Zoltan Magyar	HUN
1984		

Rings

1896	Jean Mitropoulos	GRE
1904	Hermann Glass	USA
1924	Francesco Martino	ITA
1928	Leon Stukelj	YUG
1932	George Gulack	USA
1936	Alois Hudec	CZE
1948	Karl Frei	SUI
1952	Grant Shaginyan	URS
1956	Albert Azaran	URS
1960	Albert Azaran	URS
1964	Takuji Hayata	JPN
1968	Akinori Nakayama	JPN
1972	Akinori Nakayama	JPN
1976	Nikolai Andrianov	URS
1980	Alexandr Ditiatin	URS
1984		

Vault

1896	Karl Schumann	GER
1904	Anton Heida	USA
	and George Eyser	USA
1924	Frank Kriz	USA
1928	Eugen Mack	SUI
1932	Savino Guglielmetti	ITA
1936	Karl Schwarzmann	GER
1948	Paavo Aaltonen	FIN
1952	Viktor Chukarin	URS
1956	Helmuth Bantz	GER
	and Valentin Moratov	URS
1960	Boris Shakhlin	URS
	and Takashi Ono	JPN
1964	Haruhiro Yamashita	JPN
1968	Mikhail Voronin	URS
1972	Klaus Koeste	GDR
1976	Nikolai Andrianov	URS
1980	Nikolai Andrianov	URS
1984		

Parallel Bars

1896	Alfred Flatow	GER
1904	George Eyser	USA
1924	August Guttinger	SUI
1928	Ladislav Vacha	CZE
1932	Romeo Neri	ITA
1936	Konrad Frey	GER
1948	Michael Reusch	SUI
1952	Hans Eugster	SUI
1956	Viktor Chukarin	URS
1960	Boris Shakhlin	URS
1964	Yukio Endo	JPN
1968	Akinori Nakayama	JPN
1972	Sawao Kato	JPN
1976	Sawao Kato	JPN
1980	Alexandr Tkachyov	URS
1984		

Horizontal Bar

1896	Hermann Weingartner	GER
1904	Anton Heida	USA
	and Edward Hennig	USA
1924	Leon Stukelj	YUG
1928	Georges Miez	SUI
1932	Dallas Bixler	USA
1936	Aleksanteri Saarvala	FIN
1948	Josef Stalder	SUI
1952	Jack Gunthard	SUI
1956	Takashi Ono	JPN
1960	Takashi Ono	JPN
1964	Boris Shakhlin	URS
1968	Mikhail Voronin	URS
	and Akinori Nakayama	JPN
1972	Mitsuo Tsukahara	JPN
1976	Mitsuo Tsukahara	JPN
1980	Stoyan Deltchev	BUL
1984		

GYMNASTICS (Women)

Team

1928	Holland
1936	Germany
1948	Czechoslovakia
1952	Soviet Union
1956	Soviet Union
1960	Soviet Union
1964	Soviet Union
1968	Soviet Union
1972	Soviet Union
1976	Soviet Union
1980	Soviet Union
1984	

All—Around Individual

1952	Maria Gorokhovskaya	URS
1956	Larisa Latynina	URS
1960	Larisa Latynina	URS
1964	Vera Caslavska	CZE
1968	Vera Caslavska	CZE
1972	Ludmilla Turischeva	URS
1976	Nadia Comaneci	ROM
1980	Yelena Davydova	URS
1984		

Vault

1952	Yekaterina Kalinchuk	URS
1956	Larisa Latynina	URS
1960	Margarita Nikolaeva	URS
1964	Vera Caslavska	CZE
1968	Vera Caslavska	CZE
1972	Karin Janz	GDR
1976	Nelli Kim	URS
1980	Natalia Shaposhnikova	URS
1984		

Asymmetrical Bars

1952	Margit Korondi	HUN
1956	Agnes Keleti	HUN
1960	Polina Astakhova	URS
1964	Polina Astakhova	URS
1968	Vera Caslavska	CZE
1972	Karin Janz	GDR
1976	Nadia Comaneci	ROM
1980	Maxi Gnauck	GDR
1984		

Balance Beam

1952	Nina Bocharova	URS
1956	Agnes Keleti	HUN
1960	Eva Bosakova	CZE
1964	Vera Caslavska	CZE
1968	Natalia Kuchinskaya	URS
1972	Olga Korbut	URS
1976	Nadia Comaneci	ROM
1980	Nadia Comaneci	ROM
1984		

Floor Exercise

1952	Agnes Keleti	HUN
1956	Larisa Latynina	URS
	and Agnes Keleti	HUN
1960	Larisa Latynina	URS
1964	Larisa Latynina	URS
1968	Vera Caslavska	CZE
	and Larissa Petrik	URS
1972	Olga Korbut	URS
1976	Nelli Kim	URS
1980	Nelli Kim	URS
	and Nadia Comaneci	ROM
1984		

Rhythmic Individual All–Around

1984

HANDBALL (TEAM)
Men

1972	YUG	21	CZE	16
1976	URS	19	ROM	15
1980	GDR	23	URS	22
1984				

Women

1976	URS	14	GDR	11
1980	URS	18	YUG	9
1984				

HOCKEY (Field)
Men

1908	GBR	8	IRL	1
1920	GBR	5	DEN	1
1928	IND	3	HOL	0
1932	IND	11	JPN	1
1936	IND	8	GER	1
1948	IND	4	GBR	0
1952	IND	6	HOL	1
1956	IND	1	PAK	0
1960	PAK	1	IND	0
1964	IND	1	PAK	0
1968	PAK	2	AUS	1
1972	GER	1	PAK	0
1976	NZL	1	AUS	0
1980	IND	4	SPN	3
1984				

Women

1980	ZIM	8	CZE	7 *
1984				

* Round robin tournament

JUDO

Open Class

1964	Anton Geesink	HOL
1972	Willem Ruska	HOL
1976	Haruki Uemura	JPN
1980	Dietmar Lorenz	GDR
1984		

Heavyweight

1964	Isao Inokuma	JPN
1972	Willem Ruska	HOL
1976	Sergei Novikov	URS
1980	Angelo Parisi	FRA
1984		

Half Heavyweight

1972	Shota Khokoshvili	URS
1976	Kazuhiro Ninomiya	JPN
1980	Robert Van De Walle	BEL
1984		

Middleweight

1964	Isao Okano	JPN
1972	Shinobu Sekine	JPN
1976	Isamu Sonoda	JPN
1980	Juerg Roethlisberger	SUI
1984		

Half Middleweight

1972	Toyokazu Nomura	JPN
1976	Vladimir Nevzorov	URS
1980	Shota Khabareli	URS
1984		

Lightweight

1964	Takehide Nakatani	JPN
1972	Takeo Kawaguchi	JPN
1976	Hector Rodriguez	CUB
1980	Ezio Gamba	ITA
1984		

Half Lightweight

1980	Nikolay Solodukhin	URS
1984		

Extra Lightweight

1980	Thierry Rey	FRA
1984		

MODERN PENTATHLON

Individual

1912	Gustaf Lilliehook	SWE	27.0
1920	Gustaf Dryssen	SWE	18.0
1924	Bo Lindman	SWE	18.0
1928	Sven Thofelt	SWE	47.0
1932	Johan Oxenstierna	SWE	32.0
1936	Gotthard Handrick	GER	31.5
1948	William Grut	SWE	16.0
1952	Lars Hall	SWE	32.0
1956	Lars Hall	SWE	4,833.0
1960	Ferenc Nemeth	HUN	5,024.0
1964	Ferenc Torok	HUN	5,116.0
1968	Bjoern Ferm	SWE	4,964.0
1972	Andras Balczo	HUN	5,412.0
1976	Janusz Pyciak-Peciak	POL	5,520.0
1980	Anatoly Starostin	URS	5,568.0
1984			

Team

1952	Hungary	166.0
1956	Soviet Union	13,609.5
1960	Hungary	14,863.0
1964	Soviet Union	14,961.0
1968	Hungary	14,325.0
1972	Soviet Union	15,968.0
1976	Great Britain	15,599.0
1980	Soviet Union	16,126.0
1984		

ROWING (Men)

Single Sculls

1900	Henry Barrelet	FRA	7:35.6
1904	Frank Greer	USA	10:08.5
1908	Harry Blackstaffe	GBR	9:26.0
1912	William Kinnear	GBR	7:47.6
1920	John Kelly	USA	7:35.0
1924	Jack Beresford	GBR	7:49.2
1928	Henry Pearce	AUS	7:11.0
1932	Henry Pearce	AUS	7:44.4
1936	Gustav Schafer	GER	8:21.5
1948	Mervyn Wood	AUS	7:24.4
1952	Yuri Tykalov	URS	8:12.8
1956	Vyacheslav Ivanov	URS	8:02.5
1960	Vyacheslav Ivanov	URS	7:13.96
1964	Vyacheslav Ivanov	URS	8:22.55
1968	Henri Jan Wienese	HOL	7:47.80
1972	Yuri Malyshev	URS	7:10.12
1976	Pertti Karppinen	FIN	7:29.03
1980	Pertti Karppinen	FIN	7:09.61
1984			

Double Sculls

1904	United States of America	10:03.2
1920	United States of America	7:09.0
1924	United States of America	6:34.0
1928	United States of America	6:41.4
1932	United States of America	7:17.4
1936	Great Britain	7:20.8
1948	Great Britain	6:51.3
1952	Argentina	7:32.2
1956	Soviet Union	7:24.0
1960	Czechoslovakia	6:47.50
1964	Soviet Union	7:10.66
1968	Soviet Union	6:51.82
1972	Soviet Union	7:01.77
1976	Norway	7:13.20
1980	German Democratic Republic	6:24.33
1984		

Coxless Quadruple Sculls

1976	German Democratic Republic	6:18.25
1980	German Democratic Republic	5:49.81
1984		

Coxless Pairs

1908	Great Britain	9:41.0
1924	Holland	8:19.4
1928	Germany	7:06.4
1932	Great Britain	8:00.0
1936	Germany	8:16.1
1948	Great Britain	7:21.1
1952	United States of America	8:20.7
1956	United States of America	7:55.4
1960	Soviet Union	7:02.01
1964	Canada	7:32.94
1968	German Democratic Republic	7:26.56
1972	German Democratic Republic	6:53.16
1976	German Democratic Republic	7:23.31
1980	German Democratic Republic	6:48.01
1984		

Coxed Pairs

1900	Holland	7:34.2
1920	Italy	7:56.0
1924	Switzerland	8:39.0
1928	Switzerland	7:42.6
1932	United States of America	8:25.8
1936	Germany	8:36.9
1948	Denmark	8:00.5
1952	France	8:28.6
1956	United States of America	8:26.1
1960	Germany	7:29.14
1964	United States of America	8:21.33
1968	Italy	8:04.81
1972	German Democratic Republic	7:17.25
1976	German Democratic Republic	7:58.99
1980	German Democratic Republic	7:02.54
1984		

Coxless Fours

1904	United States of America	9:53.8
1908	Great Britain	8:34.0
1924	Great Britain	7:08.6
1928	Great Britain	6:36.0
1932	Great Britain	6:58.2
1936	Germany	7:01.8
1948	Italy	6:39.0
1952	Yugoslavia	7:16.0
1956	Canada	7:08.8
1960	United States of America	6:26.26
1964	Denmark	6:59.30
1968	German Democratic Republic	6:39.18
1972	German Democratic Republic	6:24.27
1976	German Democratic Republic	6:37.42
1980	German Democratic Republic	6:08.17
1984		

Coxed Fours

1900	Germany	5:59.0
1912	Germany	6:59.4
1920	Switzerland	6:54.0
1924	Switzerland	7:18.4
1928	Italy	6:47.8
1932	Germany	7:19.0
1936	Germany	7:16.2
1948	United States of America	6:50.3
1952	Czechoslovakia	7:33.4
1956	Italy	7:19.4
1960	Germany	6:39.12
1964	Germany	7:00.44
1968	New Zealand	6:45.62
1972	German Federal Republic	6:31.85
1976	Soviet Union	6:40.22
1980	German Democratic Republic	6:14.51
1984		

Eights

1900	United States of America	6:09.8
1904	United States of America	7:50.0
1908	Great Britain	7:52.0
1912	Great Britain	6:15.0
1920	United States of America	6:02.6
1924	United States of America	6:33.4
1928	United States of America	6:03.2
1932	United States of America	6:37.6
1936	United States of America	6:25.4
1948	United States of America	5:56.7
1952	United States of America	6:25.9
1956	United States of America	6:35.2
1960	Germany	5:57.18
1964	United States of America	6:18.23
1968	German Federal Republic	6:07.00
1972	New Zealand	6:08.94
1976	German Democratic Republic	5:58.29
1980	German Democratic Republic	5:49.05
1984		

ROWING (Women)

Single Sculls

1976	Christine Scheiblich	GDR	4:05.56
1980	Sanda Toma	ROM	3:40.69
1984			

Double Sculls

1976	Bulgaria	3:44.36
1980	Soviet Union	3:16.27
1984		

Coxless Pairs

1976	Bulgaria	4:01.22
1980	German Democratic Republic	3:30.49
1984		

Coxed Quadruple Sculls

1976	German Democratic Republic	3:29.99
1980	German Democratic Republic	3:15.32
1984		

Coxed Fours

1976	German Democratic Republic	3:45.08
1980	German Democratic Republic	3:19.27
1984		

Eights

1976	German Democratic Republic	3:33.32
1980	German Democratic Republic	3:03.32
1984		

SHOOTING (Men)

Free Pistol (50 Meters)

1896	Sumner Paine	USA	442
1900	Karl Roderer	SUI	503
1912	Alfred Lane	USA	499
1920	Carl Frederick	USA	496
1936	Thorsten Ullmann	SWE	559
1948	Edwin Vascuez	PER	545
1952	Huelet Benner	USA	553
1956	Pentti Linnosvuo	FIN	556
1960	Alexey Gustchin	URS	560
1964	Vaino Markkanen	FIN	560
1968	Grigory Kosykh	URS	562
1972	Ragner Skanaker	SWE	567
1976	Uwe Potteck	GDR	573
1980	Aleksandr Melentev	URS	581
1984			

Small—bore Rifle: Prone position *

1908	A. A. Carnell	GBR	387
1912	Frederick Hird	USA	194
1920	Lawrence Nuesslein	USA	391
1924	Charles Coquelin de Lisle	FRA	398
1932	Bartil Ronmark	SWE	294
1936	Willy Rogeberg	NOR	300
1948	Arthur Cook	USA	599
1952	Iosef Sarbu	ROM	400
1956	Gerald Ouellette	CAN	600
1960	Peter Kohnke	GER	590
1964	Laszlo Hammerl	HUN	597
1968	Jan Kurka	CZE	598
1972	Ho Jan Li	PRK	599
1976	Karl Heinz Smieszek	GER	599
1980	Karoly Varga	HUN	599
1984			

* The exclusively prone position was not enforced until 1924.

Small—bore Rifle: Three positions

1952	Erling Kongshaug	NOR	1164
1956	Anatoli Bogdanov	URS	1172
1960	Viktor Shamburkin	URS	1149
1964	Lones Wigger	USA	1164
1968	Bernd Klingner	GER	1157
1972	John Writer	USA	1166
1976	Lanny Bassham	USA	1162
1980	Viktor Vlasov	URS	1173
1984			

Rapid Fire Pistol

1924	H. M. Bailey	USA	
1932	Renzo Morigi	ITA	
1936	Cornelius van Oyen	GER	
1948	Karoly Takacs	HUN	580
1952	Karoly Takacs	HUN	579
1956	Stefan Petrescu	ROM	587
1960	William McMillan	USA	587
1964	Pentti Linnosvuo	FIN	592
1968	Josef Zapedzki	POL	593
1972	Jozef Zapedzki	POL	595
1976	Norbert Glaar	GDR	597
1980	Corneliu Ion	ROM	596
1984			

Running Game Target

1972	Lako Zhelezniak	URS	569
1976	Alexandr Gazov	URS	579
1980	Igor Sokolov	URS	589
1984			

Air Rifle

1984

SHOOTING (Women)

Standard Rifle

1984

Air Rifle

1984

Pistol Match

1984

SHOOTING (Mixed)

Skeet Shooting

1968	Evgeny Petrov	URS	198
1972	Konrad Wirnhier	GER	195
1976	Josef Panacek	CZE	198
1980	Hans Kjeld Rasmussen	DEN	196
1984			

Trap Shooting

1900	Roger de Barbarin	FRA	17
1908	Walter Ewing	CAN	72
1912	James Graham	USA	96
1920	Mark Arie	USA	95
1924	Gyula Halasy	HUN	98
1952	George Genereux	CAN	192
1956	Galliano Rossini	ITA	195
1960	Ion Dumitrescu	ROM	192
1964	Ennio Mattarelli	ITA	198
1968	John Braithwaite	GBR	198
1972	Angelo Scalzone	ITA	199
1976	Donald Haldeman	USA	190
1980	Luciano Giovannetti	ITA	198
1984			

SWIMMING, DIVING & WATER POLO (Men)

100—meter Freestyle

1896	Alfred Hajos	HUN	1:22.2
1904	Zoltan de Halmay	HUN	1:02.8
1908	Charles Daniels	USA	1:05.6
1912	Duke Kahanamoku	USA	1:03.4
1920	Duke Kahanamoku	USA	1:01.4
1924	Johnny Weissmuller	USA	59.0
1928	Johnny Weissmuller	USA	58.6
1932	Yasuji Miyazaki	JPN	58.2
1936	Ferenc Csik	HUN	57.6
1948	Walter Ris	USA	57.3
1952	Clarke Scholes	USA	57.4
1956	Jon Henricks	AUS	55.4
1960	John Devitt	AUS	55.2
1964	Donald Schollander	USA	53.4
1968	Mike Wenden	AUS	52.2
1972	Mark Spitz	USA	51.22
1976	Jim Montgomery	USA	49.99
1980	Jorg Woithe	GDR	50.40
1984			

200—meter Freestyle

1900	Frederick Lane	AUS	2:52.2
1904	Charles Daniels	USA	2:44.2
1968	Mike Werden	AUS	1:55.2
1972	Mark Spitz	USA	1:52.78
1976	Bruce Furniss	USA	1:50.29
1980	Sergei Kopliakov	URS	1:49.81
1984			

400-meter Freestyle

1896	Paul Neumann	AUT	8:12.6	*
1904	Charles Daniels	USA	6:16.2	
1908	Henry Taylor	GBR	5:36.8	
1912	George Hodgson	CAN	5:24.4	
1920	Norman Ross	USA	5:26.8	
1924	Johnny Weissmuller	USA	5:04.2	
1928	Alberto Zorilla	ARG	5:01.6	
1932	Buster Crabbe	USA	4:48.4	
1936	Jack Medica	USA	4:44.5	
1948	William Smith	USA	4:41.0	
1952	Jean Boiteux	FRA	4:30.7	
1956	Murray Rose	AUS	4:27.3	
1960	Murray Rose	AUS	4:18.3	
1964	Donald Schollander	USA	4:12.2	
1968	Michael Burton	USA	4:09.0	
1972	Bradford Cooper	AUS	4:00.27	
1976	Brian Goodell	USA	3:51.93	
1980	Victor Salnikov	URS	3:51.31	
1984				

* Distance was 500 meters

1,500-meter Freestyle

1896	Alfred Hajos	HUN	18:22.2	*
1900	John Jarvis	GBR	13:40.2	†
1904	Emil Rausch	GER	27:18.2	
1908	Henry Taylor	GBR	22:48.4	
1912	George Hodgson	CAN	22:00.0	
1920	Norman Ross	USA	22:23.2	
1924	Andrew Charlton	AUS	20:06.6	
1928	Arne Borg	SWE	19:51.8	
1932	Kusuo Kitamura	JPN	19:12.4	
1936	Noboru Terada	JPN	19:13.7	
1948	James McLane	USA	19:18.5	
1952	Ford Konno	USA	18:30.0	
1956	Murray Rose	AUS	17:58.9	
1960	Jon Konrads	AUS	17:19.6	
1964	Robert Windle	AUS	17:01.7	
1968	Michael Burton	USA	16:38.9	
1972	Michael Burton	USA	15:52.58	
1976	Brian Goodell	USA	15:02.40	
1980	Victor Salnikov	URS	14:58.27	
1984				

* Distance was 1200 meters.
† Distance was 1000 meters.

100-meter Backstroke

1908	Arno Bieberstein	GER	1:24.6
1912	Harry Hebner	USA	1:21.2
1920	Warren Kealoha	USA	1:15.2
1924	Warren Kealoha	USA	1:13.2
1928	George Kojac	USA	1:08.2
1932	Masaji Kiyokawa	JPN	1:08.6
1936	Adolf Kiefer	USA	1:05.9
1948	Allen Stack	USA	1:06.4
1952	Yoshinobu Oyakawa	JPN	1:05.4
1956	David Thiele	AUS	1:02.2
1960	David Thiele	AUS	1:01.9
1968	Roland Matthes	GDR	58.7
1972	Roland Matthes	GDR	56.58
1976	John Naber	USA	55.49
1980	Bengt Baron	SWE	56.53
1984			

200-meter Backstroke

1900	Ernst Hoppenberg	GER	2:47.0
1964	Jed Graef	USA	2:10.3
1968	Roland Matthes	GDR	2:09.6
1972	Roland Matthes	GDR	2:02.82
1976	John Naber	USA	1:59.19
1980	Sandor Wladar	HUN	2:01.93
1984			

100-meter Breaststroke

1968	Donald McKenzie	USA	1:07.7
1972	Nobutaka Taguchi	JPN	1:04.94
1976	John Hencken	USA	1:03.11
1980	Duncan Goodhew	GBR	1:03.34
1984			

200-meter Breaststroke

1908	Frederick Holman	GBR	3:09.2
1912	Walter Bathe	GER	3:01.8
1920	Hakan Malmroth	SWE	3:04.4
1924	Robert Skelton	USA	2:56.6
1928	Yoshiyuki Tsuruta	JPN	2:48.8
1932	Yoshiyuki Tsuruta	JPN	2:45.4
1936	Tetsuo Hamuro	JPN	2:41.5
1948	Joseph Verdeur	USA	2:39.3
1952	John Davies	AUS	2:34.4
1956	Masura Furukawa	JPN	2:34.7
1960	William Mulliken	USA	2:37.4
1964	Ian O'Brien	AUS	2:27.8
1968	Felipe Munoz	MEX	2:28.7
1972	John Hencken	USA	2:21.55
1976	David Wilkie	GBR	2:15.11
1980	Robertas Zulpa	URS	2:15.85
1984			

100-meter Butterfly

1968	Douglas Russell	USA	55.9
1972	Mark Spitz	USA	54.27
1976	Matt Vogel	USA	54.35
1980	Par Arvidsson	SWE	54.92
1984			

200-meter Butterfly

1956	William Yorzyk	USA	2:19.3
1960	Michael Troy	USA	2:12.8
1964	Kevin Berry	AUS	2:06.6
1968	Carl Robie	USA	2:08.7
1972	Mark Spitz	USA	2:00.70
1976	Mike Bruner	USA	1:59.23
1980	Sergei Fesenko	URS	1:59.76
1984			

200-meter Medley

1968	Charles Hickcox	USA	2:12.0
1972	Gunnar Larsson	SWE	2:07.17
1984			

400-meter Medley

1964	Richard Roth	USA	4:54.4
1968	Charles Hickcox	USA	4:48.4
1972	Gunnar Larsson	SWE	4:31.98
1976	Rod Strachan	USA	4:23.68
1980	Aleksandr Sidorenko	URS	4:22.89
1984			

4 X 100—meter Medley Relay

1960	United States of America	4:05.4
1964	United States of America	3:58.4
1968	United States of America	3:54.9
1972	United States of America	3:48.16
1976	United States of America	3:42.22
1980	Australia	3:45.70
1984		

4 X 100—meter Freestyle Relay

1964	United States of America	3:33.2
1968	United States of America	3:31.7
1972	United States of America	3:26.42
1984		

4 X 200—meter Freestyle Relay

1908	Great Britain	10:55.6
1912	Australia	10:11.6
1920	United States of America	10:04.4
1924	United States of America	9:53.4
1928	United States of America	9:36.2
1932	Japan	8:58.4
1936	Japan	8:51.5
1948	United States of America	8:46.0
1952	United States of America	8:31.1
1956	Australia	8:23.6
1960	United States of America	8:10.2
1964	United States of America	7:52.1
1968	United States of America	7:52.3
1972	United States of America	7:35.78
1976	United States of America	7:23.22
1980	Soviet Union	7:23.50
1984		

Springboard Diving

1908	Albert Zurner	GER
1912	Paul Gunther	GER
1920	Louis Kuehn	USA
1924	Albert White	USA
1928	Pete Desjardins	USA
1932	Michael Galitzen	USA
1936	Richard Degener	USA
1948	Bruce Harlan	USA
1952	David Browning	USA
1956	Robert Clotworthy	USA
1960	Gary Tobian	USA
1964	Ken Sitzberger	USA
1968	Bernard Wrightson	USA
1972	Vladimir Vasin	URS
1976	Philip Boggs	USA
1980	Aleksandr Portnov	URS
1984		

Platform Diving

1904	George Sheldon	USA
1908	Hjalmar Johansson	SWE
1912	Erik Adlerz	SWE
1920	Clarence Pinkston	USA
1924	Albert White	USA
1928	Pete Desjardins	USA
1932	Harold Smith	USA
1936	Marshall Wayne	USA
1948	Samuel Lee	USA
1952	Samuel Lee	USA
1956	Joaquin Capilla Perez	MEX
1960	Robert Webster	USA
1964	Robert Webster	USA
1968	Klaus Dibiasi	ITA
1972	Klaus Dibiasi	ITA
1976	Klaus Dibiasi	ITA
1980	Falk Hoffman	GDR
1984		

Water Polo

1900	GBR	7	BEL	2	
1904	USA	6	USA	0	*
1908	GBR	9	BEL	2	
1912	GBR	6	SWE	3	
1920	GBR	3	BEL	2	
1924	FRA	3	BEL	0	
1928	GER	5	HUN	2	
1932	HUN	6	GER	2	
1936	HUN	2	GER	2	*
1948	ITA	4	HUN	3	*
1952	HUN	2	YUG	2	*
1956	HUN	2	YUG	1	*
1960	ITA	2	URS	0	*
1964	HUN	4	YUG	4	*
1968	YUG	13	URS	11	
1972	URS	3	HUN	3	
1976	HUN	6	ITA	5	
1980	URS	8	YUG	7	*
1984					

* Round robin, gold/silver game result.

SWIMMING & DIVING (Women)

100—meter Freestyle

1912	Fanny Durack	AUS	1:22.2
1920	Ethelda Bleibtrey	USA	1:13.6
1924	Ethel Lackie	USA	1:12.4
1928	Albina Osipowich	USA	1:11.0
1932	Helene Madison	USA	1:06.8
1936	Hendrika Mastenbroek	HOL	1:05.9
1948	Greta Andersen	DEN	1:06.3
1952	Katalin Szoke	HUN	1:06.8
1956	Dawn Fraser	AUS	1:02.0
1960	Dawn Fraser	AUS	1:01.2
1964	Dawn Fraser	AUS	59.5
1968	Jan Henne	USA	1:00.0
1972	Sandra Neilson	USA	58.59
1976	Kornelia Ender	GDR	55.65
1980	Barbara Krause	GDR	54.79
1984			

200—meter Freestyle

1968	Debbie Meyer	USA	2:10.5
1972	Shane Gould	AUS	2:03.56
1976	Kornelia Ender	GDR	1:59.26
1980	Barbara Krause	GDR	1:58.33
1984			

400—meter Freestyle

1924	Martha Norelius	USA	6:02.2
1928	Martha Norelius	USA	5:42.8
1932	Helene Madison	USA	5:28.5
1936	Hendrika Mastenbroek	HOL	5:26.4
1948	Ann Curtis	USA	5:17.8
1952	Valeria Gyenge	HUN	5:12.1
1956	Lorraine Crapp	AUS	4:54.6
1960	Christine von Saltza	USA	4:50.6
1964	Virginia Duenkel	USA	4:43.3
1968	Debbie Meyer	USA	4:31.8
1972	Shane Gould	AUS	4:19.04
1976	Petra Thurmer	GDR	4:08.89
1980	Ines Diers	GDR	4:08.76
1984			

800—meter Freestyle

1968	Debbie Meyer	USA	9:24.0
1972	Keen Rothhammer	USA	8:53.68
1976	Petra Thumer	GDR	8:20.59
1980	Michelle Ford	AUS	8:28.90
1984			

100—meter Backstroke

1924	Sybil Bauer	USA	1:23.2
1928	Marie Braun	HOL	1:22.0
1932	Eleanor Holm	USA	1:19.4
1936	Dina Senff	HOL	1:18.9
1948	Karen Harup	DEN	1:14.4
1952	Joan Harrison	SAF	1:14.3
1956	Judy Grinham	GBR	1:12.9
1960	Lynn Burke	USA	1:09.3
1964	Cathy Ferguson	USA	1:07.7
1968	Kaye Hall	USA	1:06.2
1972	Melissa Belote	USA	1:05.78
1976	Ulrike Richter	GDR	1:01.83
1980	Rica Reinisch	GDR	1:00.86
1984			

200—meter Backstroke

1968	Lilian Watson	USA	2:24.8
1972	Melissa Belote	USA	2:19.19
1976	Ulrike Richter	GDR	2:13.43
1980	Rica Reinisch	GDR	2:11.77
1984			

100—meter Breaststroke

1968	Djurdjica Bjedov	YUG	1:15.8
1972	Catherine Carr	USA	1:13.58
1976	Hannelore Anke	GDR	1:11.16
1980	Ute Geweniger	GDR	1:10.22
1984			

200—meter Breaststroke

1924	Lucy Morton	GBR	3:33.2
1928	Hilde Schrader	GER	3:12.6
1932	Clare Dennis	AUS	3:06.3
1936	Hideko Maehata	JPN	3:03.6
1948	Petronella van Vliet	HOL	2:57.2
1952	Eva Szekely	HUN	2:51.7
1956	Ursula Happe	GER	2:53.1
1960	Anita Lonsbrough	GBR	2:49.5
1964	Galina Prozumenshchikova	URS	2:46.4
1968	Sharon Wichman	USA	2:44.4
1972	Beverley Whitfield	AUS	2:41.71
1976	Marina Koshevaia	URS	2:33.35
1980	Lina Kachushite	URS	2:29.54
1984			

100—meter Butterfly

1956	Shelley Mann	USA	1:11.0
1960	Carolyn Schuler	USA	1:09.5
1964	Sharon Stouder	USA	1:04.7
1968	Lynn McClements	AUS	1:05.5
1972	Mayumi Aoki	JPN	1:03.34
1976	Kornelia Ender	GDR	1:00.13
1980	Caren Metschuck	GDR	1:00.42
1984			

200—meter Butterfly

1968	Ada Kok	HOL	2:24.7
1972	Karen Moe	USA	2:15.57
1976	Andrea Pollack	GDR	2:11.41
1980	Ines Geissler	GDR	2:10.44
1984			

200—meter Medley

1968	Claudia Kolb	USA	2:24.7
1972	Shane Gould	AUS	2:23.07
1984			

400—meter Medley

1964	Donna de Varona	USA	5:18.7
1968	Claudia Kolb	USA	5:08.5
1972	Gail Neall	AUS	5:02.97
1976	Ulrike Tauber	GDR	4:42.77
1980	Petra Schneider	GDR	4:36.29
1984			

4 X 100—meter Medley Relay

1960	United States of America	4:41.1
1964	United States of America	4:33.9
1968	United States of America	4:28.3
1972	United States of America	4:20.75
1976	German Democratic Republic	4:07.95
1980	German Democratic Republic	4:06.67
1984		

4 X 100—meter Freestyle Relay

1912	Great Britain	5:52.8
1920	United States of America	5:11.6
1924	United States of America	4:58.8
1928	United States of America	4:47.6
1932	United States of America	4:38.0
1936	Holland	4:36.0
1948	United States of America	4:29.2
1952	Hungary	4:24.4
1956	Australia	4:17.1
1960	United States of America	4:08.9
1964	United States of America	4:03.8
1968	United States of America	4:02.5
1972	United States of America	3:55.19
1976	United States of America	3:44.82
1980	German Democratic Republic	3:42.71
1984		

Springboard Diving

1920	Aileen Riggin	USA
1924	Elizabeth Becker	USA
1928	Helen Meany	USA
1932	Georgia Coleman	USA
1936	Marjorie Gestring	USA
1948	Victoria Draves	USA
1952	Pat McCormick	USA
1956	Pat McCormick	USA
1960	Ingrid Kramer	GER
1964	Ingrid Kramer-Engel	GER
1968	Sue Gossick	USA
1972	Micki King	USA
1976	Jennifer Chandler	USA
1980	Irini Kalinina	URS
1984		

Platform Diving

1912	Greta Johansson	SWE
1920	Stefani Fryland-Clausen	DEN
1924	Caroline Smith	USA
1928	Elizabeth Pinkston	USA
1932	Dorothy Poynton	USA
1936	Dorothy Poynton Hill	USA
1948	Victoria Draves	USA
1952	Pat McCormick	USA
1956	Pat McCormick	USA
1960	Ingrid Kramer	GER
1964	Lesley Bush	USA
1968	Milena Duchkova	CZE
1972	Ulrika Knape	SWE
1976	Elena Vaytsekhovskaia	URS
1980	Martina Jaschke	GDR
1984		

Synchronized Swimming: Duets

1984

VOLLEYBALL

Men

1964	Soviet Union
1968	Soviet Union
1972	Japan
1976	Poland
1980	Soviet Union
1984	

Women

1964	Japan
1968	Soviet Union
1972	Soviet Union
1976	Japan
1980	Soviet Union
1984	

WEIGHTLIFTING

Flyweight (52 kg)

1972	Zygmunt Smalcerz	POL	337.5 kg	744	lb.
1976	Alexandr Voronin	URS	242.5 kg	534.5	lb.
1980	Kanybek Osmanoliev	URS	245 kg	540	lb.
1984					

Bantamweight (56 kg)

1948	Joseph de Pietro	USA	307.5 kg	677.5	lb.
1952	Ivan Udodov	URS	315 kg	694.5	lb.
1956	Charles Vinci	USA	342.5 kg	755.5	lb.
1960	Charles Vinci	USA	345 kg	760.5	lb.
1964	Alexey Vakhonin	URS	357.5 kg	788	lb.
1968	Moh. Nasiri Seresht	IRN	367.5 kg	810	lb.
1972	Imre Foeldi	HUN	377.5 kg	832	lb.
1976	Norai Nurikyan	BUL	262.5 kg	578.5	lb.
1980	Daniel Nunez	CUB	275 kg	606	lb.
1984					

Featherweight (60 kg)

1920	Frans de Haes	BEL	220 kg	485	lb.
1924	Pierino Gabetti	ITA	402.5 kg	887	lb.
1928	Franz Andrysek	AUT	287.5 kg	633.5	lb.
1932	Raymond Suvigny	FRA	287.5 kg	633.5	lb.
1936	Anthony Terlazzo	USA	312.5 kg	688.5	lb.
1948	Mahmoud Fayad	EGY	332.5 kg	733	lb.
1952	Rafael Chimishkyan	URS	337.5 kg	744	lb.
1956	Issac Berger	USA	352.5 kg	777	lb.
1960	Evgeniy Minayev	URS	372.5 kg	821	lb.
1964	Yoshinobu Miyake	JPN	397.5 kg	876	lb.
1968	Yoshinobu Miyake	JPN	392.5 kg	865	lb.
1972	Norai Nurikyan	BUL	402.5 kg	887	lb.
1976	Nikolai Koleshikov	URS	285 kg	628	lb.
1980	Viktor Mazin	URS	290 kg	639	lb.
1984					

Lightweight (67.5 kg)

1920	Alfred Neuland	EST	257.5 kg	567	lb.
1924	Edmond Decottignies	FRA	440 kg	970	lb.
1928	Kurt Helbig	GER	332.5 kg	733	lb.
	& Hans Haas	AUT	332.5 kg	733	lb.
1932	Rene Duverger	FRA	325 kg	716.5	lb.
1936	Mohammed Mesbah	EGY	342.5 kg	755	lb.
	& Robert Fein	AUT	342.5 kg	755	lb.
1948	Ibrahim Shams	EGY	360 kg	793.5	lb.
1952	Thomas Kono	USA	362.5 kg	799	lb.
1956	Igor Rybak	URS	380 kg	837.5	lb.
1960	Viktor Bushuyev	URS	397.5 kg	876	lb.
1964	Waldemar Baszanowski	POL	432.5 kg	953	lb.
1968	Waldemar Baszanowski	POL	437.5 kg	964.5	lb.
1972	Mukharbi Kirzhinov	URS	460 kg	1014	lb.
1976	Zbigniew Kaczmarek	POL	307.5 kg	677.5	lb.
1980	Yanko Russev	URS	342.5 kg	755	lb.
1984					

Middleweight (75 kg)

1920	Henri Gance	FRA	245 kg	540	lb.
1924	Carlo Galimberti	ITA	492.5 kg	1085.5	lb.
1928	Roger Francois	FRA	335 kg	738.5	lb.
1932	Rudolf Ismayr	GER	345 kg	760.5	lb.
1936	Khadr El Touni	EGY	387.5 kg	854	lb.
1948	Frank Spellman	USA	390 kg	859.5	lb.
1952	Peter George	USA	400 kg	881.5	lb.
1956	Fyeodor Bogdanovski	URS	420 kg	925.5	lb.
1960	Aleksandr Kurynov	URS	437.5 kg	964.5	lb.
1964	Hans Zdrazila	CZE	445 kg	981	lb.
1968	Viktor Kurentsov	URS	475 kg	1047	lb.
1972	Yordan Mikov	BUL	485 kg	1069	lb.
1976	Yordan Mikov	BUL	335 kg	738.5	lb.
1980	Assen Zlatev	BUL	360 kg	793.5	lb.
1984					

Light–Heavyweight (82.5 kg)

1920	Ernest Cadine	FRA	290 kg	639	lb.
1924	Charles Rigoulot	FRA	502.5 kg	1107.5	lb.
1928	Said Nosseir	EGY	355 kg	782.5	lb.
1932	Louis Hostin	FRA	365 kg	804.5	lb.
1936	Louis Hostin	FRA	372.5 kg	820.5	lb.
1948	Stanley Stanczyk	USA	417.5 kg	920	lb.
1952	Trofim Lomakin	URS	417.5 kg	920	lb.
1956	Thomas Kono	USA	447.5 kg	986.5	lb.
1960	Ireneusz Palinski	POL	442.5 kg	975.5	lb.
1964	Rudolf Plyukeider	URS	475 kg	1047	lb.
1968	Boris Selitsky	URS	485 kg	1069	lb.
1972	Leif Jenssen	NOR	507.5 kg	1118.5	lb.
1976	Valeri Shary	URS	365 kg	804.5	lb.
1980	Yurik Vardanyan	URS	400 kg	881.5	lb.
1984					

Middle–Heavyweight (90 kg)

1952	Norbert Schemansky	USA	445 kg	981	lb.
1956	Arkhadiy Vorobyev	URS	462.5 kg	1019.5	lb.
1960	Arkhadiy Vorobyev	URS	472.5 kg	1041.5	lb.
1964	Vladimir Golovanov	URS	487.5 kg	1074.5	lb.
1968	Kaarlo Kangasniemi	FIN	517.5 kg	1140.5	lb.
1972	Andon Nikolov	BUL	525 kg	1157	lb.
1976	David Rigert	URS	382.5 kg	843	lb.
1980	Peter Baczako	URS	377.5 kg	832	lb.
1984					

First Heavyweight (100 kg)

1980	Ota Zaremba	CZE	395 kg	870.5	lb.
1984					

Second Heavyweight (110 kg)

1972	Yan Talts	URS	580 kg	1278.5	lb.
1976	Valentin Khristov	BUL	400 kg	881.5	lb.
1980	Leonid Taranenko	URS	422.5 kg	931	lb.
1984					

Super–Heavyweight (open)

1896	Viggo Jensen	DEN	111.5 kg	245.5	lb.
1904	Perikles Kakousis	GRE	111.6 kg	246	lb.
1920	Filipo Bottino	ITA	270 kg	595	lb.
1924	Giuseppe Tonani	ITA	517.5 kg	1140.5	lb.
1928	Josef Strassberger	GER	372.5 kg	821	lb.
1932	Jaroslav Skobla	CZE	380 kg	837.5	lb.
1936	Jozef Manger	AUT	410 kg	903.5	lb.
1948	John Davis	USA	452.5 kg	997.5	lb.
1952	John Davis	USA	460 kg	1014	lb.
1956	Paul Anderson	USA	500 kg	1102	lb.
1960	Yuri Vlasov	URS	537.5 kg	1184.5	lb.
1964	Leonid Zhabotinsky	URS	572.5 kg	1262	lb.
1968	Leonid Zhabotinsky	URS	572.5 kg	1261.5	lb.
1972	Vasily Alexeev	URS	640 kg	1410.5	lb.
1976	Vasily Alexeev	URS	440 kg	970	lb.
1980	Sultan Rakhmanov	URS	440 kg	970	lb.
1984					

WRESTLING (Freestyle Classes)

Light Flyweight (48 kg)

1972	Roman Dmitriev	URS
1976	Khassan Issaev	BUL
1980	Claudio Pollio	ITA
1984		

Flyweight (52 kg)

1904	Robert Curry	USA
1948	Lennart Vitala	FIN
1952	Hasan Gemici	TUR
1956	Mirian Tsalkalamanidze	URS
1960	Ahmet Bilek	TUR
1964	Yoshikatsu Yoshida	JPN
1968	Shigeo Nakata	JPN
1972	Kiyomi Kato	JPN
1976	Yuji Takada	JPN
1980	Anatoly Belaglazov	URS
1984		

Bantamweight (57 kg)

1904	Isaac Niflot	USA
1908	George Mehnert	USA
1924	Kustaa Pihlajamaki	FIN
1928	Kalle Makinen	FIN
1932	Robert Pearce	USA
1936	Odon Zombori	HUN
1948	Nasuk Akkar	TUR
1952	Shohaci Ishii	JPN
1956	Mustapha Dagistanli	TUR
1960	Terence McCann	USA
1964	Yojiro Uetake	JPN
1968	Yojiro Uetake	JPN
1972	Hideaki Yanagida	JPN
1976	Vladimir Umin	URS
1980	Sergei Beloglazov	URS
1984		

Featherweight (62 kg)

1904	Benjamin Bradshaw	USA
1908	George Dole	USA
1920	Charles Ackerley	USA
1924	Robin Reed	USA
1928	Allie Morrison	USA
1932	Hermanni Pihlajamaki	FIN
1936	Kustaa Pihlajamaki	FIN
1948	Gazanfer Bilge	TUR
1952	Bayram Sit	TUR
1956	Shoze Sasahara	JPN
1960	Mustafa Dagistanli	TUR
1964	Osamu Watanabe	JPN
1968	Masaaki Kaneko	JPN
1972	Zagalav Abdulbekov	URS
1976	Jung-Mo Yang	PRK
1980	Magomedgasan Abushev	URS
1984		

Lightweight (68 kg)

1904	Otto Roehm	USA
1908	George de Relwyskow	GBR
1920	Kalle Anttila	FIN
1924	Russell Vis	USA
1928	Osvald Kapp	EST
1932	Charles Pacome	FRA
1936	Karoly Karpati	HUN
1948	Selal Atik	TUR
1952	Olle Anderberg	SWE
1956	Emamali Habibi	IRN
1960	Shelby Wilson	USA
1964	Enio Valchev	BUL
1968	Abdollah Mohaved Ardabili	IRN
1972	Dan Gable	USA
1976	Pavel Pinigin	URS
1980	Saipulla Absaidov	URS
1984		

Welterweight (74 kg)

1904	Charles Erickson	USA
1924	Hermann Gehri	SUI
1928	Arve Haavisto	FIN
1932	Jack van Bebber	USA
1936	Frank Lewis	USA
1948	Yasar Dogu	TUR
1952	William Smith	USA
1956	Mitsuo Ikeda	JPN
1960	Douglas Blubaugh	USA
1964	Ismail Ogan	TUR
1968	Mahmut Atalay	TUR
1972	Wayne Wells	USA
1976	Jiichiro Date	JPN
1980	Valentin Raitchev	BUL
1984		

Middleweight (82 kg)

1908	Stanley Bacon	GBR
1920	Eino Leino	FIN
1924	Fritz Haggmann	SUI
1928	Ernst Kyburz	SUI
1932	Ivar Johansson	SWE
1936	Emile Poilve	FRA
1948	Glen Brand	USA
1952	David Tsimakuridze	URS
1956	Nikola Nikolov	BUL
1960	Hassan Gungor	TUR
1964	Prodan Gardshev	BUL
1968	Boris Gurevitch	URS
1972	Levan Tediashvili	URS
1976	John Peterson	USA
1980	Ismail Abilov	BUL
1984		

Light—Heavyweight (90 kg)

1920	Anders Larsson	SWE
1924	John Spellman	USA
1928	Thure Sjostedt	SWE
1932	Peter Mehringer	USA
1936	Knut Fridell	SWE
1948	Henry Wittenberg	USA
1952	Wiking Palm	SWE
1956	Gholamreza Tahkti	IRN
1960	Ismet Atli	TUR
1964	Alexandr Medved	URS
1968	Ahmet Ayik	TUR
1972	Ben Peterson	USA
1976	Levan Tediashvili	URS
1980	Sanasar Oganesyan	URS
1984		

Heavyweight (100 kg)

1896	Karl Schumann	GER
1904	Robert Hansen	USA
1908	George O'Kelly	GBR
1920	Robert Rothe	SUI
1924	Harry Steele	USA
1928	Johan Richtoff	SWE
1932	Johan Richtoff	SWE
1936	Kristjan Palusalu	EST
1948	Gyula Bobis	HUN
1952	Arsen Makokishvili	URS
1956	Hamit Kaplan	TUR
1960	Wilfried Dietrich	GER
1964	Alexandr Ivanitsky	URS
1968	Alexandr Medved	URS
1972	Ivan Yarygin	URS
1976	Ivan Yarygin	URS
1980	Ilya Mate	URS
1984		

Super Heavyweight (open)

1972	Alexandr Medved	URS
1976	Sosian Andiev	URS
1980	Sosian Andiev	URS
1984		

WRESTLING (Greco–Roman Classes)

Light Flyweight (48 kg)

1972	Gheorghe Berceanu	ROM
1976	Alexey Schumakov	URS
1980	Zaksylik Ushkempirov	URS
1984		

Flyweight (52 kg)

1948	Pietro Lombardi	ITA
1952	Boris Gurevich	URS
1956	Nikolay Solovyev	URS
1960	Dumitru Pirvulescu	ROM
1964	Tsutomu Hanahara	JPN
1968	Petar Kirov	BUL
1972	Petar Kirov	BUL
1976	Vitaly Konstantinov	URS
1980	Vakhtang Blagidze	URS
1984		

Bantamweight (57 kg)

1924	Edvard Putsep	EST
1928	Kurt Leucht	GER
1932	Jakob Brendel	GER
1936	Marton Lorincz	HUN
1948	Kurt Pettersen	SWE
1952	Imre Hodes	HUN
1956	Konstantin Vyrupayev	URS
1960	Olyeg Karavayev	URS
1964	Masamitsu Ichiguchi	JPN
1968	Janos Varga	HUN
1972	Rustem Kazakov	URS
1976	Petti Ukkola	FIN
1980	Shamil Serikov	URS
1984		

Featherweight (62 kg)

1912	Kalle Koskelo	FIN
1920	Oskari Friman	FIN
1924	Kalle Anttila	FIN
1928	Voldemar Vali	EST
1932	Giovanni Gozzi	ITA
1936	Yasar Erkan	TUR
1948	Mohammed Oktav	TUR
1952	Yakov Punkin	URS
1956	Rauno Makinen	FIN
1960	Muzahir Sille	TUR
1964	Imre Polyak	HUN
1968	Roman Rurua	URS
1972	Gheorghi Markov	BUL
1976	Kazikierz Lipien	POL
1980	Stilianos Migiakis	GRE
1984		

Lightweight (68 kg)

1908	Enrico Porro	ITA
1912	Eemil Vare	FIN
1920	Eemil Vare	FIN
1924	Oskari Friman	FIN
1928	Lajos Keresztes	HUN
1932	Erik Malmberg	SWE
1936	Lauri Koskela	FIN
1948	Karl Freij	SWE
1952	Shazam Safin	URS
1956	Kyosti Lehtonen	FIN
1960	Avtandil Koridze	URS
1964	Kazim Ayvaz	TUR
1968	Muneji Munemura	JPN
1972	Shamil Khisamutdinov	URS
1976	Suren Nalbandyan	URS
1980	Stefan Rusu	ROM
1984		

Welterweight (74 kg)

1932	Ivar Johansson	SWE
1936	Rudolf Svedberg	SWE
1948	Gosta Andersson	SWE
1952	Miklos Szilvasi	HUN
1956	Mithat Bayrak	TUR
1960	Mithat Bayrak	TUR
1964	Anatoly Koleslov	URS
1968	Rudolf Vesper	GDR
1972	Vitezlav Macha	CZE
1976	Anatoli Bykov	URS
1980	Ferenc Kocsis	HUN
1984		

Middleweight (82 kg)

1908	Fritjof Martensson	SWE
1912	Claes Johansson	SWE
1920	Carl Westergren	SWE
1924	Edvard Westerlund	FIN
1928	Vaino Kokkinen	FIN
1932	Vaino Kokkinen	FIN
1936	Ivar Johansson	SWE
1948	Axel Gronberg	SWE
1952	Axel Gronberg	SWE
1956	Guivi Kartozia	URS
1960	Dimitar Dobrev	BUL
1964	Branislav Simic	YUG
1968	Lothar Metz	GDR
1972	Csaba Hegedus	HUN
1976	Momir Petkovic	YUG
1980	Gennady Korban	URS
1984		

Light Heavyweight (90 kg)

1908	Verner Weckman	FIN
1920	Claes Johansson	SWE
1924	Carl Westergren	SWE
1928	Ibrahim Moustafa	EGY
1932	Rudolf Svensson	SWE
1936	Axel Cadier	SWE
1948	Karl Nilsson	SWE
1952	Kaelpo Grondahl	FIN
1956	Valentin Nikolayev	URS
1960	Terfik Kis	TUR
1964	Boyan Radev Alexandrov	BUL
1968	Boyan Radev Alexandrov	BUL
1972	Valeri Rezantsev	URS
1976	Valeri Rezantsev	URS
1980	Norbert Nottny	HUN
1984		

Heavyweight (100 kg)

1896	C. Schuhnann	GER
1908	Richard Weisz	HUN
1912	Yrjo Saarela	FIN
1920	Adolf Lindfors	FIN
1924	Henry Deglane	FRA
1928	Rudolf Svensson	SWE
1932	Carl Westergren	SWE
1936	Kristjan Palusalu	EST
1948	Ahmed Kirecci	TUR
1952	Johannes Kotkas	URS
1956	Anatoli Parfenyov	URS
1960	Ivan Bogdan	URS
1964	Istvan Kozma	HUN
1968	Istvan Kozma	HUN
1972	Nikolai Martinescu	ROM
1976	Nikolai Bolboshin	URS
1980	Gheorgi Raikov	BUL
1984		

Super Heavyweight (open)

1972	Antoly Roschin	URS
1976	Alexandr Kolchinski	URS
1980	Alexandr Kolchinski	URS
1984		

YACHTING

Soling

1972	United States of America
1976	United States of America
1980	Denmark
1984	

Star

1932	United States of America
1936	Germany
1948	United States of America
1952	Italy
1956	United States of America
1960	Soviet Union
1964	Bahamas
1968	United States of America
1972	Australia
1980	Soviet Union
1984	

Flying Dutchman

1960	Norway
1964	New Zealand
1968	Great Britain
1972	Great Britain
1976	German Federal Republic
1980	Spain
1984	

470

1976	German Federal Republic
1980	Brazil
1984	

Finn

1956	Paul Elvstrom	DEN
1960	Paul Elvstrom	DEN
1964	Willi Kuhweide	GER
1968	Valentin Mankin	URS
1972	Serge Maury	FRA
1976	Jochen Schumann	GDR
1980	Ekso Rechardt	FIN
1984		

Tornado

1976	Great Britain
1980	Brazil
1984	

Boardsailing

1984	

AUTHORS' BIOGRAPHIES

Bill Toomey began his gold medal bid in Mexico City with a swift 10.36 secs, the fastest 100 meters in decathlon history.

Author's wife Mary Toomey set a world record to win long jump gold in Tokyo 1964.

BILL TOOMEY

Bill Toomey earned one of the highest distinctions in sports when he won the decathlon title in the 1968 Olympic Games in Mexico City. *Time Magazine* said, "Of all the Olympic competitions, the decathlon most closely reflects the original Greek ideal of all- round athletic excellence. An entire track and field meet in miniature, its ten events in two days add up to the toughest individual test of speed, stamina, strength and spirit ever devised. The man who wins the Olympic decathlon well deserves to be known as the finest athlete in the world. That man last week was William Anthony Toomey."

The following year he set a world record of 8417 points and won the coveted Sullivan Award, as the athlete who had done the most to advance the cause of sport in 1969.

Toomey was graduated from the University of Colorado and received his M.A. in Journalism from Stanford University. He served on the Presidential Commission on Olympic Sports, which restructured the organization of amateur sport in the United States. For eight years, Bill served on the Board of Directors of the United States Olympic Committee.

He has worked for all three networks as a television commentator and covered the 1972 Olympics with ABC. Together with co-author Barry King, Toomey founded Sports Directions, a prominent sports public relations company.

Bill and his wife, Tokyo gold medalist Mary Rand Toomey, reside in Laguna Niguel, California, with their two daughters, Sarah and Samantha, both natural athletes who enjoy all sports. Bill says, "I will expose my children to every aspect of sports life, but I won't push too hard. They are going to realize that physical activity is an integral part of good living. Having a sound body is not a game that ends when you do not make the high school team, any more than it ends when you win a gold medal at the Olympic Games."

Author Barry King prepares to heave the shot, third of the decathlon's ten events.

BARRY KING

Born in England, Barry King was educated at the University of Colorado as a foreign student-athlete, and now makes his home in Southern California.

He represented Great Britain in the 1972 Olympics and held national records for the decathlon and pentathlon, as well as gaining bronze and silver medals in the Commonwealth Games.

King became Associate Dean of Students at the University of California, San Diego. Then, in 1971, he and Bill Toomey founded Sports Directions, one of the nation's most prestigious sports consulting firms. Subsequently, he traveled extensively in the administration of international sports development programs in South and Central America, the Middle East, and Asia. More recently, Barry King has developed programs for U.S. corporate clients.

Of *The Olympic Challenge,* he says, "The book recounts past Olympic highlights and previews those to come in 1984. We answer the need for essential information to enable the reader to enjoy the upcoming Olympics to the fullest."

At 38, he still runs regularly, although easy jaunts along the beach are preferred to those around the track. He resides in Laguna Niguel with wife Deanna and his six-year-old daughter, Andrea.